THE HEIR AND THE SAGE

SUNY series in Chinese Philosophy and Culture

Roger T. Ames, editor

The Heir
and the Sage

DYNASTIC LEGEND IN EARLY CHINA

revised and expanded edition

Sarah Allan

SUNY
PRESS

Cover art: *Taigong Wang fishing*, Nicol Allan, ca. 1968

Published by
STATE UNIVERSITY OF NEW YORK PRESS
Albany

© 2016 State University of New York

All rights reserved

Printed in the United States of America

For information, contact
State University of New York Press
www.sunypress.edu

Production and book design, Laurie D. Searl
Marketing, Anne M. Valentine

Library of Congress Cataloging-in-Publication Data

Names: Allan, Sarah.
Title: The heir and the sage : dynastic legend in early China / Sarah Allan.
Description: Revised and expanded edition. | Albany : State University of
   New York Press, [2016] | Includes bibliographical references and index.
Identifiers: LCCN 2016005984 (print) | LCCN 2016008006 (ebook) | ISBN
   9781438462257 (hardcover : alk. paper) | ISBN 9781438462240 (pbk. : alk.
   paper) | ISBN 9781438462264 (e-book)
Subjects: LCSH: Legends—China. | China—History—To 221 B.C.
Classification: LCC GR335 .A43 2016 (print) | LCC GR335 (ebook) | DDC
   398.20951—dc23
LC record available at http://lccn.loc.gov/2016005984

10   9   8   7   6   5   4   3   2   1

to Nicol Allan

Contents

Preface to the Revised and Expanded Edition

The Heir and the Sage was first published in 1981. It is now being republished on the heels of a new book, *Buried Ideas: Legends of Abdication and Ideal Government in Early Chinese Bamboo-slip Manuscripts*. *The Heir and the Sage* serves as the foundation for that new work, which discusses the materials that have come to light in the intervening years and how they pertain to the ideas discussed in this one. Accordingly, I have not made substantive changes to the new edition. In any case, I believe that the work retains its integrity as a comprehensive account of how legends of change of rule operated in transmitted texts of the fifth to first centuries BC.

I have, nevertheless, made some minor changes. These include the correction of minor errors and the addition of some translations and original Chinese text of passages that were only cited briefly in the earlier edition. I have also added an "Introduction" in which I comment on structuralist theory and the method I used herein and outline how I now understand the development of historical paradigms in early China. I have also appended my article, "The Identities of Taigong Wang in Zhou and Han Literature," first published in *Monumenta Serica* XXX (1972–73), because it provides supporting evidence for the role of history as a means of thinking about social conflict that is the thesis of this book. It is unchanged except for minor corrections.

Acknowledgments

This book originated as my doctoral dissertation at the University of California at Berkeley (awarded in 1974). I owe much to my teachers at Berkeley, especially Peter Boodberg (1903–1972) and Wolfram Eberhard (1909–1989). Boodberg and Eberhard were as different as the proverbial chalk and cheese. Boodberg was Russian, a philologist, and an idealist about the value of humanistic scholarship, who published very little, preferring to circulate his work in the form of mimeographed sheets. Eberhard was German, a folklorist and sinologist, who was proud to be considered a social scientist, and published prolifically. They agreed on very little, but each encouraged me to learn from the other, and they both supported my efforts to find my own intellectual trajectory. I also owe a great deal to Chen Shih-hsiang (1912–1971), who imparted his love for and gave me a solid training in early Chinese literature. And, to Cyril Birch, who managed to persuade a reluctant department to accept an unorthodox dissertation after the death of two of the original members of the committee, Chen Shih-hsiang and Peter Boodberg, I am eternally grateful. I began teaching at the School of Oriental and African Studies in 1972, and I also owe much to my colleagues there, D. C. Lau and Paul Thompson, for their criticisms and assistance. David N. Keightley also read a draft and offered many useful comments.

The book was first published by Chinese Materials Center in 1981. I am grateful to Robert L. Irick, who was willing to publish it at a time when mainstream sinology was unsympathetic to the use of structuralist method, as well as for returning the copyright to me before the first Chinese translation was published by Beijing University Press in 2001.

The Appendix, "The Identities of Taigong Wang in Zhou and Han Literature," originated as my Master's thesis. It was first published in *Monumenta Serica* 30 (1972–73): 57–99. It is reproduced here by kind permission of the Monumenta Serica Institute.

I would also like to thank, William French III, who as an undergraduate at Dartmouth, produced the electronic edition for me, and Claire V. Beskin, who proofread it. I am also grateful to Yu Jia 余佳, who, in retranslating the book into Chinese for the Commercial Press edition (*Shixi yu shanrang* 世襲與禪讓, 2010), pointed out mistakes and omissions in the original English text that I have corrected herein.

My husband, Nicol Allan, made the sumi ink drawing of Taigong Wang fishing (with a straight hook) on the cover of this book to amuse and encourage me when I was a graduate student at Berkeley. It is, as it was when it was first published, dedicated to him.

Preface to the Original Edition

Ancient Chinese literature contains few myths in the traditional sense of stories of the supernatural, but much history. This has long puzzled scholars who have generally attributed the lack of myth to an aversion of the literati to folk cults and a rationalistic tendency to present mythological figures as if they were human in written texts. The Chinese have frequently been called the most history-conscious people in the world. Their record keeping begins with divinations inscribed on bone and shell in the Shang Dynasty. Confucius is said to have considered that his reputation would be determined by a dry chronicle of his native state of Lu. And by the first century BC, Sima Qian had compiled a lengthy and complex universal history, the *Shi ji*.

But what is history and what is myth? In the following work, I will apply a method derived from the structuralist school of myth analysis to some of the history that occurs in ancient Chinese texts. I will be particularly concerned with stories surrounding the transfer of rule and the formation of dynasties from the time of Yao and Shun to the Zhou Dynasty as recorded in texts written from the fifth to the first centuries BC. My purpose is to show that these accounts are structured, and that they serve, like myth, to mediate an inherent social conflict—a conflict between the interests of kinship and those of community. This conflict is embodied in the theory of the dynastic cycle, which I interpret as a conflict between rule by virtue and rule by heredity; it also appears in myth in various transformations—heir and sage, king and minister, minister and recluse, regent and rebel. Each period will be related to the next, and the themes will be shown to repeat themselves in the same structural configuration, though the stories, contrary to common belief, are seldom mere replicas of one another.

The texts on which this study is based were written in the Warring States and early Han periods. This is the classical period of Chinese philosophy, and the frequent brief references to history in the philosophical texts are taken as source material together with the more lengthy historical accounts. The stories vary and are frequently contradictory, but I will not be concerned with determining historical accuracy. Rather, by analyzing the range of possible variation and its meaning, I hope to show that "history" in these texts could be transformed, at least within a certain range, and that ancient Chinese writers used these transformations as a means of expressing political and social attitudes.

These texts and the world in which they were written are vastly different from the oral accounts and tribal societies studied by Claude Lévi-Strauss and his followers. Thus, although my theoretical assumptions derive largely from Lévi-Strauss's early theoretical work, I have developed my own methodology by means of which I hope to shed light on the nature and meaning of references to history in early Chinese texts. At the same time, I hope to show the validity and usefulness of a structural method, if interpreted flexibly, to validate certain principles of Lévi-Strauss's method of analysis, and to offer certain revisions or extensions of that method.

In chapter 1 the problem is set out and the theory discussed. In chapters 2 through 5, legend sets surrounding the critical periods of transfer of rule are discussed individually, and the relationships among events and figures of different periods are charted. These include (1) the transfer of rule from Yao to Shun, (2) the transfer of rule from Shun to Yu, (3) the succession of Qi and the foundation of the first hereditary dynasty, the Xia, (4) the foundation of the Shang Dynasty, and (5) the foundation of the Zhou Dynasty. In chapter 6 philosophic texts—*Mozi, Lun yu, Mengzi, Xunzi, Hanfeizi,* and *Zhuangzi* —are analyzed to determine whether a given philosophic attitude implies a consistent pattern of transformations in the historical accounts. Chapter 7 is a brief discussion of the importance of these legend sets for later China. The scope of the work is limited. Many important changes occurred during and after the Han Dynasty, but the themes and motifs discussed here, as well as the general approach to the past they embody, continued to influence Chinese history, historiography, and historical fiction.

La conviction que le tout et chacune des totalités qui le composent ont une nature cyclique et se resolvent en alternance, domine si bien la pensée que l'idée de succession est toujours primée par celle d'interdependance. . . . Ce qu'on se plait à enregistrer, ce ne sont pas des causes et des effets, mais . . . des manifestations concues comme singulières.

—Marcel Granet, *La Pensée Chinoise*

There is now more to gain from trying to situate our own exoticism as one particular case within a general grammar of cosmologies rather than continuing to attribute to our own vision of the world the value of a standard by which to judge the manner in which thousands of civilizations have managed to acquire some obscure inkling of that vision.

—Philippe Descola, *Beyond Nature and Culture*

Introduction

Since the publication of the first edition of this book, three groups of well-preserved Warring States Period bamboo-slip manuscripts that include philosophical and historical texts have been discovered. The first group was excavated from Guodian 郭店 Tomb One, near Jingmen 荊門 City, in Hubei Province in 1993. The other two groups were looted, presumably from tombs, and are now in the collections of the Shanghai Museum and Tsinghua University. The manuscripts are written in a similar script, that of the southern state of Chu. The Guodian tomb dates to around 300 BC. The Shanghai and Tsinghua manuscripts are also thought to have been buried around this date. Most of the manuscripts included in these three groups were previously entirely unknown and it is not clear whether they were ever widely circulated. However, they provide us with a glimpse of the broader intellectual world in which the transmitted texts discussed in the previous pages were composed. Moreover, in recent years, archaeological evidence, including changing patterns of burial, has confirmed the reality of the breakdown of the noble lineages in the Warring States Period and the rise of a newly empowered *shi* 士-class who achieved status and authority through literary culture and appointment to official office.[1]

In *Buried Ideas: Legends of Abdication and Ideal Government in Early Chinese Bamboo-slip Manuscripts* (SUNY Press, 2015), I discuss this new ✳

---

1. Allan, *Buried Ideas*, 12–13; Hsü Cho-yun. *Ancient China in Transition*, 38; Lothar von Falkenhausen, *Chinese Society in the Age of Confucius (1000–250 BC)*, 70, 395.

archaeological evidence and introduce these three groups of bamboo-slip manuscripts. I also provide a detailed analysis of four manuscripts that discuss the legend of Yao and Shun. These manuscripts present a much more meritocratic stance than any of the transmitted texts discussed herein and it is clear from them that some philosophers advocated abdication as a means of succession. Because I reexamine the issues discussed in this book in the light of these new finds in *Buried Ideas*, I will use the following pages to reflect on the structuralist theory, explain how I arrived at the method used in the previous pages, and outline my current thinking about the development of historical thinking in pre-Han China.

Structuralism in Retrospect

The use of anthropological theory for the study of ancient China is almost always problematic. Although such theory aims at universality, the intellectual historical context is inevitably European/American, particularly as the analysis is usually applied to cultures of indigenous peoples without an extensive written tradition. This tends to create a dichotomy between "them" and "us," with "them" interpreted through concepts derived from our own intellectual tradition. Even though Lévi-Strauss insisted on the intellectual equality of the indigenous peoples, he does not avoid this dichotomy. This is most obvious in his use of "nature" and "culture." He takes this opposition as fundamental to the thinking of indigenous societies, but he also uses it to define an overarching division between those cultures which represent "the mind in its untamed state" and European civilization in which the "mind (is) cultivated or domesticated for the purpose of yielding a return."[2] The former are thus defined as "cold" societies, "peoples without history" that use classification to annul the effects of history, and the latter, as "hot" ones that "have elected to explain themselves by history."[3]

The universality of this dualism has been called into question by Philippe Descola, a student of Lévi-Strauss and his successor as director of the Laboratoire d'anthropologie sociale. Descola takes the nature/culture dualism as fundamental to the conception of theoretical anthropology, but argues that this dualism is contingent upon the

---

2. Claude Lévi-Strauss, *The Savage Mind*, 219.

3. Ibid., 232–34.

grammar of a particular cosmology. His argument is striking because it is based upon his fieldwork among an Amazonian people, the Achuar, and the peoples of this region were Lévi-Strauss's primary subject in his *Mythologiques*. Descola points out that the Achuar had no word for "nature" and even the forest was not understood as a "wild space" but as an immense garden cultivated by a spirit. Humans' perceived understanding of their relationship with the nonhuman is integrally related to their cosmology, and the Achuar regard most plants and animals as having souls similar to those of humans. Thus, the distinction between "nature" and "culture" is not meaningful to them.[4]

Early China does not fit neatly into this dichotomy of hot and cold societies. Moreover, there is also no word for "nature" in ancient China. In *The Way of Water and Sprouts of Virtue* (SUNY, 1997), I argued that the root metaphors of many of the philosophical concepts used in the Warring States period are founded in imagery deriving from what we would consider the natural world; that is, water and plant life. Early Chinese philosophers believed that all living things, including plants, animals, and humans, were governed by similar principles. Thus, one could learn the correct principles for human conduct by studying, for example, the intrinsic tendencies of water or the growth of plants. This cosmological structure is different from that of the Achuar, but it also negates the distinction between human and nonhuman.

An important consequence of the role of plants as a root metaphor was that historical time was understood as having seasonal patterns; thus, dynasties arose, flourished, and died down, to be followed by other ones, just as plants did.[5] The predominant view among sinologists has long been that Chinese cosmology was understood as continuous, with no idea of creation or rupture. Concomitantly, there was no discontinuity between nature and culture. This view has been challenged by Michael Puett, who argues for the importance of the idea of creation in early China.[6] I think that Puett's consistent translation of *zuo* 作 as "create" rather than "make" or "start" distorts the meaning of the word and tends to project an idea of creation into the texts that is not evident in them. Nevertheless, Puett is certainly correct that the role of innovation and artifice (things made by human effort) in human history was an

---

4. Philippe Descola, *Beyond Nature and Culture*.

5. Sarah Allan, *The Way of Water and Sprouts of Virtue*.

6. Michael Puett, *The Ambivalence of Creation*.

important question in the Warring States period, as was the relationship between human culture (customary practices, values, and institutions) and the spontaneous workings of the natural world. Some thinkers of the Warring States period were interested in a dualism between making (*zuo*) or acting (*wei* 為) and things that are so of themselves (*ziran* 自然) or without action (*wuwei* 無為). However, in spite of its superficial resemblance, this dualism—between things that happen spontaneously and those that are the product of human artifice—does not have the same social or cosmological implications as the nature/culture dualism implicit in Lévi-Strauss's myth analysis.

I originally assumed that the reason a nature/culture dualism did not play the same role in early Chinese thought that it did in hunter-gathering societies might be because of the advanced stage of social development—by the fifth century BC, China was already a highly developed society with a literate elite and urban centers. In retrospect, there is little evidence that categories denoting "nature" and "culture" (or "wild" and "domesticated") were ever a defining dualism in early Chinese thought.

My hypothesis that rule by hereditary right and rule by virtue were contradictory principles resulted from my analysis of the patterns of opposition between heir and sage, king and minister, minister and recluse, regent and rebel, etc., in the texts that I analyzed, as I shall discuss further below. I also suggested that these contradictory principles represent a universal; that is, the conflict between obligation to one's kinship group (or self) and responsibility to the larger social group that is inherent in any complex human society. I still think that a contradiction between obligation to kin and obligation to the larger social group is intrinsic in the organization of human societies because they inevitably divide into kinship groups. However, as with nature and culture, the terms in which such a dualism is conceived and its significance will differ according to the intellectual history of that culture.

Method

The discovery of early structuralist theory, then at its height (around 1970), provided me with a means for understanding how the system of classification and permutations I had already discovered in the ancient texts might have worked. For me, the primary value of structuralism remains that it provides a method for analyzing relationships within a system—of language, myth, or society. My primary influences herein were the French anthropologist Claude Lévi-Strauss and the American linguist Noam Chomsky. What I took from Noam Chomsky was primarily the idea of a deep structure that could systematically generate a range of statements. This enabled me to describe the relationships between contradictory versions of what seemed to be the same legend without regarding them as chronological developments. It also removed transformations of a legend from considerations of historical authenticity. What I took from Claude Lévi-Strauss was primarily the idea of myth as a way of thinking about irresolvable social contradictions. This explained not only why the texts classified historical figures of different periods together, but also the system of contrasts and permutations that I found in the texts.

My research on historical legend began with my master's thesis, the published version of which is included herein as an appendix. I decided on the topic of Taigong Wang, after two of my teachers, Wolfram Eberhard and Peter Boodberg, had independently mentioned him, but I knew very little about him. My first problem was to figure out who he was. I soon realized that he not only had a number of different names, but also different personas, which tended to be associated with particular names. In some accounts, he was described as a military leader. In these accounts, he was usually identified with an archaic style of name, not used after the Western Zhou Dynasty. He also had a surname that identified him as a member of a tribe, the leaders of which were related to the Zhou kings by a system of cross-cousin marriage. In other accounts, he had different names and personas. He might be a fisherman, butcher, or boatman, but he was always an unknown man of humble position whose worth was recognized by King Wen of Zhou, who raised him up to a position of power, after which he assisted the Zhou in the foundation of their new dynasty. I concluded that the idea of dynastic change required what Marcel Granet had called a "founding minister" and that different regional legends about his humble position before he achieved power had been attached to a historical personage.

Gu Jiegang observed that historical actors in the Chinese tradition appear like the painted actors in Chinese opera, with the same roles showing up in successive eras. Whereas roles in Chinese opera are signaled by costumes and painted faces, those in early texts are signaled by a literary device whereby the figure is introduced with a series of parallel statements. In these, Taigong Wang is grouped with singularly wise and talented men from successive eras, all of whom had been discovered in obscurity and raised to power by a future king or hegemon.

This discovery that historical figures in different eras were classified in categories that could be exposed by tracing the manner in which the figures and their actions were paralleled or juxtaposed to one another in the texts was the impetus for a larger study of the figures that surrounded transfer of rule.

An unusual feature of this study is its use of short references to legend figures and events embedded within philosophical discussion. These are much more common than historical narratives in the literature, but their significance was—and remains—largely ignored, presumably because they are not particularly useful in reconstructing historical narratives. This was a consequence of my method. Personal computers were not available in the early 1970s, but there were concordances and indexes of the major texts. I used these to find references to Taigong under his various names and then an expanding list of related figures, which I copied on punch cards, making no distinction between types of reference or genre.

By sorting the legendary references with the punch cards, I was able to discover who could be grouped with whom; that is, which figures were, in Lévi-Strauss's terminology, "operators of the same class." I could also discover who acted upon or was contrasted with whom and the range of verbs used to describe the relationships between people. In other words, I could map the synchronic and diachronic relationships of each historical figure. Since my parallel series consistently began with the time of Yao and his transfer of power to Shun, I put that succession at the beginning. Since the Zhou Dynasty was the last change of rule before most of my texts were presumably composed, it served as the endpoint.

Since the discovery of Warring States period bamboo-slip manuscripts, many scholars, including myself, have stressed the composite nature of early transmitted texts.[7] This is because the bamboo manuscripts provide evidence that small sections of text circulated independently. The idea that philosophical texts are composites is not new. Indeed, I observed in chapter 6 of this book that philosophical works included diverse and inconsistent materials. This was "not a simple matter of forgery but rather of conception. The works included sayings, teachings, arguments, and stories associated with the founder of the school, but the attribution of a work to a philosopher did not mean that he himself wrote

---

7. See *Buried Ideas*, 46–49.

it" (see p. 120). In this light, the consistency of the pattern of transformations of legends in the transmitted philosophical texts is surprising. The reason for this coherency is not entirely clear. It could be the product of purposeful selection and editing, which suggests that the logic of the transformations was clearly understood. There is also some evidence of written "histories" that reflected different philosophical stances, and these may have been associated with different schools of thought.

One example is the *Bamboo Annals*. When historical accounts are taken as legend, we find that the transformations of the legends found in the "old text" *Bamboo Annals* (*Guben zhushu jinian*) are generally coherent with those found in the *Hanfeizi* 韓非子.[8] The *Bamboo Annals* were buried around the time of the recently discovered Chu-script bamboo-slip manuscripts, namely, around 300 BC. When they were compiled is not clear, but we have no reason to believe that they are much earlier than this. Nevertheless, the *Annals* are often taken as factual records. In my opinion, the primary reason that they have been given such credence is that their descriptions of the use of force for dynastic change seem more realistic to modern scholars than the historical patterns attributed to a morally ordered cosmos found, for example, in the *Mencius*. However, the consistency of the manner in which the legends have been transformed in the *Hanfeizi* and the *Annals* suggests that the texts had a shared understanding of history and the role of human behavior in political change. In other words, the *Annals* was a Legalist history. Thus, the legend transformations that stress the role of force found in both texts are not a reflection of historical reality but a philosophical response to the idea of the supremacy of a morally ordered cosmos.

Rongchengshi 容成氏, a Warring States period bamboo-slip manuscript in the Shanghai Museum collection, provides another example of a history that expresses a philosophical viewpoint. It takes the form of a narrative that begins in high antiquity and ends with the foundation of the Zhou Dynasty. It opens with a utopian era before the time of Yao and Shun in which a list of sage kings, many of whom are unknown in transmitted literature, abdicated to one another and everyone was employed in the manner most suitable to their abilities, after which, with the introduction of governmental measures, human society began to decline. Although there is a high degree of intertextuality with transmitted texts, its historical paradigm and implicit philosophical stance contrast sharply

---

8. See pp. 131–34.

with those found in other texts of the period. The literary style and philosophical stance of this manuscript are very different from the *Bamboo Annals*. Moreover, the legend transformations are not consonant with the works of any transmitted philosophers. Nevertheless, the "history" is probably also the product of a thinker or "master" (*zi* 子) rather than that of a historian or "scribe" (*shi* 史), and it may have been intended to serve as the basis for philosophical arguments.[9]

The Development of Ideas about the Ancient Past

The structuralist method of analysis that I use herein is essentially a synchronic tool. Although I included some works from the Western Han period in my analysis, the system of legend transformations that I have describe in the following chapters is essentially one of the Warring States period. In the intervening years, much of my research has been concerned with attempting to understand the development of ideas about the ancient past. In the following, I will briefly review my current thinking about the historical development of historical paradigms.

In this book, I took the "history" recorded in early texts as "myth" because I found that ostensibly historical accounts had a similar role in early Chinese thought to that of myth as understood by Lévi-Strauss; that is, it served as a means of thinking about the society in which the authors lived. Because this "history" did not have obvious supernatural elements, I used the term *legend*. However, the structure of early Chinese religion is such that history and myth are not readily distinguishable.[10] Chinese ancestor worship, from at least as early as the Shang Dynasty and probably earlier, was based upon a belief that people continued to exist in some form after death, to exercise power over their descendants, and to require sustenance from the living. Accordingly, the spirits were the ancestors of the living and the stories told about them were stories about what they did as living human beings. Because the spirits required food from their descendants, their ritual relationships were with the living and there is no evidence that they interacted with one another in another world.

---

9. See *Buried Ideas*, 181–262.

10. For my earliest iteration of this idea, see "Shang Foundations of Modern Chinese Folk Religion." See also *The Shape of the Turtle*, 19–21.

There is, however, some evidence of the supernatural in references to births of lineage founders and culture heroes. These are found in pre-Qin transmitted texts, as well as Warring States period manuscripts. According to the *Shi jing*, the founders of the Shang and Zhou dynasties were supernaturally engendered and I have argued that the myth of the birth of the first Shang ancestor from the egg of a black bird originated as a Shang myth of the birth of the royal ancestors from the sun(s).[11] Thus, there may have been an early belief in a period before chronological time. Nevertheless, these ancestors were worshipped because of their ritual significance to their descendants, and the period in which they supposedly lived is vague.

In *The Shape of the Turtle: Myth, Art and Cosmos in Early China*, I argued that the Shang not only claimed birth from the sun(s) but also had a myth of a people who were their opposite—identified with moons rather than suns, darkness rather than light, water rather than sky, dragons rather than birds—and who had been defeated by their ancestors. When the Zhou conquered the Shang, around 1050 BC, they continued many Shang ritual practices and they needed the cooperation of the Shang elite. In order to establish legitimacy, the Zhou argued that they were repeating a pattern established by the Shang ancestors when they defeated these previous people, known in Western Zhou texts as the Xia.[12] The Zhou justified their overthrow of the Shang on moral grounds, that the last ruler of the Shang was so morally debased that he had lost the support of the Lord on High. By thus transforming a Shang myth of an earlier people who were their opposite into "history," a repeating cycle of three dynasties was established. This cycle incorporated the conflicting principles of hereditary rule and rule by virtue. Thus, as discussed at the beginning of this book, there was a paradox—hereditary right could be challenged on the basis of loss of virtue, but dynastic overthrow could also be categorized as regicide.

The Western Zhou idea of dynastic cycle did not include rulers before the beginning of the Xia Dynasty and it is not clear when Yao and

---

11. Allan, "Sons of Suns" and *The Shape of the Turtle*, ch. 3. The supernatural births of the first ancestors of the Xia, Shang, and Zhou are also described in the Warring States period bamboo-slip manuscript, the *Zi Gao* 子羔. See *Buried Ideas*, 143–70; Sarah Allan, "Not the *Lun yu*: The Chu Script Bamboo Slip Manuscript, *Zi Gao*, and the Nature of Early Confucianism."

12. Allan, *The Shape of the Turtle*, 63–71. See also Allan, "The Myth of the Xia Dynasty."

Shun came to be regarded as rulers who preceded the foundation of the Xia Dynasty. In *The Shape of the Turtle*, I suggested that a myth of the appointment of the first Shang ancestor by Shang Di, the Lord on High, was the source of the legend of Yao and Shun. Yu seems to have a distinct origin as a flood hero.[13] If this reconstruction is correct, then Yao, Shun, and Yu all had long histories before they were included in framework in which they were successive nonhereditary rulers over all-under-heaven. Although the paucity of textual evidence makes it impossible to trace the early development of this new conceptual framework in which there was a period of nonhereditary succession before the foundation of the Xia Dynasty, by the end of the Spring and Autumn and early Warring States period, history conventionally began with the time of Yao.

Abdication was not a significant issue for Confucius in the *Analects*, but the legend of Yao's nonhereditary transfer of rule to Shun in its various transformations was pervasive in the other philosophical texts of the Warring States period. In these texts, the legends of predynastic nonhereditary succession are linked by textual parallels and the repetition of legend motifs to the legends of dynastic change in the later era. Thus, the archetypal figures and dualisms associated with ruler and founding minister, regent and ruler, refusers of rule or office and rebels are found in the same structural relationships in both eras. Because of this structural repetition, the nonhereditary transfers of rule in the predynastic era appear to support the idea of dynastic cycle and do not threaten the principle of hereditary rule.

From the bamboo-slip manuscripts, we now know that there was a countervision and philosophers who advocated abdication as the ideal means of political succession, not simply an ancient prototype that encompassed the same principles as dynastic change. There was even an actual abdication of a ruler to his minister in the state of Yan around 316 BC. The most explicit expression of this viewpoint is *Tang Yú zhi dao* 唐虞之道 ("The Way of Tang (Yao) and Yú Shun"), a Warring States period manuscript excavated from Guodian Tomb One. *Tang Yú zhi dao* advocates abdication as essential to preserving cosmic and social harmony—the ideal form of succession for any age. Significantly, even though the manuscript advocates abdication as a system of succession, it recognizes the

---

13. See chapter 1, 30. The names Yao and Shun are not found in any Western Zhou text or inscription. Yu, who appears to have a separate origin as a flood hero, is first found in late Western Zhou bronze inscription; See Allan, "Some Preliminary Comments on the X Gong Xu"; Constance A. Cook, "The Sage King Yu and the Bin Gong *xu*."

dual principles of virtue and hereditary right that I have described in this work. Accordingly, Yao and Shun "loved kin" (*ai qin* 愛親) *and* "honored worthies" (*zun xian* 尊賢), Although "loving one's kin" would seem to correlate naturally with hereditary succession, the manuscript argues that filial piety results in "loving everyone-under-heaven." Thus, loving one's kin leads to abdication to a sage rather than hereditary succession.[14]

As I noted above, one reason for the rise of legends of abdication in this period was the breakdown in the lineage system established at the beginning of the Western Zhou and the rise of the *shi* class. Another reason was an ideological crisis that resulted from the failure of the idea of dynastic cycle alone as an explanatory paradigm. This paradigm was established when the Zhou claimed legitimacy by arguing they were following the example of the Shang founders, who had defeated a previous dynasty. In so doing, they inadvertently created the expectation that their rule would eventually be overthrown and replaced by another one. However, history did not happen as expected. Zhou power declined, but defeating the Zhou king was insufficient in itself to establish a new dynasty. And this was not because of the virtue of the Zhou rulers; the Zhou had the famously evil kings Li 厲 (r. 878–828 BC) and You 幽 (795 −771 BC), but this did not lead to the replacement of the Zhou king by a good man from another lineage.[15] This combination of social conflict and ideological crisis was the stimulus for the outpouring of philosophical argumentation that has made this the "golden age" of Chinese philosophy. It was also the impetus for the creation of new historical paradigms. These included, but were not limited to the legend of Yao's abdication and Shun.

Although the nonhereditary succession of Yao and Shun normally stands at the beginning of history in transmitted texts of the Warring States period, the bamboo-slip manuscripts provide evidence of a greater diversity of predynastic historical scheme than previously known. One reason is that the distinction between first ancestors and ancient "rulers" was vague. For example, in the Shanghai Museum collection manuscript, *Zi Gao*子羔, the first ancestors of the Xia, Shang, and Zhou dynasties, rather than the founders of those dynasties, are called *tianzi* 天子, "sons of heaven," a term usually reserved for rulers.[16] Besides these figures

---

14. *Buried Ideas*, 98–102.

15. Ibid., 318–20.

16. In *Buried Ideas*, I take this to mean that they were literally born of heaven by their supernatural births, see 153–63.

who were associated with the three "dynasties," there were presumably also a great many other lineage ancestors and cultural heroes who were regarded locally as former rulers. In *Rongchengshi*, for example, there is a long list of abdicating rulers, many of whom are unidentifiable, before the time of Yao and Shun.

With the application of five-phase (*wu xing* 五行) theory, the historical scheme that began with Yao, Shun, and Yu was expanded to include five predynastic rulers or *di* 帝. Thus, the official Han scheme began with Huang Di 黃帝, the "Yellow Emperor," and Zhuan Xu 顓頊, followed by Yao, Shun, and Yu. Once this all-encompassing cosmological system was generally accepted, the fluidity in the formulation of historical paradigms found in the Warring States period was curtailed. Moreover, the addition of Huang Di and Zhuan Xu and the stress upon five cosmic forces as the motive power for change of rule tempered the significance of the abdications of Yao and Shun. Nevertheless, the idea of dynastic cycle with its inherent paradox of rule by hereditary right and rule by virtue remained until the twentieth century.

1

Problem and Theory

Chinese history was traditionally seen as a succession of dynasties. Each dynasty had a cyclical pattern. The first king established his right to rule by his virtue. This right was then transferred hereditarily as long as the king's descendants were virtuous—or at least not overtly immoral. If they did engage in improper behavior or oppressed the people, the dynasty came to an end, the king was overthrown, and a virtuous man of another family became ruler and passed the rule to his own descendants.

Closely related to the cyclical interpretation of history was the theory of *tian ming* 天命, a heavenly decree or "mandate of heaven" (as it is conventionally translated). According to this theory, heaven's command determined the ruler. Heaven normally transferred its mandate hereditarily, but if a king violated the principles of heaven, he lost his moral imperative, and the right to rule was bestowed on another (regardless of whether the ruler's heir was virtuous).

The idea of a dynastic cycle and the theory of a changing mandate of heaven occur in the earliest historical texts available to us, those chapters of the *Shang shu* 尚書 thought to have been written in the early Western Zhou.[1] These chapters not only contain references to the virtue of the first

---

1. *Da gao* 大誥, *Kang gao* 康誥, *Jiu gao* 酒誥, *Luo gao* 洛誥, *Duo shi* 多士, *Jun shi* 君奭, *Duo fang* 多方. For the dating of these seven chapters, see Homer H. Dubs, "The Archaic Royal Jou Religion," 224, 227–29, n. 2; and H. G. Creel, *The Origins of Statecraft in China*, vol. 1, 449–53. In *Early Archaic Chinese*, W. A. C. H. Dobson uses the first five of these chapters and the *Shao gao* 召誥 as samples of texts from the first sixty years of the Zhou dynasty.

Shang king,[2] the immoral behavior of the last Shang kings, and their consequent loss of mandate,[3] they refer to this sequence of normative events
as part of a repeated pattern that occurred in the Xia, Shang, and Zhou.[4]
In the *Duo shi* 多士 and *Duo fang* 多方 chapters, the Zhou appealed to
historical precedent in order to persuade the Yin people of the legitimacy
of their rule. The following speech, for example, is traditionally attributed
to Zhougong 周公, who speaks in lieu of Cheng Wang 成王:

> The king has spoken to you thus: You, Yin's remaining many
> officers! The merciless and severe heaven has greatly sent
> down destruction on the Yin. We Zhou have assisted the
> .decree, and taking heaven's bright majesty we effected the
> royal punishment and rightly disposed the mandate of Yin: it
> was terminated by [the Lord on High]. . . .
>
> You know that the earlier men of Yin had documents and
> records of how Yin superseded the mandate of Xia.[5]

> 王若曰。爾殷遺多士。弗弔旻天大降喪于殷。我有周佑命。
> 將天明威致王罰。敕殷命。終于帝. . . .
>
> 惟爾知惟殷先人有冊有典殷革夏命。

Although various scholars have advanced the view that the theory
of *tian ming* was a Zhou innovation,[6] to the extent that such speeches

---

2. *Kang gao*, vol. 20; *Jiu gao*, vols. 9–11; *Shao gao*, vol. 10; *Duo shi*, vols. 6–7; *Jun shi*, vols. 7–9;
Duo Fang, vols. 8–10—all in B. Karlgren, "The Book of Documents," 40, 45, 49, 55, 61, 64.

3. *Jiu gao*, vol. 11; *Duo fang*, vols. 12–17 (Karlgren, "Documents," 45, 64). A parallel is made
here with the last Xia ruler.

4. *Shao gao*, vols. 11, 17, 23; *Duo shi*, vols. 5–7 19–20; *Duo fang*, vols. 4–19 (Karlgren,
"Documents," 49, 51 55 62–65).

5. *Duo shi*, vols. 2, 19 (Karlgren, "Documents," 54–56). Emended translation. I have changed
the romanization in this and other quotations to *pinyin* for the sake of uniformity throughout the text.

6. Qi Sihe 齊思和, "Xi Zhou shidai zhi zhengzhi sixiang" 西周時代之政治思想, 37, stated
that it was the "most distinctive aspect of Zhou thought." Dubs, 236–37, attributes it to
Wen Wang because Wen Wang is "stated to have received the mandate," and Wu Wang and
Zhougong speak with a unanimous voice. However, Creel, *Statecraft*, 82, states, "We cannot
tell how early the doctrine of the Mandate of Heaven was in existence," and remarks (n.
82) that he cannot see the force of Dubs's argument.

were effective as propaganda, the Shang must have accepted their basic premises. The stress on the transferability of the mandate was undoubtedly new in that age, as it would not have been in the interests of the hereditary rulers of Shang to promote that aspect of the theory, but they may have believed their rule depended on the grace of Shang Di 上帝 and that, as suggested in the *Shang shu*, a Xia Dynasty had preceded the Yin.[7] Whether or not the theory had its roots in Shang thought, it was generally accepted after the Western Zhou, and it became a fundamental theorem of Chinese political thought until modern times.

The cyclical interpretation of history embodies an inherent contradiction between the principles of rule by hereditary right (represented by dynastic continuation) and rule by virtue (represented by dynastic change). The theory of a mandate of heaven attempted to explain this contradiction and to regulate its manifestations, but in any manifestation there was always the potential for conflict with the opposing principle. Any new ruler might be considered a usurper for having breached the hereditary right of the former ruler. Similarly, any hereditary ruler could be accused of having lost his moral authority. In practical political terms, the hereditary ruler had to contend with the possibility that a rebel or usurper would claim that the mandate had been transferred. On the other hand, the rebel had to show not only that he was worthy of the rule, but also that the previous hereditary cycle had come to an end. The new ruler stressed the principle of rule by virtue; the entrenched ruler, hereditary right. But the alternative principle was always present as a possibility.

Hypothesis

In the following paper, I will examine the sets of legends that surround the crucial periods of change or continuation of rule from Tang Yao 唐堯

---

7. See Tsung-tung Chang, *Der Kult der Shang Dynastie im Spiegel der Orakelinschriften*, 239, for discussion of Di 帝 as an impartial god. Chang holds that although the theory of the Mandate of Heaven was given form by the Zhou, its origin lay in the Shang. Similarly, David N. Keightley, reviewing Creel, *Statecraft*, in *Journal of Asian Studies* 30, no. 3 (May 1971): 658, states, "The doctrine of the Mandate of Heaven (though not the moral content, which was apparently a Zhou contribution) thus has its origin in pre-Chou times." The supposition that the Shang accepted the tradition of a prior Xia Dynasty must rest with the interpretations of the early chapters of the *Shang shu*. For my later considerations of this issue, see Sarah Allan, "The Myth of the Xia Dynasty," and *The Shape of the Turtle: Myth, Art and Cosmos in Early China*, 63–64.

to Cheng Wang as recorded in Chinese texts from the fifth to the first centuries BC. The periods under consideration include: (1) the transfer of rule from Yao 堯 to Shun 舜, (2) the transfer of rule from Shun to Yu 禹, (3) the succession of Qi 啓 to Yu (the establishment of a hereditary Xia Dynasty), (4) the transfer of rule from Jie 桀 to Cheng Tang 成湯 and the succession of Tai Jia 太甲 (the defeat of the last Xia king and the establishment of a hereditary Shang Dynasty), and (5) the transfer of rule from Zhòu 紂 to Wu Wang 武王 and the succession of Cheng Wang (the defeat of the last Shang king and the establishment of a hereditary Zhou Dynasty).

A legend set will include all accounts of the transfer of rule or the establishment of hereditary succession at any one period and any other legends that are related to this passage of rule in the texts (for the major figures in each legend set, see Chart A).

The study begins with the legend set surrounding the transfer of rule from Yao to Shun because these are the first legends in which our texts discuss the transfer of rule. Earlier rulers do occasionally occur in the texts, but their manner of succession is not described, nor are they included in the parallels the texts make with the later transfers of rule. The study closes with the legend set surrounding the founding of the Zhou Dynasty because this is the last dynasty founded before the first of the texts was written.

The texts will include the philosophic texts *Lun yu* 論語, *Mozi* 墨子, *Zhuangzi* 莊子, *Mengzi* 孟子, *Xunzi* 荀子, and *Hanfeizi* 韓非子; the anthologies *Guo yu* 國語, *Zuo zhuan* 左傳, *Zhanguo ce* 戰國策, *Lüshi chunqiu* 呂氏春秋, and *Huainanzi* 淮南子; the historical texts *Guben zhushu jinian* 古本竹書紀年 and *Shi ji* 史記; and the "Tian wen" 天問 and "Li sao" 離騷 sections of the *Chu ci* 楚辭 corpus. These comprise the major works within the period of the fifth to first centuries BC.[8] Legendary material in ancient Chinese texts is always difficult to date because it is frequently copied from one text to another. The texts themselves are usually composite works compiled from various sources or by more than one hand rather than the product of a single author. However, almost all of the material in these texts can reasonably be assumed to have come from the designated period, most of it from the Warring States period (475–222 BC).

---

8. Other texts, including texts from before and after the designated period, have of course, been consulted and will occasionally be cited in the notes. These are listed with the designated texts in the bibliography under primary sources. However, these texts are used as supportive material rather than as a basis for establishing transformations.

The heart of the corpus is the philosophic texts compiled by Warring States philosophers and their disciples. These will be discussed individually in chapter 6. Although there are later insertions in many of these texts, the insertions are almost entirely from the Western Han. The references to history in these texts are sometimes in the form of anecdotes, but more frequently historical examples are encapsulated and placed within philosophic and political arguments. The encapsulated examples have usually been ignored in other studies of Chinese historical legend because they provide little if any factual information that is not in the anecdotes or other narrative material. But they do provide information about what the author considers to be the meaning of the legend, and because they are frequently set side by side to show similarity or contrast, they reveal the underlying structure of the legends. The analysis of these encapsulations will be an essential part of this study.

I have supplemented the philosophic texts with similar material from anthological texts and from the *Zuo zhuan*. The authorship of the *Guo yu*, *Zhanguo ce*, and *Zuo zhuan* is subject to question, but most scholars agree they include mainly material from the Warring States period. At the latest, insertions were made during the Xin Dynasty (6 BC–AD 24).[9] The *Lüshi chunqiu* was compiled under the patronage of Lü Buwei 呂不韋 (290–235 BC); the *Huainanzi*, in the court of Liu An 劉安, Prince of Huainan (d. 122 BC).[10] Both works are eclectic, but the absence of Han names in the passages under consideration indicates that these too

9. The arguments concerning the nature and authorship of these three works are voluminous and have been summarized by Cho-yün Hsü, *Ancient China in Transition*, 183–86, 191–92, and Creel, *Statecraft*, 475–78. The theory of Kang Youwei 康有為 that the *Zuo zhuan* and *Guo yu* were forgeries of Liu Xin 劉歆 during the Xin Dynasty (see *Xinxue weijing kao* 新學偽經考) has been largely discounted, though it does not seem impossible that Liu Xin may have changed or added an occasional passage. Other opinion places these two texts in the fourth or third, or at latest, second centuries BC. On the basis of grammatical analysis, Karlgren ("On the Authenticity and Nature of the Tso Chuan," 64–65) dates the *Zuo zhuan* to the period 468–300 BC, and the *Guo yu* to roughly the same period. On the basis of content, Liu Rulin 劉汝霖 (Zhang Xincheng 張心澂, *Weishu tongkao* 偽書通考, 408–409) dates the *Zuo zhuan* to 375–340 BC. William Hung (*Chunqiu jingzhuan yinde* 春秋經傳引得, xcii–xcv, lxxxii–lxxxvi), dates the *Zuo zhuan* to the second century BC and the *Guo yu* to the third. Probably neither text was compiled from a single source at a single time, but both may be reasonably assumed to belong to the designated period. Similarly, the *Zhanguo ce* probably derives from various sources, but was compiled by Liu Xiang 劉向, from Warring States sources (see Zhang Xincheng, 543–44, Hsü, 194).

10. These dates (and those of other pre-Qin philosophers given in this paper) are from Qian Mu 錢穆, *Xian Qin zhuzi xinian* 先秦諸子繫年.

derive mainly from the Warring States period. The "Li sao" and "Tian wen" from the *Chu ci* corpus include references to myths and legends from the southern state of Chu. The "Li sao" was written by the fourth century poet Qu Yuan 屈原 and the "Tian wen" is also attributed to him. The origin of this unusual work is uncertain, as is its interpretation, but it probably reached its present form near the time of Qu Yuan, and the questions often reveal paradoxes in the legends.[11]

The historical texts provide further interpretations of the legends. The *Guben zhushu jinian*, often called the "authentic Bamboo Annals," was originally buried with a ruler of the state of Wei in 296 BC. When it was compiled is not known, but it too is probably of Warring States origin.[12] It will be discussed in chapter 6 together with the *Hanfeizi*, which includes similar references to the legends. Finally, no interpretation of references to historical legend would be complete without recourse to the more extended narratives in the *Shi ji* of Sima Qian 司馬遷 (145?–90? BC). I have taken this as the final work of the corpus.

By analyzing the textual references to these periods of dynastic change and continuation, I will demonstrate that the contradiction between rule by hereditary right and rule by virtue represents an inherent structural conflict, repeatedly expressed and mediated by the legends that surround these crucial periods of Chinese "history." The conflict appears in the texts in various transformations: between such figures as heir and sage, king and minister, minister and recluse, regent and rebel; and between such concepts as aristocratic privilege and appointment by merit, and obligation to kin and responsibility to the state. Actual social conflicts other than those between the contradictory principles of rule also underlie these transformations. The ruler, who usually achieved his power by heredity, shared it with a prime minister and other officials who were increasingly appointed by merit during this period. The officials came in turn from clans, tribes, and extended families with hereditary interests which often conflicted with those of the state. During the Warring States period, from which most of the material comes, the rising *shi* 士 class competed for office with the established nobility.[13]

The period from the fifth to the first century BC was critical in Chinese history. It was the classical period of Chinese philosophy in which

---

11. David Hawkes, *Ch'u Tz'u: The Songs of the South*, 45.

12. H. G. Creel, *Statecraft*, 484–85.

13. Hsü Cho-yün, 34–52.

"one hundred schools of thought" contended for favor first in numerous small states and then in a few large kingdoms, each school hoping to find the key to the establishment of a new and lasting dynasty. It was also a period of great social change. The pre-imperial dynasties, the Shang and Zhou, were tribal in origin and tended to rely on kinship ties, the system of ancestral reverence, and the loyalty of aristocratic families to maintain their power. New states such as Qin introduced mechanical and legalistic means of organizing the state that eroded the power of the noble families. In all parts of China the crisis of the Warring States allowed an unusual amount of social mobility as ambitious and able men took advantage of the opportunities that unsettled conditions offered them. Some of the philosophers promoted this new mobility; others saw it as a threat and stressed the familial ties of the traditional order. Even after the beginning of the Han Dynasty, forces that looked back to the familial patterns of the pre-imperial period contended with those that favored the new system.[14]

Changing social patterns in the Warring States period contributed to the philosophers' concerns, but in any society that differentiates one kinship group from another there is an inherent conflict between the obligation to one's own family or kinship group and the obligation to the larger community or state that includes other kinship groups. The texts continually poise and counterpoise these principles of heredity and worth in attempted resolution of this conflict. History, then, as it appears in these texts, will be shown to function like myth to expose a logical contradiction and mediate between conflicting principles.

Of all the texts under consideration, only the *Shi ji* and the *Guben zhushu jinian* record the events of these periods as part of a chronological sequence. The other texts usually encapsulate the events and present them as the medium of philosophic thought or political argument. These encapsulations are often listed in parallel form to demonstrate an underlying principle, which may then be made explicit. At other times, they are juxtaposed as contrasting possibilities in a similar situation or alternative answers to a given problem. As the political and philosophic attitudes of the writers differ, so too do the encapsulations of the events. The variation, however, is limited and reflects an underlying structure.

The contrasts between the *Shi ji* and the *Guben zhushu jinian* are the most marked. In the *Shi ji* Yao abdicated to Shun twenty-eight years

---

14. Michael Loewe, *Crisis and Conflict in Han China* (London: 1974).

before Yao died; in the *Guben zhushu jinian* Shun imprisoned Yao in the last years of Yao's life. The other texts include a full range of positions from voluntary cession of the throne by Yao to forceful overthrow by Shun, but they maintain a certain consistency, and the variation is limited: all of the texts agree that the rule passed from Yao to Shun, and that Shun was not Yao's son but his son-in-law married to his two daughters.

Furthermore, the variants are not arbitrary, but represent regular transformations within a larger system. The account that a writer gives of one event in one period necessarily determines his approach to other events. For example, a writer who states that Yao abdicated to Shun will, if he happens to mention the next transfer of rule, also state that Shun abdicated to Yu; he will never say that Yu overthrew Shun. If he adds that Yao raised up Shun from the fields before abdicating to him, he may also say that Tang raised up Yi Yin 伊尹 from the kitchen, and that Wen Wang 文王 raised up Taigong Wang 太公望 from the butcher's market or fishing banks. If he holds the opinion that Shun went to farm at Li Shan in a deliberate attempt to transform the people who had quarreled over the boundaries of their fields, he will also hold the opinion that Yi Yin and Taigong Wang were eremitic gentlemen waiting for a true king.

These limitations and the regularity of variation within an apparent system I take as evidence of structure, defined by Jean Piaget as follows:

> We may say that a structure is a system of transformations. Inasmuch as it is a system and not a mere collection of elements and their properties, these transformations involve laws: the structure is preserved and enriched by the interplay of its transformation laws, which never yield results external to the system nor employ elements that are external to it. In short, the notion of structure is comprised of three key ideas: the idea of wholeness, the idea of transformation, and the idea of self-regulation.[15]

My hypothesis, then, is that the sets of legends surrounding each crucial period of change or continuation of rule serve as models to resolve the opposition between the conflicting principles of rule by heredity and rule by virtue. These legends are furthermore part of a larger system in which a change or transformation of any one legend will effect regu-

---

15. J. Piaget, *Structuralism*, 5.

lar changes in the entire system, the structural balance of the system remaining the same.

In accordance with the idea of wholeness, I will make no distinction between myth and history, but regard all textual references as equally valid manifestations of the same structure. I use the term *legend* for this historical myth—or mythical history, as the case may be—to avoid confusion. In so doing, I do not mean to imply that none of the events actually happened as recorded. Indeed, history may have been enacted in accordance with the structure as well as interpreted in its light. My purpose is simply to show that the records are structured.

Theory

My hypothesis that these legends provide a model to resolve a contradiction is derived from the theories of the structuralist school of myth analysis founded by the French anthropologist Claude Lévi-Strauss. However, the theories and methods of this school are not directly transferable to the Chinese materials, which are different in both type and level of sophistication from the primitive tribal myths normally subjected to structuralist analysis. Therefore, I turn to the early theoretical formulations of Lévi-Strauss for exegesis, which may shed light on the Chinese materials.[16]

The world in which the Chinese writers lived and worked was possibly as different from that of the modern African, Australian, and American tribal cultures studied by Lévi-Strauss as it is from the European-American society in which I live and think today, and its concerns are correspondingly different. Since in some areas agriculture had been practiced for thousands of years and the writers mainly lived in urban centers, they were primarily interested in the organization of society or in the relationships between man and man rather than in the relationship of man to nature. Nor were they concerned with metaphysics, but rather with ethics and politics. These concerns are reflected in the texts. Nevertheless, as Lévi-Strauss implies, there are certain elemental ways of thought universal to all mankind. Principles that he establishes with relation to the "mythical thought" of primitive societies can be used to illuminate the meaning and function of "history" in these Zhou and Han texts.

---

16. The most useful of Lévi-Strauss's works for my purposes is *The Savage Mind*.

According to Lévi-Strauss, the logic of mythical thought is as rigorous as that of modern science, but it differs from scientific thinking in the nature of the things to which it is applied and in its purpose.[17] Lévi-Strauss explains the material of mythical thought by analogy with the treasury of a French *bricoleur,* a type of odd-job man who collects things because they may "come in handy."[18] In working on a project, the bricoleur surveys his treasury for things he can use. He is limited, however, by the extent of his treasury and by the features of his pieces, already determined by their previous history and use in another context. The significance of his choice lies in the possible alternatives and in the structural reorganization implied by the choice of placing any one piece in any one place. Mythical thought also builds its projects from a treasury of preconstrained elements—"the remains and debris of events: in French 'des bribes et des morceaux,' or odds and ends in English, fossilized evidence of the history of an individual or society."[19] Like the bricoleur and unlike the scientist who could at least attempt to design new elements in conjunction with a preconceived plan, mythic thought is limited by the characteristic features and previous history of its elements, and the significance of its choices also lies in rejected alternatives and in the consequent effect of both what is chosen and what is rejected on the resultant structure.

Lévi-Strauss borrows the term *sign* from linguistics (Saussure) to further explain the nature of mythical thought. He speaks of *bricolage* and signs:

> Each represent a set of actual and possible relations; they are "operators" but they can be used for any operations of the same type.
> The elements of mythical thought similarly lie half-way between percepts and concepts. It would be impossible to separate percepts from the concrete situations in which they appeared while recourse to concepts would require that

---

17. "The Structural Study of Myth," in *Structural Anthropology,* 202–27 (226–27).

18. Lévi-Strauss, *The Savage Mind,* 17, translator's note: "The 'bricoleur' has no precise equivalent in English. He is a man who undertakes odd jobs and is a jack-of-all trades or a kind of professional do-it-yourself man, but as the text makes clear, he has a different standing from, for instance, the English 'odd-job man' or handyman."

19. Lévi-Strauss, *The Savage Mind,* 21–22.

thought could at least provisionally put its projects (to use Husserl's expression) "in brackets." Now there is an intermediary between images and concepts, namely signs; . . . images and concepts play the part of signifying and signified respectively.

Signs resemble images in being concrete entities but they resemble concepts in their powers of reference. Neither concepts nor signs relate exclusively to themselves; either may be substituted for something else. Concepts, however, have an unlimited capacity in this respect, while signs have not.[20]

Concepts, in other words, have an infinite power of reference whereas the permutations of signs are limited by the possible uses of the images that signify them.

Mythical thought uses these signs to build up slates, each different from the other and from any instrumental set. By their repetitions, however, they make their structure apparent. Lévi-Strauss states:

A myth exhibits a "slated" structure, which comes to the surface, so to speak, through the process of repetition. However, the slates are not absolutely identical. And since the purpose of myth is to provide a logical model capable of overcoming a contradiction (an impossible achievement if, as it happens, the contradiction is real), a theoretically infinite number of slates will be generated, each one slightly different from the others.[21]

Science, which has recourse to concepts, builds up structures that are one step removed from reality. By its hypotheses and theories, it creates its own events and continually tries to go beyond the boundaries of its particular state of civilization, but "mythical thought for its part is imprisoned in the events and experiences which it never tires of ordering and reordering in its search to find them a meaning."[22] The difference is not qualitative, but lies in the means and the purpose.

In applying Lévi-Strauss's theory to the Chinese materials, the manner in which the philosophers and persuaders manipulated the structure

---

20. Ibid., 18.

21. Lévi-Strauss, *Structural Anthropology*, 226.

22. Lévi-Strauss, *The Savage Mind*, 22.

must be distinguished from the structure itself. The Chinese philosophers and persuaders manipulated the legends according to the transformation laws of the system. They were at least intuitively aware that the legends were structured and deliberately brought out the repeating themes of legends of different periods in order to derive principles from them. These principles, formulated by the writers in conceptual terms, were then used as the medium of philosophical and political argument. The manner in which the legends were manipulated, however, implies structure, and within this structure the legends function as mythical thought.

The ancient Chinese philosopher or persuader who wished to make an argument may be compared to the bricoleur at work on a specific project. We may suppose that he would begin by surveying his treasury of legend for pieces which he could use. His treasury, like that of the bricoleur, was limited, and each piece was preconstrained by its previous history and connotations. If he referred to Yao and Shun, for example, he would bring to mind various legends about their background and relationship (e.g., that Shun was the son of the blind man Gu Sou 瞽瞍, that he married Yao's two daughters) and a network of related legends (e.g., that Yu succeeded Shun). He might define the legend in various ways, but he could not exceed these preconstraints. He could say that Yao yielded or abdicated to Shun, that Shun forced the rule from Yao, that the people turned to Shun, but he could never say that Shun was really Yao's son. The significance of his choice, like that of the bricoleur, lay in the possibility of alternatives, and he too would have to reorganize his entire structure accordingly (if he stated that Yao yielded to Shun, he would also have to state that Shun yielded to Yu).

The Chinese writer's references to legend fit Lévi-Strauss's definition of signs, but they are one step farther removed from the concrete than the narrative units that Lévi-Strauss and other structural anthropologists take as the elements of mythical thought in their analyses of primitive societies, and they are used in conjunction with thought forms which Lévi-Strauss associates with scientific thought. In saying that "Yao gave the rule to Shun," the writer is using a concrete image to signify a concept. That image is as valid for the sophisticated society of ancient China as the statement "the jaguar gave the girl meat" is for the Bororo Indians, and as relevant to its concerns. Neither statement is likely to be a direct account of history, but both are made up of the "remains and debris of events."

However, the Chinese writer seldom places his statement in a narrative context. Rather than telling a story, he refers to one or two events and lets these stand for the entire legend. He indicates his permutation by his manner of reference (e.g., Yao gave the rule to Shun, the people went from Yao to Shun) and may further bring the conceptual signifi- cance of his permutation to the forefront by paralleling his statement with a reference to another legend of another period. This will be an "operator of the same type" similarly permuted (e.g., Yao gave the rule to Shun, Shun gave the rule to Yu). Or he may contrast the sign with one of opposite significance from the same or another period (e.g., Yao gave the rule to Shun, but Tang took the rule from Jie). He may even draw a conclusion using conceptual terms (e.g., "these were [examples of] cession"; "this was [due to] heaven"; "this was fate").

The relationship of these concepts to the signs, however, is not precisely that which would be expected in Western logic. In "The Logic of Confucian Dialogues," A. S. Cua compared the role of concepts and historical examples in the dialogues of certain Confucian texts to their role in the Socratic dialogues. He states:

> In the Socratic dialogues, concepts are determined not by particular examples of their uses or denotation. It is the con- cept that must ultimately determine the significance and clas- sification of examples. . . . The Confucian methodology, on the other hand, regards the examples as inherent in the use or understanding of concepts. . . . The so-called examples are not really exemplifications of concepts or general principles, but are exemplars.[23]

This distinction between the Socratic and Confucian uses of concepts resembles Lévi-Strauss's distinction between scientific and mythical thought. He argued that science builds up its own events by its theories and hypotheses, whereas mythical thought is imprisoned in the events and experiences of the past, which it never tires of reordering. When the legends are used in the Chinese manner to illuminate expressed concepts, the concepts are bound by the possible permutations of the legends. They are nevertheless concepts and not signs, for they are not tied to any particular representations or imagery, but they may be used for events past, present, or future.

That the Chinese had recourse to forms of thought that fit Lévi-Strauss's definition of scientific thought may be seen most clearly

---

23. In John K. Ryan, ed., *Studies in Philosophy and the History of Philosophy*, 29–30.

in the logical arguments of the Neo-Mohists and Logicians. The esoteric arguments about whether a white horse is a horse, for example, were neither an attempt to classify horses nor a story of mythical ancestors, but an exercise in logical method, "thought put in brackets." Questions of argumentation were discussed in these and other texts, and rules of logic not unlike those of the West were recognized and formulated.[24]

Thus, scientific and mythical thought were not mutually exclusive in ancient China. In using myth in political and philosophical argumentation, the Chinese writer operated at a higher level of abstraction and with greater self-consciousness than is normally associated with mythical thought. He did not narrate legend but abstracted from it. Aware that the legends were structurally similar, he paralleled them to make the repeating themes apparent and continually sought to derive the concepts associated with the signs.[25]

Underlying the writer's manipulation of the legends, however, is a level at which the signs function as the elements of mythical thought and the legends serve as myth. To borrow terminology from Chomsky and the transformational-generative linguists, the references to the legends in the texts are "surface structures."[26] These surface structures may be used in a manner that is far removed from their meaning within the system of mythical thought, and this is not my concern. The limited range of the

---

24. See Chung-ying Cheng, "Aspects of Classical Chinese Logic," 213–35, and Janus Chmielewski, "Notes on Early Chinese Logic," for recent studies on the formulation of logical method in classical Chinese texts.

25. In *The Raw and the Cooked*, 11, Lévi-Strauss states, "Although the possibility cannot be excluded that the speakers who create and transmit myths may become aware of their structure and mode of operation, this cannot occur as a normal thing, but only partially and intermittently." However, in a discussion with John Weightman ("A Visit to Lévi-Strauss," 39–40), he implies that the final test of his interpretation would be its acceptance by the Indians themselves and states that a native's explanation would be couched in different terms, but that he was capable of grasping the underlying philosophy of his myths. The question cannot be tested with regard to the ancient Chinese. Nevertheless, I have attempted to make a formulation that accords with that indicated by the grammatical relations to the texts themselves.

26. I use these terms borrowed from transformational-generative linguistics with some caution. To my knowledge, Lévi-Strauss never mentions the work of Chomsky or the other structural linguists. Chomsky, on the other hand, doubts the validity of the theories expressed by Lévi-Strauss in the *Savage Mind* (*Language and Mind*, 65–66). However, I use this terminology as the simplest manner of describing the relationship between the basic elements of the legends and the variants that actually appear in the texts, i.e., that the variants are transformations generated from the deep structures.

variation of the references implies underlying "deep structures," a level from which specific variations of the legends may be derived, but only according to certain transformation laws. These deep structures are in turn generated from the themes of heredity and virtue, which are constant in each legend set. These sets, then, are like Lévi-Strauss's "slates"; they continually repeat the same themes in the same structural order, but are different in their factual details.

By analyzing the deep structures of the legends as well as the surface structures, we may begin to see "how myth operated in men's minds without their being aware of the fact" rather than "how men think in myth."[27] The analogy of the bricoleur is again applicable, but here the treasury includes all of the odds and ends of history and not simply the events of an already determined system of legend. The bricoleur deals in mythical thought; he is not an individual thinker, and the signs function in mediating the conflict between heredity and virtue rather than in extraneous argument. The choice that the bricoleur makes of a sign again implies others, and the significance lies in the possible alternatives. If, for example, the transfer of rule from Yao to Shun is nonhereditary and includes a ritual declining of the throne from Yao to Shun, this signifies giving precedence to virtue, especially when Yao's son Dan Zhu 丹朱 is described as bad. This choice implies others, since unless the system is one in which virtue is given precedence over heredity, equivalent stress must be given to the principle of heredity—hence the other legends of the set (Shun was Yao's son-in-law. Shun was devoted to his own father). Each choice further requires others, and the set is built up in this manner. Any particular representation at the surface structure level also has implications for the rest of the set, but the transformations will remain within the possibilities of the set. If, for example, the people went from Yao to Shun, the transfer is still nonhereditary and still signifies giving precedence to virtue, but since Yao did not abdicate and Shun did not accept his abdication, Shun did not need to rid himself of the taint of breach of heredity by further yielding the throne to the recluse Shan Juan 善卷.

In the present paper, I will demonstrate the manner in which these legends do indeed operate as signs within a structure. They will be shown to be concrete entities, permutable within a limited range and significant of concepts. Furthermore, they will be shown to fulfill the purpose of

---

27. Lévi-Strauss claims to show the former but not the latter (which is more properly the study of logic), in *The Raw and the Cooked*, 12.

myth, defined by Lévi-Strauss as "to provide a logical model capable of overcoming a contradiction," in this case the contradiction between hereditary right and rule by virtue. Since the contradiction is real and can never be totally overcome, the model is continuously repeated with slates of different myths at each period of change, but the same structural elements are maintained.

Closely related to Lévi-Strauss's distinction between mythical and scientific thought is a parallel distinction between "cold" and "hot" societies, "the former seeking by the institutions they give themselves, to annul the possible effects of historical factors on their equilibrium and continuity in a quasi-automatic fashion; the latter resolutely internalizing the historical process and making it the moving power of their development."[28] Natural cycles present no problem to the cold societies because they are "periodically repeated in duration without their structures necessarily undergoing any change." The overall sweep of history, however, is not recognized by these societies. Instead, they postulate a period of mythical history in which there were ancestors whose nature was different from that of modern man. In modern times, these ancestors are imitated and ritual conjoins past and present, but the intervening passage of time is obliterated by the repetitiousness of all of man's acts.

At first glance, the Chinese would appear to be in polar opposition to these primitive "peoples without history." They have frequently been called the most history-conscious people in the world. The number of their historical texts remaining is greater than any other ancient civilization, and the accuracy of much of the material has recently been attested by archaeological discovery. On the other hand, the texts include an extreme paucity of the truly mythological (in the traditional sense of the supernatural). There are only enough references to myth and ritual to posit an earlier period of supernatural belief. Wolfram Eberhard, using later material as well as the early texts, has tied these references to local cultures, which, he believes, were joined together to become what we now recognize as Chinese culture.[29] Henri Maspero has attributed the paucity of myth to euhemerization, a process by which mythical figures are historicized and their supernatural features made to appear human.[30]

---

28. *The Savage Mind*, 234.

29. Wolfram Eberhard, *Local Cultures in South and East China* and *Lokalkulturen im Alten China*.

30. Henri Maspero, "Legendes mythologiques dans le Chou King."

However, the texts not only include euhemerizations of supernatural figures, they also include mythologized (euhemerized in the traditional rather than in Maspero's sense of the term) versions of ancient history. In a previous study, "The Identities of Taigong Wang 太公望 in Zhou and Han Literature," I compared the historical evidence concerning this minister of Wen Wang and Wu Wang of the Zhou Dynasty with the many references to him in Zhou and Han texts, and found these to be entirely contradictory.[31] Historically, he was a nobleman of the Jiang 姜 clan, which traditionally intermarried with the Zhou royal family, and was possibly the uncle of Cheng Wang. In the popular tradition, however, he was always a poor man raised up from obscurity by Wen Wang to be his minister, though there are several completely different regional legends to this effect.

My theory is that Chinese writers from the fifth to the first centuries B.C. dealt with the problem of history neither by positing a mythical past and continuous indivisible present nor by viewing time as simply progressive, but by subjecting all of past time to cyclical laws. The cycles are similar in structure and provide a model to overcome the logical contradictions of the society, but since this society is the highly sophisticated and politicized world of the Warring States and the Han philosophers and persuaders, the legends reflect this world rather than presenting supernatural accounts taken from the remains and debris of a primitive history. Chinese society was, of course, still diverse. The occasional references to noneuhemerized myth are evidence that outside the courts and groups of literati, peasants and local cultures continued to build other structures more applicable to their own lives. However, for those who were concerned with political questions, this cyclical history came to function as myth.

This theory allows me to explain some phenomena that previously appeared confusing. For example, Karlgren has applied a "historical method" to much of this same material.[32] This method enabled him to trace the development of the legends in time. However, certain types of legend variants, such as those concerning the transfer of rule from Yao to Shun, which range from Yao's voluntary cession to Shun to Shun's

---

31. This study was presented as my master's thesis at the University of California, Berkeley, in June 1966 and later published in *Monumenta Serica* 30 (1972–73): 57–99. It is included herein as Appendix 2, pp. 149–89.

32. Bernhard Karlgren, "Legends and Cults in Ancient China."

overthrow of Yao, coexist in the texts and cannot be adequately explained in terms of chronological development. Nonetheless, they can be understood as transformations of the same deep structure.

Maspero has effectively demonstrated that many of the predynastic figures which appear in the texts as though they were historical persons were originally supernatural creatures. Valid though this approach is, it does not provide a means for explaining why the legends were combined or euhemerized in the manner in which they occur in their later versions. The legends of Gun 鯀 and Yu, for example, were originally separate local flood myths, but when they were combined and the figures euhemerized, Yu became Gun's son. This manner of joining the legends meant that Yu came to serve his father's killer. This cannot be explained as a projection of social norms or ideals, since it violates them, but it can be effectively explained as a breach of heredity necessary to fulfill the structural requirements of the set.

The closest forerunner of this work is Marcel Granet's *Danses et Legendes de la Chine Ancienne*.[33] Granet was particularly concerned with the relationship between myth or legend and ritual. He also demonstrated that there are certain paradigms in ancient Chinese legends, such as the *minister-fondateur* or "founding minister," a term I have borrowed from him. My purpose in this work is to show the system or structure that underlies the paradigms and gives them their meaning. I have been influenced in my approach by Granet, who also influenced Claude Lévi-Strauss. But my analysis is based entirely on the texts themselves, from which I have tried to build up a system uninfluenced by the theories of later writers. Thus, I have deliberately refrained from reference to secondary sources except where they shed light on specific problems.

Finally, with regard to my own study of the identities of Taigong Wang, the difference between history and legend and the existence of several local legends with similar themes but totally different details can now be explained more clearly. The different local legends were "operators of the same type" that grew up independently, though in contradiction to historical fact, to fulfill the requirements of the legend set surrounding the founding of the Zhou Dynasty.

By suggesting that the Chinese subjected history to a cyclical interpretation, I do not mean to imply that they were unaware of chronological or progressive time. The situation is similar to that discussed above

---

33. Marcel Granet, *Danses et Legendes de la Chine Ancienne*.

with respect to signs and concepts. The ancient Chinese made use of the forms of mythical thought, although at a higher level of abstraction than in primitive societies, but they also had recourse to thought forms associated with logic. The Mohists, for example, discussed questions of universal and particular time.[34] Mythically, the idea of a life cycle was extended over long periods of time, and historical change was subjected to its laws. This is not only a question of interpretation but also of institutions, for dynastic change was a reality as well as an idea.

The ancient Chinese did assume that there was a period in the mythical past in which their ancestors were different from modern men. There are many culture heroes and supernatural feats and features associated with the mythical past. The earliest figures in our legend sets— Yao, Shun, and Yu of the predynastic period—are all heroes of this era. However, the structural model of dynastic change is projected onto these figures so that the transfers of rule from Yao to Shun and Shun to Yu are structurally identical to the changes of rule at the beginning of the Shang and Zhou. Each period follows the other in a progressive sequence (in this sense, chronological time is assumed), but the structure does not change. By this means, then, the mythical past is conjoined with the present, and the present acts of men are given legitimacy.

Method and Procedure

In the following study, I will use three primary methods in determining the meaning and structural configuration of the legends. First, I will attempt to determine the "deep structure" of each individual legend by examining the full range of textual variations and defining the common semantic elements within these variations. Second, I will determine the scope and structural configuration of each legend set by examining the manner in which the texts relate the legends surrounding each critical period of change of rule to one another—thus, a "legend set" is defined as the full range of legends that are related textually to the accounts of transfer of rule at any one period. My primary key in this respect is the manner in which the ancient Chinese texts present legend figures of the same period as contrasting examples. I assume that figures so juxtaposed are in structural opposition but have some common element. By this

---

34. Joseph Needham, *Time and Eastern Man*, 1–9.

means I will be able to show that each set contains a pattern of structural opposition in which the rulers function as mediatory figures between two extremes. Finally, I will determine the relationship between the legend sets by examining the manner in which the legends of one period are paralleled in the texts to legends of another period. Here I assume that the legend figures thus paralleled are structurally equivalent. I will thus be able to build up a system of structural relations.

Procedurally, I will begin by examining the legend set surrounding the transfer of rule from Yao to Shun and then proceed chronologically. In so doing I do not mean to imply priority of origin—this is merely an organizational device which could as easily have been reversed. Having determined the structural configuration and relations between each set, I will then examine the specific transformations of structure that appear in individual philosophic texts. For the convenience of the reader, I have also appended a series of charts describing the relationships between the major figures of each legend set. Occasional reference to these will be made in the following discussion, and the key to the charts includes a list of symbols used in both the texts and the charts. Since the number of figures discussed is large and the relationships complex, the reader may want to look these over before beginning the following discussion. All of the material contained in the charts, however, also appears in the text.

All references with a solidus (/) refer to the *juan* and page numbers of the *Sibu congkan* 四部叢刊 editions as originally published in Shanghai in 1919–1922. Other editions consulted are listed in Bibliography A.

2

Legend Set I: Tang Yao to Yú Shun

Yao to Shun: The Transfer of Rule

During the period under consideration, Tang Yao 唐堯 to early Zhou 周, there are four occasions in which the rule is transferred from a member of one family to a member of another. The rulers and their successors may be described as a parallel series:

Yao : Shun :: Shun : Yu :: Jie : Tang :: Zhòu : Wu Wang

堯 : 舜 :: 舜 : 禹 :: 桀 : 湯 :: 紂 : 武王

Yao, Shun, Jie, and Zhòu are rulers and Shun, Yu, Tang, and Wu Wang are subjects who became rulers. (See Chart B; the formula A : B :: X : Y means A *is to* B *as* X *is to* Y). In each case, there is an apparent violation of the heredity principle.

The first such transfer of rule with which we will be concerned is that between Yao and Shun. This is most often characterized as a voluntary transfer devoid of violence, an "abdication." The characterization is expressed syntactically in our texts. In most cases the transfer from Yao to Shun, like that from Shun to Yu, is described in the form "Yao *verb* Shun," in which Yao gives, cedes, or abdicates the throne to Shun but, whatever the verb, remains the actor while Shun is the recipient of the action.[1] This

---

1. I am including in this classification of grammatical transformation, such as *Shun shou Yao zhi tianxia* 舜受堯之天下 and *Shun shou Yao zhi chuan* 舜受堯之傳, in which Shun is the passive recipient and Yao the implied actor. I regard these as structurally identical to *Yao yi tianxia shou Shun* 堯以天下授舜 and *Yao chuan Shun* 堯傳舜.

contrasts with the descriptions of the nonhereditary transfers of rule at the beginning of the Shang and Zhou Dynasties in which Cheng Tang and Wu Wang are characterized as taking the rule from Jie and Zhòu by force. In this case; the new rulers are the actors and the former rulers the recipients of the action—i.e., "Tang *verb* Jie" or "Wu Wang *verb* Zhòu."

When the legends are so interpreted, the verbs used for the predynastic and dynastic eras are correspondingly different. The verbs used for the predynastic era imply peaceful and orderly transfer of the rule, though there is a range in the degree of pressure by Shun or active choice by Yao implied. They include such verbs as *rang* 讓 "yield" or "ritually decline,"[2] *shan* 禪 "abdicate," *chuan* 傳 "transmit" (all-under-heaven or the rule), *shou* 授 "bestow," *yu* 與 "give," and *li* 立 "establish" (as son-of-heaven). Those for the dynastic era imply force or violence, but vary according to the authority and moral right of the preceding or succeeding king. They range from *shi* 弒 "kill one's superior" (or "commit regicide") to *zhu* 誅 "punish" (usually by execution, implying that the succeeding king has already assumed the moral authority or ruler) and commonly include such verbs as *fa* 伐 "smite," *fang* 放 "banish," and *sha* 殺 "kill."

Accordingly, there is a distinction in form and meaning which I graph as:

a) Yao → Shun, Shun → Yu
b) Jie ← Tang, Zhòu ← Wu Wang

Both (a) and (b) are nonhereditary transfers of rule, but (a) is distinguished from (b) by the absence of violence. In this transformation, the transfers of rule can only be made parallel by omitting the grammatical object (the recipient of the action) and contrasting as well as comparing the two transfers:

---

2. *Rang* 讓 is often translated as "yield" or "cede" and may connote yielding to superior force, either military or moral. *Xunzi* 12/10b, for example, argues that Yao and Shun could not have abdicated (擅讓) because their authority was so venerated. "They had no enemies on earth. To whom could they have yielded?" 無敵於天下夫有誰與讓矣. Their virtue was all-encompassing, so "there were no eremitic sages or neglected good men" 天下無隱士無遺善. "How could they abdicate all-under-heaven?" 夫有惡擅天下矣. *Rang* may also mean "refuse" or "decline" (as in *ci rang* 辭讓), with the sense of ritual declamation (cf. *rang* 讓 and *shan rang* 禪讓). Marcel Granet has discussed the word's ritual connotations at some length, particularly stressing its value as a rite of expiation (*Danses et légendes*, especially vol. 1, 88–89, 293–97).

a) Yao and Shun yielded 堯舜讓

b) Tang and Wu contended 湯武爭 (*Zhuangzi* 6/17a–b)[3]

In both eras, the rule was passed from a member of one family to a member of another. In the predynastic era, however, the rulers gave the rule to their subjects in an orderly manner, though they may have responded to pressure. In the dynastic era, the new rulers had to apply some degree of force, although they may have obtained the moral authority befitting a ruler before applying that force.

There are two other transformations in which there is no grammatical distinction between the predynastic and dynastic types of transfer of rule. In these transformations, all of the transfers of rule become parallel, demonstrating the link between the two types of nonhereditary transfer. Nevertheless, even in these transformations the transfer of rule from Yao to Shun may be derived from the same deep structure; Yao made a gesture of ritual abdication in which he appointed Shun his successor. The first transformation exaggerates the force used by Shun and Yu to the extent that they rather than Yao and Shun become the primary actors. Hence, there is no longer a grammatical contrast in the portrayals of the two periods:

Shun forced (*bi* 偪) Yao; Yu forced Shun:

Tang banished (*fang* 放) Jie; Wu Wang smote (*fa* 伐) Zhòu.

These four kings were all subjects who committed regicide (*shi* 弒) on their rulers. (*Hanfeizi* 17/8b)

Shun and Yu are the primary actors in this passage, equivalent in their "regicide" to Jie and Zhòu. The use of the term *shi* is probably not meant literally. No other text accuses Shun, Yu, or Tang of actually murdering the ruler. It simply shows that all of the acts were of the same regicidal type. The use of the term *bi* 偪, "compel" or "force," however, implies a response by Yao and Shun, presumably a gesture of ritual abdication, as well as resistance.

---

3. All references with a solidus (/) refer to the *juan* and page numbers of the *Sibu congkan* editions; "a" and "b" mean obverse (*shang* 上) and reverse (*xia* 下) sides of the page.

A similar transformation occurs in the *Guben zhushu jinian*. The *Bu* 補 compiled by Fan Xiangyong 范祥雍 includes the following fragments:

> In Yao's last years, his virtue declined and he was imprisoned by Shun.

> 堯之末年, 德衰, 為舜所囚。

> Shun imprisoned Yao.

> 舜囚堯。

> Shun usurped Yao's position.

> 舜簒堯位。

> After Yao abdicated the throne, Shun became king; after Shun abdicated the throne, Yu became king.

> 堯禪位後, 為舜王之, 舜禪位後, 為禹王之。[4]

In the first three references, Shun is the actor and forces the rule from Yao. In the last, Yao abdicates to Shun, but the term used, *shan* 禪, refers specifically to the ritual performance of abdication. If the gathered fragments are not inconsistent, Yao must have been forced into the act of abdication by Shun.

The other transformation removes both ruler and subject from the position of actor by inserting a third determiner, either the people or heaven. The rule does not change because of any overt action on the part of either person; it changes because heaven changes the mandate or the people go from one ruler to the other. The *Mengzi*, for example, stresses the role of heaven that manifests its mandate in the acceptance of the

---

4. *Guben zhushu jinian jijiao dingbu*, 6–7. The text of the fourth fragment appears to be corrupt and I have only been able to translate it by taking 為 as 惟. Another possibility is that 王 should be 囚. The fragment derives from the *Sushi yanyi* and reads as given by Fan Xiangyong in the *Han hai ben* and *Rongyuan congshu* editions. The *Gujinzhu zhonghua gujinzhu sushi yanyi* however, gives this fragment as 堯為舜囚之舜為禹囚之. This would give further support to the second fragment quoted above.

people. The ruler may "commend" or "present" (*jian* 薦) his successor to heaven, but this is not the determining factor. Yao commended Shun to heaven, and after his death, the people followed him, but after Yu's death, they went to Yu's son Qi rather than to Yi, whom Yu had commended.[5] Similarly, heaven set aside Jie and Zhòu, and so the people turned from them to Tang and Wu.[6] The *Xunzi*, on the other hand, defines kingship by the obedience of the people. The people will obey the heir if he is worthy, or turn to a sage if he is not. Thus, Yao and Shun could not have voluntarily abdicated, nor Tang and Wu forcefully usurped the throne.[7]

This transformation removes the onus for breaching the rule of heredity from both the ceding kings of the predynastic era and the rebel kings of the dynastic era by regarding all transfers of rule, both hereditary and nonhereditary, as equally valid manifestations of heaven's will or as determined by the allegiance of the people. This insertion of an outside force as the causal factor means that the new rulers are no longer responsible for the breach of heredity, but the basic elements remain the same. Yao must have commended Shun to heaven, or Shun could not have become king; Jie and Zhòu must have been evil, or Tang and Wu Wang could not have become rulers.

The transfer of rule from Yao to Shun, then, is the first of a series of nonhereditary transfers of rule, which includes the transfers from Shun to Yu, Jie to Tang, and Zhòu to Wu Wang. This transfer, like that from Shun to Yu, includes a ritual gesture of appointment of a successor by the preceding ruler, though this may not be the causal factor. It is distinguished from the transfers of the dynastic era in that it may be attributed to the action of the preceding rather than the succeeding ruler and may be characterized as devoid of violence, whereas the transfers from Jie to Tang and Zhòu to Wu Wang never include even the gesture of abdication, are always attributed to the actions of the succeeding rulers, and always include some degree of violence.

A closer examination of Legend Set 1 shows that the succession of Shun does not simply symbolize the breach of heredity, but involves a mediation between the principles of heredity and virtue. In later periods this mediation takes place by combining a period of violent overthrow

---

5. *Mengzi* 9/9a–12b (5A.5, 6).

6. *Mengzi* 7/7b–8a (4A.9).

7. *Xunzi* 12/2b–6a, 10b–15a.

with a succeeding period of regency, but in the legendary era the major
themes of both periods are telescoped into a single model whose possible absence of violence tends to legitimize the transformations of the
dynastic period. The mediatory role of Shun may be seen by examining
the figures with which he is contrasted, the principles established for
later times by examining the parallels.

Shun, in accepting the throne from Yao, is contrasted in our texts
with two other figures. On the one hand, he is contrasted with Dan
Zhu 丹朱, the son of Yao who should have obtained the throne by the
principle of heredity but was disqualified by his lack of virtue. On the
other, he is contrasted with Xu You 許由, the eremitic sage who qualified by his virtue but refused because he had no hereditary right to the
throne. Between these two figures is Shun, the son-in-law but not the
legitimate heir of Yao. Shun, though a sage, was nevertheless willing to
breach the rules of heredity and take the throne.

I have graphed Legend Set 1 as follows:

By my positioning of Shun I mean to show that in the nonhereditary
transfer of rule from Yao to Shun, which may be attributed to positive
action by Yao, Shun serves as a mediator between the conflicting principles of virtue without hereditary (represented by Xu You) and hereditary
without virtue (represented by Dan Zhu).

Shun and Dan Zhu: The Sage and the Heir

Dan Zhu was the eldest son of Yao, who according to some texts had
ten sons altogether.[8] His character, where delineated, is always negative,
and the texts cite him as an example of a bad man who could not be

---

8. *Lüshi chunqiu* 1/11b, 22/8b. The *Mengzi* 9/1b (5A.1), *Huainanzi* 20/5a, and the *Shi ji, juan*
1, 33, refer to Yao's nine sons being made to serve Shun, apparently omitting Dan Zhu.

transformed by the most worthy of kings.[9] In the *Shi ji* account (derived from the *Shang shu, Yao dian*), Yao states that Dan Zhu is "headstrong and truculent. I will not use him."[10] Other texts call him "unworthy" (*bu xiao* 不肖).[11]

Dan Zhu is linked in the texts with a series of rebellious members of the royal family:

> Yao had Dan Zhu; and Shun had Shang Jun; Qi had the Wu
> Guan; the Shang had Tai Jia; Wu Wang had Guan and Cai.
> Those punished by these five rulers were all related to them
> as father to son or younger to elder brother.

堯有丹朱而舜有商均啓有五觀商有太甲武王有管蔡五王之所
誅者皆父兄子弟之親也 (*Hanfeizi* 17/8a)

Dan Zhu, Shang Jun 商均, the Wu Guan 五觀, Tai Jia, and Guan 管 and Cai 蔡 were all members of the ruling family who upset the peace.[12] This is usually represented as rebellion, but according to the transformation, all of them may also be regarded as fighting to protect the hereditary interests of the ruling family.

Although Dan Zhu was bad, he is well known as Yao's son, and no text ever questions that he was the legitimate heir. There is no suggestion in any text of an alternative heir nor of the possibility of a fraternal succession as practiced by the Shang. In choosing to replace Dan Zhu with Shun, Yao made a clear choice between hereditary legitimacy and worth. This choice is emphasized when all ten of Yao's sons are men-

---

9. *Huainanzi* 19/5b; *Xunzi* 12/5a. These passages are particularly revealing because the writers are not speaking of succession and would not have biased their account for that reason.

10. 頑凶不用. See *Shi ji, juan* 1, 20.

11. 不肖. See *Shi ji, juan* 1, 30; *Mengzi* 9/11a (5A.6).

12. This series also appears in the *Guo yu* (Chu yu 楚語) 17/1a in a passage concerned with the problem of replacing the heir with a minister. In this passage the *er* 而 before Shun is omitted, Tang 湯 is substituted for Shang 商, and the concluding remarks are, "These five kings all had depraved sons though their virtue was of the highest quality." The manner of Dan Zhu's rebellion is somewhat uncertain. The *Guben zhushu jinian jijiao dingbu* (8) mentions that Dan Zhu was banished by Hou Ji 后稷, and the *Lüshi chunqiu* (20/6b–7a) that Yao fought a battle at Dan Shui 丹水 and subdued the Southern Man 南蠻. B. Karlgren ("Legends and Cults," 291) thinks the latter were the supporters of Dan Zhu.

tioned, since the accounts of unworthiness only refer to Dan Zhu. In the *Lüshi chunqiu*, for example, the choice between heredity (i.e., "sons") and virtue or "worth" (i.e., *xian* 賢) is made quite explicit:

> Yao had ten sons; he did not give [the throne] to his sons, but bestowed it on Shun.

堯有子十人不與其子而授舜 (*Lüshi chunqiu* 1/11b)

> Yao and Shun were virtuous rulers. They both made men of worth their successors and were unwilling to give [the throne] to their descendants.

堯舜賢主也皆以賢者為後不肯與其子孫 (*Lüshi chunqiu* 3/11a)

Similarly, the *Xunzi* (18/4b) states that Yao "yielded to a man of worth" (*rang xian* 讓賢) and "bestowed the throne on the capable" (*shou neng* 授能). The breach of his hereditary obligations, however, cannot be concealed. The *Zhuangzi, Huainanzi,* and *Lüshi chunqiu* all point out that Yao was "unfatherly" or, muting it slightly, "had a reputation for being unfatherly." Another passage from *Zhuangzi* goes so far as to state that Yao "killed his eldest son."[13]

Yao's choice of an outsider over his sons presents a dangerous precedent to hereditary interests, not only within the ruling family but to the entire nobility. The *Hanfeizi* decries the transfer on the grounds that Shun was a commoner rather than simply because he was not the heir:

> When Yao wanted to transmit all-under-heaven to Shun, Gun remonstrated [with him] saying, "This is inauspicious! Who has ever transmitted all-under-heaven to an ordinary fellow?" Yao did not listen. He raised an army to punish him and killed him in the environs of Feather Mountain. Gong Gong also remonstrated and said, "Who has ever transmitted all-under-heaven to an ordinary fellow?" Yao did not listen and again raised an army and punished Gong Gong at the

---

13. For 不慈 see *Zhuangzi* 9/38a (*pian* 29); for 不慈之名 see *Huainanzi* 13/5a, *Lüshi chunqiu* 11/8a, 19/18b; for 殺長子, see *Zhuangzi* 9/42a (*pian* 29).

city of You Zhou.[14] Then no one in all-under-heaven dared to speak against all-under-heaven being transmitted to Shun. Zhong Ni heard of this and said, "For Yao to know Shun's worth was not the difficult thing; the difficulty was to realize that by punishing the remonstrants all-under-heaven would inevitably be transmitted to Shun."

堯欲傳天下於舜鯀諫曰不祥哉孰以天下而傳之於匹夫乎堯不聽舉兵而誅殺鯀於羽山之郊共工又諫曰孰以天下而傳之於匹夫乎堯不聽又舉兵而誅共工於幽州之都於是天下莫敢言無傳天下於舜仲尼聞之曰堯之知舜之賢非其難者也夫至乎誅諫者必傳之舜乃其難也 (*Hanfeizi* 13/8a)

This passage is particularly interesting because the first figure remonstrating with Yao is Gun. Gun was the father of Yu, to whom Shun later passed the throne, and consequently is a symbol of hereditary interests, a point that will be discussed in more detail in the following chapter. Most texts state that Gun was killed because he was unable to allay the flood. Here his concern for hereditary right is used to further emphasize the breach of hereditary interests by Yao.

In the *Shi ji*, Sima Qian attempts to explain the conditions that necessitated Yao's choice. In doing so, he appears to recognize the potential threat implied by Yao's breach of heredity:

Yao knew that his son Dan Zhu was too unworthy to bestow all-under-heaven upon; so, he weighed the question of bestowing it on Shun. In bestowing it on Shun, all-under-heaven would be benefited and Dan Zhu would suffer. In bestowing it on Dan Zhu, all-under-heaven would suffer and Dan Zhu would be benefited. Yao said, "I could never benefit one man to the detriment of all-under-heaven." In the end, he bestowed all-under-heaven on Shun.

---

14. There is a lack of parallelism and apparently a character missing from this line. Chen Qiyu *Hanfeizi jishi* 韓非子集釋 (v. 2, 741), noting earlier corrections of *zhu* 誅 to *liu* 流 on the basis of citations of the *Mengzi* and *Shang shu* in the *Taiping yulan*, suggests that *liu* should follow *zhu*. In this case the line would read, "Yao raised an army to punish him, and banished him to You Zhou."

堯知子丹朱之不肖不足授天下, 於是乃權授舜, 授舜則天下得
其利而丹朱病; 授丹朱則天下病而丹朱得其利。堯曰終不以
天下之病而利一人, 而卒授舜以天下。 (*Shi ji, juan* 卷 1, 30)

The contrast between Shun and Dan Zhu points up the breach
of hereditary succession by Yao, who has set his own son aside in favor
of a stranger. Sima Qian justifies the ritual violation by Yao in terms of
virtue (for the good of all-under-heaven) but carefully limits the conditions under which this precedent might be followed: only when the heir
is so unworthy that his rule would be detrimental. That Sima Qian finds
it necessary to theorize in this manner betrays a problem, the conflict
between the principles represented by Shun and those represented by
Dan Zhu. More abstractly, the conflict is between virtue and heredity,
between the sage and the heir.

However, Shun is not simply a symbol of virtue as opposed to
heredity. Although in contrast to Dan Zhu he is the sage rather than
the heir, he also has a limited kinship relation to Yao similar to that of
an adopted son. When Yao discovered Shun, he made him his minister,
gave him his two daughters in marriage,[15] and subordinated his sons to
Shun's authority.[16] In this manner Shun became Yao's son-in-law and
assumed the role of eldest son. He is still opposed to Yao's sons in principle—as sage versus heir—but at the same time he was linked to them
as adopted brother and brother-in-law. He is thus a figure of mediation
between the positions of kin and non-kin rather than simply a figure in
opposition to the hereditary principle.

Shun's mediatory role with respect to the principle of heredity is
further confirmed by his relationship to his own father. Shun was the
son of the Blind Man, Gu Sou 瞽瞍. After Shun's mother died, his
father remarried and had a son, Xiang 象, by his second wife. Gu
Sou and Xiang, like Dan Zhu, are always described in negative terms
so bad that they could not even be transformed by the virtue of the
best of kings.[17] They hated Shun and tried several times to kill

---

15. *Shi ji, juan* 1, 21, 32 (after the *Shang shu*, "Yao dian"); *Mengzi* 9/1b (5A.1); *Lüshi chunqiu*
22/8b; *Chu ci* 3/19b ("Tian wen" in Hawkes, 94).

16. *Lüshi chunqiu* 22/8b mentions ten sons. *Shi ji, juan* 1, 32; and *Mengzi* 3/1b (2A.1) both
mention nine sons. See note 8 above.

17. *Xunzi* 12/15a; *Mengzi* 11/5b (6A.6).

him,[18] but Shun only responded with filial and brotherly behavior, so his devotion became proverbial.[19] The Blind Man, by attempting to kill his son, violated the father-son relationship in the most extreme manner possible, but Shun exceeded the requirement of right conduct, thus confirming his filial piety in spite of the violation.

In all likelihood, the function of this story was to abrogate Shun's further responsibility to Gu Sou and allow him to serve Yao in a son-like relationship. Shun's assumption of a filial role toward Yao implies a violation of his obligation to Gu Sou. The *Mengzi* points to the inherent contradiction in the ritual obligations of a nonhereditary successor who has a living (and especially a bad) father. One disciple questions Mencius about whether Gu Sou faced north and served Shun as a subject while Shun faced south as ruler, and quotes Confucius as stating that the state was endangered when Shun looked upon his father, presumably because he might recognize the evil Gu Sou as his father while he was ruler.[20] Another asks what Shun would have done if Gu Sou had committed a murder, for a son could not punish his father.[21] The paradox between Shun's position as ruler and son is inherent, and the conflict between obligation to kin and state is manifest.

The passages quoted above, which label Yao as "unfatherly," also call Shun "unfilial" (or "of a low father").[22] This is surprising, since Shun is ordinarily regarded as the essence of filial piety (*zhi xiao* 至孝), but the commentators refer us to "Tian wen":

> If Shun had a wife in his house, how could his father consider him unmarried?

---

18. *Shi ji, juan* 1, 32–33; *Mengzi* 9/3b–4b (5A.2).

19. See *Shi ji, juan* 1, 32; *Mengzi* 7/17a (4A.28), 9/3a–6a (5A.2, 3) for descriptions of Shun's fraternal love and filial devotion.

20. *Mengzi* 9/6b (5A.4).

21. *Mengzi* 13/14a–b (7A.35).

22. For 不孝 see *Zhuangzi* 9/38a (*pian* 29), *Lüshi chunqiu* 11/8a; for 以卑父之號 see *Lüshi chunqiu* 19/18b. The other two passages that refer to Yao's unfatherly behavior speak of Shun's banishment of his brother (放弟, *Huainanzi* 20/11b) and mother and brother (流母弟, *Zhuangzi* 9/41b, *pian* 29). These passages do not appear to be derived from one another. The surrounding text is in each case different, the list of figures is not identical, and the language used to describe them often differs even when the intent is the same.

If Yao did not tell Shun's family, how could his two daughters be married to him?[23]

舜閔在家父何以鰥堯不姚告二女何親 (*Chu ci* 3/19b)

Although the first question is unclear, it seems to mean that Shun's father refused to accept or was unaware of Shun's marriage to Yao's daughters. The second question, of Shun's ritual violation in marrying without his father's consent, is also raised in the *Mengzi*.[24] Whether or not this is the referent of the term *unfilial* in the other texts cannot be ascertained, but the epithet and question confirm my theory that Shun assumed a particularly close relationship to Yao in violation of his normal relationship to Gu Sou. The questions further imply that Shun's residence was matrilocal, another indication that his role was that of an adopted son to Yao.

Dan Zhu, then, is the legitimate heir of Yao according to the principle of heredity but unworthy because of his lack of virtue. The only other figure regularly contrasted in the texts with Shun is Xu You, a recluse who refused the rule when offered it by Yao. Xu You is a sage who was qualified to rule by right of virtue but of such pure integrity that he could not assume that which was not his hereditary due. As a sage, totally without hereditary right, he is the opposite of Dan Zhu, the unworthy heir. Shun is contrasted with Dan Zhu as sage rather than heir, but is also linked to him in the filial role which he assumed toward Yao. Similarly, he is contrasted with the perfect sage Xu You, who would not compromise his integrity, but also linked with him as a man of worth offered the throne by Yao.

Shun and Xu You: The Ruler and the Refuser

According to the *Shang shu* (*Yao dian*), Yao disapproved of his son Dan Zhu, so he offered the throne to the chief of the four mountains (*si yue*

---

23. After Hawkes, 51, lines 93–94. I have followed Hawkes in taking 閔 as a loan meaning woman or wife (see his Notes, 188–89), but I have not been able to find textual justification for his interpretation of 父 as 夫 and have retranslated the second part of line 93 accordingly. This makes better sense than Hawkes's "How could he be unmarried?" and accords with other accounts of the legend.

24. *Mengzi* 9/3a–b (5A.2).

四嶽). The chief of the four mountains felt unworthy and recommended Shun, whom Yao subsequently appointed. The chief of the four mountains does not appear outside of this text and the *Shi ji* account derived from it, but other texts include various other persons who refused rule when offered it by Yao, the most prominent of whom is Xu You.[25]

Shun and Xu You are similar in that they are both sages to whom Yao ceded the throne, but they differ in their responses to Yao's action. The texts use identical language to describe Yao's cession: Yao "yielded" (*rang* 讓) to Xu You,[26] "gave" (*yu* 與) the throne to him,[27] or "transmitted" (*chuan* 傳) it to him,[28] just as he did with Shun. However, Xu You's response contrasts with that of Shun. He "did not receive" the throne,[29] "fled from" Yao,[30] and "went to the foot of Mount Ji 箕, on the southern bank of the Ying River, fed himself by plowing and had no lust for the realm."[31]

The texts link the two men as "men of worth" (*xian* 賢) and the concept signified in both cases is "exalting men of worth" (*shang xian* 尚賢),[32] but they also contrast their actions:

> A man who accepted all-under-heaven and was yet a man of worth is Shun. . . . A man who refused it and was yet a man of worth is Xu You.

> 夫受而賢者舜也. . . . 夫辭而賢者許由也 (*Lüshi chunqiu* 18/14a)

---

25. Besides Xu You, Yao tried to cede the throne to Zi Zhou Zhi Fu 子州支父 (*Zhuangzi* 9/18a, *pian* 28) and Nie Xie 齧缺 (*Zhuangzi* 5/5a, *pian* 12).

26. *Shi ji, juan* 61, 2121; *Hanfeizi* 8/2b; *Zhuangzi* 1/9b, 9/18a; *Zhanguo ce* 7/23a, 9/12a; *Shenzi* 72 (translated in Thompson), or *Yiwen leiju* 藝文類聚 (Shanghai, 1965), 379.

27. *Zhuangzi* 9/11a (*pian* 26).

28. *Lüshi chunqiu* 18/14a.

29. 弗受 *Huainanzi* 12/17b; 不受 *Zhuangzi* 9/18a (*pian* 28).

30. For 逃 see *Zhuangzi* 8/37a (*pian* 24), 9/11a (*pian* 26); *Hanfeizi* 8/2b; for 不受恥之逃 隱 ("did not receive it, was ashamed, and fled into seclusion") see *Shi ji, juan* 61, 2121.

31. For 遂之箕山之下穎水之陽耕而食終身無經天下之色, see *Lüshi chunqiu* 22/9b. 經, glossed in this passage as 治 or 橫理, may be a copyist's mistake for 理. See *Lüshi chunqiu jiaoshi*, 129; and *Lüshi chunqiu jishi, juan* 22, 14b.

32. *Xunzi* 18/4b. See also *Lüshi chunqiu* 18/14a and *Zhuangzi* 9/46a (*pian* 29) for references to Xu You as a *xian*.

Shun and Xu You were both sages, although their conduct
was different.

舜許由異行而皆聖 (*Huainanzi* 20/7a)

Yao chose both men as sages, but Shun accepted the throne when Xu
You would not.

Xu You, in refusing (*ci* 辭) the throne offered to him by Yao, is
the first in a series of sages who either would not accept the throne or
refused to serve under a king who had violated propriety by depriving
the rightful heir of his throne. The most prominent of these are given
in this series:

Yao : Xu You :: Shun : Shan Juan::

Tang : Wu Guang and Bian Sui :: Wu Wang : Bo Yi and Shu
Qi.[33]

堯: 許由: : 舜: 善卷: :

湯: 務光, 卞隨: : 武王: 伯夷, 叔齊

Other figures that may be substituted in some positions will be identified by reference to the legend set as they occur. Indeed, the ease with
which the names and personalities of many of these may be substituted
for one another is evidence of their importance as signs rather than as
specific historical figures.

The precise legends about the figures of the different sets differ
according to the configuration of the set in which they appear. Bo Yi
伯夷 and Shu Qi 叔齊, for example, first refused to rule their own state
and then refused to serve Wu Wang of the Zhou Dynasty. In each set,
however, they are juxtaposed with the nonhereditary successors (and
with their founding ministers in the dynastic era) as examples of true
sages. The rulers and ministers are linked to them as men of worth but
are also shown to represent mediations of the principle of rule by virtue.

---

33. There is no single passage that includes all six of these refusers in parallel order.
However, they are all paralleled with the others (or their equivalent substitutes) in various combinations.

The refusers thus balance the rebel members of the ruling family, who are juxtaposed both with the nonhereditary successors in the predynastic era and with their heirs and regents in the dynastic era, and who function to point up the mediation of the hereditary principles (See Chart E).

The principle illustrated by the sages who refuse the position offered to them is "righteousness" or "integrity" (yi 義) as opposed to "benefit" or "profit" (li 利). *Xunzi* (19/4b), for example, states that Xu You and Shan Juan "valued integrity and thought little of profit" (*zhong yi qing li* 重義輕利). This implies that to accept the throne would be to think little of integrity and to value profit. Shun's position with respect to the sages is once again mediatory. He is a man of worth but compromises his integrity in accepting the throne and depriving the true heir of his right, just as he was the son-in-law and adopted son of Yao but not the true heir. On the side of virtue he is juxtaposed with Xu You, on the side of heredity with Dan Zhu. Both Xu You and Dan Zhu can be further contrasted with each other as figures of opposition representing the positions of non-kin and non-virtue respectively. Shun, however, is similar to both of them and mediates between the conflicting principles which they represent.

The refuser, in declining the throne, implies, covertly at least, greed on the part of the accepter. The *Hanfeizi* (7/5a) goes so far as to directly accuse Tang of deliberately trying to transfer the stigma of his greed (*tan* 貪) to Wu Guang 務光 by offering the throne to him after he had overthrown Jie.[34] In the predynastic era the rulers who accept an abdication offer the throne to someone else in order to moderate the violation of virtue and the stigma associated with having accepted the throne to which they had no right. The ritual value associated with declining the throne in this manner is evident in the rather cynical machinations of the Warring States period in which persuaders advised rulers to yield the throne to a minister in order to gain the reputation of a Yao declining the throne to a Shun, assuring them all the while that the minister would in turn refuse and thereby gain the reputation of a Xu You.[35] Shun, having accepted the throne from Yao, then offers the throne to Shan Juan and

---

34. See M. Granet, *Danses et légendes*, v. 1, 295–96.

35. *Zhanguo ce* 9/12a; *Shi ji, juan* 34, 1555–56 (鹿毛壽 advises 燕王 to abdicate to Zi Zhi 子之). *Zhanguo ce* 7/23a (the 犀首 advises the king to abdicate to Zhang Yi 張儀). *Lüshi chunqiu* 18/13b–14a (魏惠王 tries to abdicate to 惠子).

finally to Yu. These offers then affect the configuration of the next legend set in which the figures again appear.

When the cause of the transfer of rule is not Yao's abdication but Shun's use of force or the mandate of heaven, this affects the entire form of the legend set. In the transformation in which Shun forced Yao to give up the throne, he also used force to prevent Dan Zhu from obtaining the rule. The *Guben zhushu jinian* states that when Shun imprisoned Yao, he also blocked off Dan Zhu and prevented him from seeing his father.[36] Whether or not Yao abdicated to Xu You in this transformation of the legend cannot be definitely ascertained, but there are no references that simultaneously mention Shun's use of force on Yao and Yao's abdication to Xu You, though this may be due to chance.

In the transformation in which the transfer was caused by heaven and demonstrated by the loyalty of the people, Yao recommended Shun to heaven. After Yao's death Shun ruled for three years but then retired from the capital and yielded to Dan Zhu. The people, however, turned from Dan Zhu to Shun. In this transformation, neither Yao nor Shun caused the change of rule; so, Yao was not unfatherly nor Shun unfilial. Shun did not accept an abdication, so there is no structural function for a contrasting refuser, nor were any refusers recommended by Yao. Similarly, Shun did not yield to another refuser but to the son, Dan Zhu, so this contrast is also negated.

Shun as Founding Minister

The inclusion of force as a necessary aspect of nonhereditary transfers in the dynastic period results in a restructuring of the legend sets. This restructuring is characterized by a division into two periods, a period of overthrow in which the themes of virtue are mediated and a period of regency in which the themes of heredity are mediated. The refusers are contrasted to the new rulers and their ministers in the legends about the first period, the rebellious members of the ruling family to the regents in those about the second. In the predynastic era, Shun and Yu also play dual roles as king and minister. They first are discovered by Yao and Shun, are made ministers, then serve as regents, and finally succeed to the throne. In the dynastic era, however, the roles of minister and regent are

---

36. *Guben zhushu jinian jijiao dingbu*, 6.

separated from the succeeding king and assigned to distinct figures who serve the new king and his hereditary successor: minister and regent are combined in one in the Shang but are two separate figures in the Zhou.

The manner in which this transformation takes place can be seen by examining the parallels to Shun that occur in the texts. Aside from his role as successor to the throne, Shun is paralleled by two series of ministers, signs of the same type as Shun but representing more specific aspects of concepts encompassed in his role. The first series includes the "founding ministers," the men who aided the first kings of the Shang and Zhou to found their dynasties.[37] The second are the "regents" who ruled temporarily in place of the founding kings' hereditary successors.

I observed above that in order for the predynastic and dynastic transfers of rule to be made parallel, the recipient of the action must be omitted and contrast as well as similarity shown—e.g., Yao and Shun yielded, Tang and Wu contended. In the ruler : founding minister series, the dynastic founders are again paralleled with the preceding rulers of the predynastic era (see chart C):

Yao : Shun :: Shun : Yu :: Yu : Yi ::
Tang : Yi Yin :: Wen and Wu Wang : Taigong Wang
堯 : 舜 :: 舜 : 禹 :: 禹 : 益 ::
湯 : 伊尹 :: 文王, 武王 : 太公望

Certain other ministers are also paralleled with these figures. In the Shang Dynasty the convict-laborer Fu Yue 傅說, who was raised up by Wu Ding 武丁, the king who renewed the Shang Dynasty, is often included. There are also the ministers of the hegemons—Ning Qi 甯戚 and Guan Zhong 管仲, who served Huan Gong of Qi 齊桓公; Sunshu Ao 孫叔敖, who served Zhuang Wang of Chu 楚莊王; Boli Xi 百里奚, who served Mu Gong of Qin 秦穆公. Hong Yao 閎夭 and Tai Dian 泰顛 are also substituted for Taigong Wang in the Zhou Dynasty.

The most obvious feature of the founding minister is his initial poverty or obscurity before he meets the ruler or would-be ruler who

---

37. I discuss this theme at some length with particular reference to its meaning in the foundation of the Shang and Zhou Dynasties and the hegemonies in "The Identities of Taigong Wang in Zhou and Han Literature," see Appendix 2. The term *founding minister*, which I have borrowed from M. Granet's "minister-fondateur" (*Danses et légendes*), is perhaps more suitable to the dynastic era than to the appointment of Shun and Yu, but I have risked a small confusion for the sake of consistency.

raises him up and makes him minister. The *Shi ji* gives Shun an illustrious ancestry but states that the family had been commoners (*shu ren* 庶人) for seven generations before Shun met Yao.[38] Other texts refer to Shun as an "ordinary fellow" (*pi fu* 匹夫)[39] and a "wearer of hemp clothing" (*bu yi* 布衣).[40] His father Gu Sou tried to burn him to death while he repaired the granary and to bury him alive in a well, so they were evidently farmers, though wealthy enough to have a granary.

The ruler's discovery and appointment of his minister usually takes a standard form. The minister initially has a position of little status or engages in some menial occupation, the ruler "gets" (*de* 得) him (the place where he meets him is usually recorded), "raises him up" (*ju* 舉), yields the power of government to him, and thus brings all-under-heaven peace. The principle is the same as that involved in the cession of the throne, yielding to a man of worth, and the same terms may be used (*yu* 與, *shou* 授), though there is no offer of actual transfer of rule. The following passage from the *Mozi*, a text which stresses the concept of "exalting men of worth," provides an example:

> In former times, Shun plowed at Mount Li, potted on the bank of the [Yellow] River, and fished at Lei Marsh. Yao got him on the south side of Fu Marsh and raised him up as son-of-heaven. He gave the government of all-under-heaven over to him to rule its people. Yi Zhi [i.e., Yi Yin] was the personal servant of the woman of the You Shen family and was himself a kitchen worker. Tang got him and raised him up as prime minister. He gave the government of all-under-heaven over to him to rule its people. Fu Yue wore hemp clothing and a rope girdle; he worked as a forced laborer at Fu Yan; Wu Ding got him and raised him up as [one of the] Three Dukes. He gave the government of all-under-heaven over to him to rule its people.

> 古者舜耕歷山陶河瀕漁雷澤堯得之服澤之陽舉以為天子與接
> 天下之政治天下之民伊摯有莘氏女之私臣親為庖人湯得之舉

---

38. *Shi ji, juan* 1, 31.

39. *Mengzi* 9/11b (5A.6); *Huainanzi* 9/9a; *Hanfeizi* 13/7b, 17/1a.

40. *Lüshi chunqiu* 19/12b.

以為己相與接天下之政治天下之民傅說被褐帶索庸築乎傅巖
武丁得之舉以為三公與接天下之政治天下之民

(*Mozi* 2/9b–10a)

In this passage, Shun's plowing, potting, and fishing are paralleled with Yi Yin's position as a servant and cook and Fu Yue's as a forced laborer. In each case the ruler or would-be ruler raises up the minister from an initial position of very low social status. The ruler recognizes the worth of the sage and is willing to give him power because he is a sage, regardless of his social status. This act signifies the placing of merit over birth, and the extent of emphasis on the minister's low social status and the extent of emphasis on this concept are in correspondence.

This special power to recognize worth is characteristic of the true king and is one way in which the founder of a dynasty manifests his legitimacy. *Huainanzi*, for example, contrasts Yao with the ordinary man of little perception:

> To realize a man's worth before he has accomplished anything, this is the way in which Yao knew Shun. Knowing his worth when his merit was achieved and his affairs completed, this is how the men in the market knew Shun.

> 未有功而知其賢者堯之知舜攻成事立而知其賢者市人之知舜
> 也 (*Huainanzi* 13/15b)

Zhanguo ce is even more explicit in describing this instantaneous recognition of Shun by Yao and parallels it to Yi Yin meeting with Tang:

> Yao met Shun among the reeds.[41] They spread the mat on an embankment and took shade from a sheltering mulberry tree. Before the shadow had moved, he [Shun] had received the transmission of all-under-heaven. Yi Yin carried the *ding*-tripod and sacrificial stand on his back and went to Tang.

---

41. *Mao* 茅 refers to reeds or rushes as used in thatch; hence it usually signifies humble living conditions. The context here, however, indicates that the reeds must be growing rather than used as thatch.

Before his name and surname became well known, he
received [the position of one of] the Three Dukes.

堯見舜於草茅之中席隴畝而廕庇桑陰移而受天下傳伊尹負鼎
俎而干湯姓名未著而受三公 (*Zhanguo ce* 6/80a)

The corollary to the ruler's ability to recognize worth and his willingness to yield power to men of worth is his ability to attract sages
into his service. The two themes occur together, but they tend to be
stressed in inverse proportion. Certain texts stress the king's recognition
of virtue even in poverty. Others moderate the degree of poverty, making it simple obscurity but not necessarily low birth, and emphasize the
luster of the king's virtue, which attracts the sage into his service. The
most extreme emphasis on the king's virtue rather than the minister's
poverty occurs together with the denial of the king's ability to abdicate
and the attribution of the power of change to heaven or the people. In
this case, the founding minister is not a man of low birth but a recluse
waiting for a true king.

Shun's initially low position is moderated in transformations in
which his menial tasks are regarded as deliberate attempts to transform the people. For example, the *Hanfeizi* quotes the following passage
somewhat sarcastically to show the logical contradiction between the
Confucianist's belief in the perfect transforming virtue of Yao, and Shun's
ability to transform the people:

> The farmers of Mount Li encroached upon each other's
> boundaries. Shun went and plowed there, and at the end of
> the year the drainage ditches dividing the fields were cor-
> rected. The fishermen on the banks of the [Yellow] River dis-
> puted about the shoals. Shun went and fished there, and at
> the end of the year they deferred to the elders. The potters
> of the Eastern Yi made poor quality vessels. Shun went and
> potted there, and at the end of the year the vessels were made
> sturdy. Zhong Ni sighed and said, "Plowing, fishing and mak-
> ing pottery were not Shun's official business. However, that
> Shun went and did them was to rescue them from distress."[42]

---

42. A similar but shorter passage occurs in *Shi ji*, *juan* 1, 33–34.

歷山之農者侵畔舜往耕焉朞年甽畝正河濱之漁者爭坻舜往漁
焉朞年而讓長東夷之陶者器苦窳舜往陶焉朞年而器牢仲歎曰
耕漁與陶非舜官也而舜往為之者所以救敗也 (*Hanfeizi* 15/2a)

This transformation of the initial low social status of Shun evades the
issue of his low birth and emphasizes the attraction of his virtue. As
a man of transforming virtue, Shun is parallel to the first king of the
new dynasties rather than to their founding ministers. This parallel is
less prevalent in the texts than that between Shun and the founding
ministers, but it does occur:

Shun finished at Lei Marsh; Tang stopped at Bo.

舜漁於雷澤, 湯止于亳 (*Shi ji, juan* 129, 3266)

Bo, like Hao 亳 of the Zhou Dynasty, is a small fief from which the new
king was able to extend his power and gain control of all-under-heaven.
In the transformations in which the people go from one ruler to another,
the small amount of territory and small number of chariots ("one hundred li," "one hundred chariots") with which the new ruler began are
stressed to show the importance of the new king's virtue rather than
his military might. Since the founding minister is particularly associated
with the military strategy of a new king, his role is also deemphasized.

Elsewhere Shun's transforming virtue is given an added twist so
that it appears as a type of sedition:

Yao's worth was the most excellent of the six kings. Yet as soon
as Shun became his follower, he gathered everyone about
him, and Yao no longer had all-under-heaven.[43]

夫堯之賢六王之冠也舜一從而咸包而堯無天下矣 (*Hanfeizi* 16/3a)

Presumably, this interpretation is associated with the transformation in
which Shun forced the rule from Yao.

---

43. I have attempted to translate this passage according to the sense of the received text,
taking the graph 一 in its meaning of "as soon as." However, the text may be corrupt,
and Chen Qiyu has suggested 一徒而成邑 for 一徒而咸包 on the basis of the *Guanzi* 管子
(舜一徒而成邑二徒而成都三徒而成國); see *Hanfeizi jishi*, vol. 2, 853.

As stated above, Shun in his acceptance of the rule from Yao was contrasted with Xu You, whose integrity was too great to accept the rule which did not belong to him. Both men were regarded as worthies (*xian* 賢), but Shun's virtue was less because of his violation of the hereditary principle. Xu You, however, not only refused the rule but refused to serve Yao as chieftain of the nine states. Similarly, in the dynastic era, when a founding minister is distinguished from the new ruler and aids him to overthrow the previous dynasty, the sages Wu Guang and Bian Sui 卞隨 and Bo Yi and Shu Qi may be contrasted either to the new ruler or to the founding minister. In raising up a founding minister, as in breaching the hereditary line, the question is the supremacy of merit over birth, sage over heir, or commoner over nobility. Yao, in raising up Shun and passing the rule to Shun, establishes the precedent for this breach at the beginning of the Shang and Zhou Dynasties.

After Shun is raised up, he becomes Yao's minister. This might be regarded as the next stage in his life, encapsulated in the following forms:

| 1) Yao *you* Shun | 堯有舜 | Yao *had* Shun (as his minister) |
| *yong* | 用 | *used* |

| 2) Shun *xiang* Yao | 舜相堯 | Shun *was minister to* Yao |
| *shi* | 事 | *served* |

The change of grammatical subject from Yao to Shun may even symbolize the changing power position. However, when I attempted to establish parallel series for this stage in Shun's life, no definite or single series occurred. Instead, there were two series, one of the "founding ministers" and the other of the regents (discussed below). The former tends to be stated in the first form (Yao *verb* Shun), the latter in the second (Shun *verb* Yao). The former may imply a moderation of the founding minister theme and a lessening of the gap between ruler and minister (Yao *had* Shun) or it may simply refer to the time when the minister served his ruler after he had been raised up. The latter may also signify moderation and occur in cases in which the writer regards regency as ministership rather than actual rule because he rejects the concept that the ruler might abdicate.[44] The minister then replaces the son only after the death of the father. Thus, "Shun ruled in Yao's place" becomes "Shun served Yao."

---

44. As in the *Xunzi*, which speaks of having ministers but never of raising them up from poverty.

Alternatively, it may simply be a stage before the abdication in which the minister proves his ability.

Shun as Regent

The next parallel is between Shun and the "regents"—Yu, Yi, Yi Yin, and Zhougong Dan. The series of regents and rulers is as follows (see Chart D):

> Shun : Yao :: Yu : Shun :: Yi : Yu :: Yi Yin : Tai Jia :: Zhougong Dan : Cheng Wang

> 舜 : 堯 :: 禹 : 舜 :: 益 : 禹 :: 伊尹 : 太甲 :: 周公旦 : 成王

All of the regents in this series ruled during the lifetime of the recognized ruler and in place of him (the predynastic regents ruled during the lifetime of the former ruler, the dynastic regents during the lifetime of the hereditary successor).

I have based this series on the similarity of the relationships between regent and ruler and on the identity of language used to describe these relationships. Shun ruled in Yao's place in Yao's old age. Yu ruled in Shun's. Yi Yin ruled for Tai Jia when he had strayed from the principles established by his grandfather. Zhougong ruled for the young King Cheng. The term most commonly used to describe all of these relationships is *she* 攝 "to hold the reins of government," "act in the place of" (e.g., Shun *she* Yao).[45] *Dai* 代 "to replace," *bing* 屛 "to put aside," and *jia (wei)* 假（位）"to assume (the throne)"[46] are also used for Yi Yin and Zhougong Dan and their rulers.

---

45. *She* 攝, with a basic sense of "to take up," means, in this context, to take up the authority of government, but temporarily or in the place of another without being regarded as the true ruler. See, for example the *Zuo zhuan* (Yin 1) 1/2a: 不書既位攝也 "[The *Chunqiu*] does not record that [Lu Yingong] was on the throne because he [only] held the reins of government."

46. The term *jia* 假 is difficult to translate. It appears in these texts as a technical term for regency, often glossed as *she* 攝, and means that the regent "assumes" the throne but is not the true ruler. See *Shi ji, juan* 92, 2621: 大丈夫定諸侯即為真王耳何以假為. He is a false ruler, a "pretender," but need not claim legitimacy as the English term would imply. See also chapter 4, note 25.

The texts do not actually parallel the predynastic and dynastic regents. There are, in fact, few direct references to the predynastic rulers as regents. This may be because regency is implied in the statements concerning abdication. If Yao passed the rule to Shun during his life-time, Shun then, by definition, ruled in his stead. This interpretation is supported by a passage from the *Zhanguo ce* in which the transfers of rule to Shun and Yu are paralleled with the regency of Zhougong Dan:

> Yao transmitted [the throne] to Shun, Shun transmitted it to Yu, Cheng Wang of Zhou entrusted it to Zhougong Dan, and in subsequent generations they were called enlightened rulers.
>
> 堯傳舜舜傳禹周成王任周公旦而世世稱曰明主 (*Zhanguo ce* 4/14a)

The relations between Yao and Shun, Shun and Yu, and Cheng Wang and Zhougong are regarded as similar in this passage, although there is also a distinction in the verb used, presumably because Zhougong returned the rule to Cheng Wang.

Although all of the texts agree that these regents replaced their rulers, their intent in so doing is subject to various transformations. Most commonly, their purpose is to protect the ruler or the interests of the ruling house. This transformation is associated with voluntary transfer during the predynastic era. In this case, Shun ruled as regent at Yao's behest when the latter was old and weak:

> When Yao was old, he ordered Shun to act as son-of-heaven in his stead in order to observe the heaven's command.
>
> 於是帝堯老命舜攝行天子之致以觀天命 (*Shi ji, juan* 1, 25)

Similarly, Yi Yin ruled as regent for Tang's grandson Tai Jia when he had strayed from the principles established by his grandfather, but returned the rule to him when he had reformed, thus preserving the ancestral principles as well as the hereditary line. Zhougong Dan ruled as regent for the young King Cheng in order to consolidate the rule of Zhou and protect him against his uncles Guan and Cai, who rebelled in conjunction with the deposed Shang people.

Potentially, however, all regents can also be regarded as usurpers. The transformations in which Yi Yin and Zhougong are usurpers rather than regents will be discussed in detail with respect to Legend Sets 4 and 5. In Legend Set 1, when Shun forced Yao to abdicate, then he ruled as a usurper (*cuan wei* 篡位) during the period in which Yao was still alive rather than as regent. When the regents are considered usurpers, the rebellious members of the ruling family with whom they are juxtaposed in the texts protect rather than violate the hereditary interests of the ruling house.

The question of whether the regent was actually the ruler or simply acted in his place is also subject to transformation. This is discussed in the texts in terms of whether Shun "faced south" as ruler and Yao north as subject, and whether Zhougong faced south and Cheng Wang north.[47] The attitude that the regents could not have actually been rulers during the lifetime of the former ruler tends to occur in conjunction with transformations in which the people went from one ruler to the other.[48] In either case, however, the regent aids the hereditary ruler and subordinates himself to the ruler's cause, even though the regents of the dynastic era might expect to become rulers by the principles of predynastic transfer.

In summary, the transfer of rule from Yao to Shun is the first in a series of nonhereditary transfers. This transfer of rule, like that from Shun to Yu, is characterized by a gesture of ritual abdication and the possible absence of violence. Shun, in receiving the rule from Yao, is juxtaposed in the texts with two figures, the recluse Xu You, who refuses to accept the throne from Yao, and the son Dan Zhu, whom he replaces. Xu You represents pure virtue and is contrasted with Shun, who is willing to compromise his integrity in accepting the throne. Dan Zhu represents pure heredity and is contrasted with Shun, who breaches hereditary right. Shun's position is mediatory. He is a sage, like Xu You, and appointed as a man of worth. He is Yao's son-in-law and, like Dan Zhu, assumes a filial role toward him.

The nonhereditary transfers of the dynastic era, on the other hand, must include some element of force and never include a ritual abdication.

---

47. *Mengzi* 9/6b (5A.4); *Xunzi* 4/1b-2a; *Lüshi chunqiu* 22/8b.

48. Both the *Mengzi* and the *Xunzi*, in which these transformations are dominant, deny that the regents could have been rulers during their regencies (see note 44 above).

That change in the manner of nonhereditary transfer of rule in the dynastic period causes a restructuring of the legend sets into two periods, a
period of overthrow in which the themes of rule by virtue are mediated
and a period of regency in which the themes of rule by heredity are
mediated. There is a further thematic division: the theme of king and
founding minister characterizes the first period, of regent and ruler the
second. Both themes, however, also occur in the predynastic era. Shun
was a farmer before Yao met him and raised him up. He then served
him as regent in his old age. When Shun acted as founding minister,
Yao yielded to his merit; when Shun acted as regent, he in turn yielded
to Yao's position. In both roles, however, he is parallel in role with the
ministers of the dynastic era, and the combination of the two includes
a further mediation of the themes of rule by virtue and hereditary right.

3

Legend Sets 2 and 3:
Yú Shun to Xia Yu and the
Foundation of the Xia Dynasty

Shun to Yu, Yu to Qi:
From Nonhereditary to Hereditary Transfer

Shun succeeds Yao and then, in the same style of nonhereditary transfer, Yu succeeds Shun. At this point, however, the pattern changes, for Yu is succeeded not by his minister, the worthy Yi 益, but by his son Qi 啓. From Qi on, the rule is passed on hereditarily. Jie, the last king of the Xia Dynasty, is replaced by the first of the Shang, who begins a new hereditary cycle. The Xia, then, is the first hereditary dynasty in Chinese history and is followed by a standard pattern of hereditary continuation of political control interrupted at intervals by dynastic change or overthrow.

Because hereditary succession appears as a new phenomenon in Chinese history, a radical change in the legends and the introduction of new themes and explanations might be expected. However, such a change does not occur. Not only does the transfer from Shun to Yu include a transformation of the same themes that occurred in Legend Set 1, the transfer from Yu to Qi is also cast in the same mold. Although there are new motifs and transformations which establish a different mediation of the principles of heredity and virtue when the rule becomes primarily hereditary rather than by virtue, in both periods mediation is obtained by a complex set of legends related to and offsetting one another, and the structure remains the same.

When the rule was transferred from Yao to Shun, both rule by heredity and rule by virtue were manifest, and a balance was maintained

between them. The same themes occur in Legend Set 2, which surrounds a nonhereditary transfer, and in Legend Set 3, which surrounds
a hereditary one. Each set maintains the same balance. There is much
interplay between the sets, and occurrences in one set may influence the
form of the next. In this respect, it is important to remember that the
sets are artificial divisions in a continually evolving scheme. An equilibrium should be maintained at any one point, but this equilibrium may
include elements that also occur in another set. At any point of definition,
however, heredity and worth are never isolated phenomena but occur in
continual interplay, projected in various transformations into a pattern
of structural opposition and mediation.

Yu as a Culture Hero

After the rule passed from Shun to Yu, Yu became the founder of the
first hereditary dynasty, the Xia, but he is perhaps even better known
as a flood hero who dredged the rivers and drained the land, thereby
allowing human habitation of all-under-heaven and the development
of agriculture. This legend has been studied in detail by Henri Maspero
and others, with two primary analytic results: (1) The accounts of flood
legends in the extant texts are found to be an amalgam of several local
traditions, and those concerning Yu and his father Gun may have been
originally distinct; (2) Yu was originally a mythical figure of supernatural proportion, but he appears in the Zhou dynasty texts as a ruler in
euhemerized, or historicized, form.[1]

The results of these studies are not directly relevant to a structural
analysis since structural analysis presupposes that whatever their origins,
the myths or legends will be changed or combined according to the principles of an underlying structure. Structurally, Yu's identity as a culture
hero remains distinct from his identity as the founder of the Xia Dynasty.
As a culture hero Yu is frequently paralleled in the texts with Shen Nong
神農 and Hou Ji 后稷, the great heroes of agriculture. However, this

---

1. Maspero, especially 47–94; Eberhard, *Local Cultures*, 292, 349–62 (Chain 33); Eberhard,
Lokalkulutren, Chains 29, 34. In the *Gu shi bian* 古史辨 (Peking and Shanghai, 1926–1941),
v. 1, 105–50, Gu Jiegang 顧頡剛 demonstrates that although Yu appears in Western Zhou
texts as a heavenly spirit (in which Gu includes Yu's roles as a culture hero and as an animal
or bear spirit), he does not appear as a king until the Eastern Zhou, and the references to
abdication do not appear in texts before the Warring States period.

parallel does not occur in passages that mention succession from Shun to Yu or Yu to Qi, nor do Shen Nong and Hou Ji occur in discussions of secession in other periods. The only other person within the succession scheme who made a great contribution to the cultural development of mankind is Yu's minister Yi, who aided him in preparing the land for agriculture by burning the forests and clearing the land, but this happened during the reign of Yao or Shun and does not appear as a factor in the succession from Yu to Yi or to his son Qi. This theme thus remains extraneous to the problem of succession and affects it structurally only to the extent that it implies certain limitations and peculiarities on the characterization of Yu as founding minister.

Legend Set 2: From Shun to Yu

Shun to Yu: The Transfer of Rule

The transfer of rule from Shun to Yu is the second transfer of rule during the period under consideration and forms the core of the second legend set. In Legend Set 1, Shun was juxtaposed with both Yao's son Dan Zhu and the sage Xu You. His violation of the hereditary principle was mediated by his filial role as Yao's son-in-law and adopted son, his violation of virtue in accepting the throne, which was not rightfully his, and by his offering the throne to Shan Juan 善卷 (綣) and other refusers after he had accepted the rule from Yao. Shan Juan and the other refusers then reappear as part of Legend Set 2, a phenomenon that creates a bias toward nonhereditary transfer in this legend set.

Yu, in accepting the rule from Shun, is also juxtaposed with the sage Shan Juan and the other refusers to whom Shun offered the rule, and to Shun's son Shang Jun. The basic form of the set is the same as that of Legend Set 1:

Shan Juan
|
Shun → Yu
|
Shang Jun

However, the manner in which the themes of heredity and virtue are mediated differs from that of Legend Set 1. Although Yu declined the throne in favor of other ministers, that was before he was willing to accept it himself. The refusal mediates Yu's breach of virtue, but his role as rule-refuser is not projected into the next legend set because of his ultimate acceptance of the throne. Furthermore, he passed the rule to his own son rather than to his minister. This mediates Yu's breach of heredity but creates the bias toward hereditary transfer in Legend Set 3.

The transfer of rule from Shun to Yu follows the basic form established in Legend Set 1. Like the transfer from Yao to Shun, it is usually considered voluntary and devoid of violence but may undergo transformations ranging from active and willing abdication by Shun to forceful overthrow by Yu. Most of the same verbs are used here as in the previous legend set—*shou* 授, *chuan* 傳, *rang* 讓, and *shan* (*wei*) 禪 (位)—all indicating various forms of cession by Shun; *bi* 偪, indicating active force by Yu; and *jian* 薦, indicating commendation or presentation by the son-of-heaven and the transfer directed by heaven.

The two transfers are frequently paralleled. Whenever this occurs, the verb is the same in both sequences:[2]

Yao bestowed [the throne] on Shun; Shun bestowed [it] on Yu.

堯授舜舜授禹 (*Lüshi chunqiu* 20/4a)

After Yao abdicated his position, Shun became king; after Shun abdicated his position, Yu became king.

堯禪位後為舜王之舜禪位後為禹王之 (*Guben zhushu jinian jijiao dingbu*, 7)

Shun forced Yao; Yu forced Shun.

舜偪堯禹偪舜 (*Hanfeizi* 17/8b)

This parallelism indicates that a transformation in either legend set must be repeated in the other set. If a writer regards Yao as abdicating to Shun, he will also regard Shun as abdicating to Yu. If he regards Yu

---

2. One possible exception to this rule is *Xunzi* 18/4b–5a which first states 堯讓賢以為民 and then, several times later, 舜授禹以天下. However, the parallel is not direct, and the passage does not seem to be coherent.

as forcing the throne from Shun, he will also regard Shun as forcing the rule from Yao.

Yu and Shan Juan: The Ruler and the Refuser

Before yielding the throne to Yu, Shun ceded it (*rang* 讓) to several sages who refused and retired from the world or committed suicide in response. The most prominent of these is Shan Juan, a "gentleman who had achieved the Way"[3] but lived simply, farming the land and following the seasons in their natural order. When offered the throne by Shun, he retired to the mountains and was never seen again.[4] Shun also offered the throne to the "Farmer of the Stone Door,"[5] the "Northerner Wu Ze,"[6] and Zi Zhou Zhi Bo,[7] none of whom would accept.

Yu's acceptance of the throne from Shun contrasts with the refusal of Shan Juan and the other sages. The texts do not actually juxtapose Yu and Shan Juan as they did Shun and Xu You. However, Yu and the other refusers are again linked as the recipients of the ruler's cession (*rang*) and implicitly juxtaposed through their differing responses. Shan Juan's refusal is also paralleled in the texts with that of Xu You.[8] There is only one passage concerning the figures of this legend set in which a sage's refusal is juxtaposed with an acceptance. In the *Zhuangzi* (9/29a), the northerner Wu Ze responded with contempt to Shun's offer of the throne:

> How strange a man is this ruler. When he dwelt among the fields, he loitered about Yao's gate, but that is not all. He also wishes to taint me with his disgraceful actions.

異哉后之為人也居於畎畝之中而遊堯之門不若是而已又欲以
其辱行漫我

---

3. *Lüshi chunqiu* 15/8b.

4. *Zhuangzi* 9/18b (*pian* 28).

5. For 石戶之農 see *Zhuangzi* 9/19a (*pian* 28).

6. For 北人無擇 see *Zhuangzi* 9/29a (*pian* 28).

7. For 子州支伯 see *Zhuangzi* 9/18b (*pian* 28).

8. *Huainanzi* 11/13b; *Zhuangzi* 9/46a (*pian* 29); *Xunzi* 18/4b; *Shenzi*, 72 (*Yin wen lei ju*, 379).

Wu Ze compares himself in this passage to Shun rather than to Yu, since Yu had yet to be offered or to accept the throne, but the contrast with Yu is implicit since Yu subsequently sullies himself by doing precisely what Wu Ze has refused, accepting the throne from Shun.

Both Shun and Yu, who obtained the rule nonhereditarily, are contrasted, therefore, to true sages whose virtue is too great to accept the throne, which does not belong to them. In Legend Set 1 Shun was able to partially allay his disgrace and mediate the opposition by subsequently yielding the throne to other men of worth. They are then contrasted in Legend Set 2 with Yu. Yu, however, is the founder of a hereditary dynasty, and the rule goes from him to his son Qi rather than to a member of another family. This implies a restructuring in Legend Set 3 which does not contain a rule-refuser in contrast to a rule-accepter. Nevertheless, the opposition must still be mediated. This mediation is performed not by Yu's declining the throne after accepting it but by his first giving way to Shun's other ministers—Hou Ji, Xie 契, and Gao Yao 皋陶—before he is willing to accept the rule.[9] In this manner the mediation between ruler and refuser takes place within the same legend set and a similar bias toward nonhereditary transfer in Legend Set 3 is avoided.

Yu and Shang Jun: The Sage and the Heir

At the other end of the virtue/heredity axis, Yu is contrasted to Shang Jun or to the nine sons of Shun, just as Shun was contrasted to Dan Zhu or the ten sons of Yao. *Lüshi chunqiu* (1/11b), for example, follows the statement "Yao had ten sons; he did not give the throne to his sons but bestowed it on Shun" with its parallel "Shun had nine sons; he did not give the throne to his sons, but bestowed it on Yu." Similarly, in the *Mengzi* where the determination is made by heaven and manifested in the loyalty of the people, the people turn from Shun's son to Yu after a period of three years' mourning, just as they had turned earlier from Dan Zhu to Shun.[10]

In Legend Set 1, this contrast between heir and sage was mediated by Shun's role as Yao's son-in-law and adopted son. Here, although Yu's breach of ritual with respect to his own father is even more emphatic

---

9. *Shi ji, juan* 1, 38, *juan* 2, 50. (The same story occurs in the *Shang shu,* "Yao dian" (1/9b), but there it is the job of controlling the waters that Yu declines, not the throne.

10. *Mengzi* 9/11a (5A.6).

than Shun's breach with respect to Gu Sou, his violation of the hereditary principle is not mediated by his relation to Shun but by his subsequently passing the rule to his own son. Whereas in the first legend
set the refuser-ruler opposition was mediated by projecting a symbol of
virtue into the next legend set and the sage-heir opposition was mediated within the same set, here the sage-heir opposition is mediated by
the projection of a symbol of heredity into the next legend set and the
refuser-ruler opposition is mediated within the same set.

Yu's father was Gun. Gun, like Yu, was a flood hero and may have
been a local cult figure. Indeed, more than one local mythological tradition seems to underlie the euhemerized figure of the traditional history.[11]
My concern here, however, is the meaning of the manner in which the
two figures have been combined in the central tradition rather than the
origins of the legends or even their precise details. The legends vary, but
Gun always appears as a symbol of heredity and functions to point up
the breach of heredity by Shun and Yu.

All texts agree that Gun was Yu's father, that he was himself the
son of Zhuan Xu 顓頊 (one of the five predynastic rulers in the historical
scheme found in the *Shi ji*), and that he was put to death at Yu Mountain. Beyond this, though there is considerable variation, two principal
traditions can be recognized. The first and most generally accepted is
that Gun was appointed by Yao to allay the flood. He built dams and
dikes but could not control the water. Therefore, when Shun became
Yao's minister, he began his tasks by executing Gun. The *Shi ji* states:

> Yao sought someone who could control the water. The court
> officials and the chiefs of the four mountains all said that Gun
> could do it. Yao said, "Gun's character is such that he rejects
> orders and destroys his tribe. He is not the right person."
> [The chiefs of the] four mountains said, "In any case, there
> has not yet been anyone more worthy than Gun. We desire
> your lord to try him." Thereupon Yao heeded the [chiefs of
> the] four mountains and employed Gun to control the water.
> After nine years the water did not desist and his task was
> not fulfilled. Thereupon Di 帝 ("Thearch") Yao again sought
> someone and further obtained Shun. Shun was promoted in
> his employment, took the reins of government in hand to act

---

11. Maspero, 72–73.

as thearch [in Yao's stead], and conducted a tow of inspection. On his travels he saw that Gun's regulation of the water was without good results, so he had Gun put to death at Feather Mountain. Everyone under heaven considered Shun's punishment correct.

堯求能治水者，群臣四嶽皆曰鯀可。堯曰：「鯀為人負命毀族，不可。」四嶽曰：「等之未有賢於鯀者願帝試之。」於是堯聽四嶽，用鯀治水。九年而水不息，功用不成，於是帝堯乃求人，更得舜。舜登用，攝行天子之政，巡狩。行視鯀之治水無狀，乃殛鯀於羽山以死。天下皆以舜之誅為是。[12]

Sima Qian's statement that everyone considered the punishment correct immediately opens it to suspicion since, if this were the case in Sima Qian's time, there would be no need to make the assertion. There is also much evidence that the contrary was true. In the "Li sao," Gun is held up as an example of a misunderstood but upright minister who was punished for his integrity:

"Gun in his stubbornness took no thought for his life,and perished, as a result, upon the moor of Yu. Why be so lofty with your passion for purity?"

曰鯀婞直以亡身兮。終然殀乎羽之野。汝何博謇而好脩兮。[13]

Here Gun is an example of a pure man, unjustly punished, with whom the author would compare himself.

The "Tian wen" challenges the propriety of the punishment even more directly:

If Gun were not fit to allay the flood, why was he given this charge? All said, "Never fear! Try him out and see if he can do it." When the bird-turtles linked together, how did Gun follow their sign? And if he accomplished work according to his will, why did the High Lord punish him? Long he lay cast off on Yu Shan. Why did he not rot for three years?

---

12. *Shi ji, juan* 2, 50 (this account is based in part on *Shang shu, Hong fan*).

13. Translated in Hawkes, 26, lines 66–68. Chinese text from *Chu ci tongshi, juan* 1, 10).

不任汩鴻。師何以尚之。僉曰何憂。何不課而行之。鴟龜曳
銜。鯀何聽焉。順欲成功。帝何刑焉。永遏在羽山。夫何三
年不施。[14]

Three problems are raised here. First, if Yao knew that Gun would
be unsuccessful, he should not have appointed him and it seems wrong
to have punished him. This is particularly true when we remember that
Shun was also appointed to allay the flood but was unsuccessful.[15] Second, Gun made a sincere attempt to allay the flood and accomplished
a plan of building dikes and dams successfully even though the flood
was not allayed until Yu drained the floodwaters out through the rivers
and built the canals.[16] That he followed a pattern indicated to him by
bird-turtles implies that the plan was heaven-directed. Third, there are
numerous traditions about Gun's death, but in all of them Gun does not
really die despite his having been "put to death." The various traditions
that his body did not putrefy and that it turned into an animal—dragon,
turtle, or bear, as the case may be—all indicate that he was considered
a wronged spirit.[17]

If Shun acted improperly in executing Gun, Yu's willingness to serve
his father's killer was even more improper. A filial relationship is implied
in the very act of succession. In the case of Shun this was evident in the
contradictions that arose between his responsibilities toward his father
as son and as ruler and led to speculation in the texts about whether
his father could have served him as a subject (face north while he faced
south) and about what he would have done if his father had committed
a crime while he was ruler. Shun mediated the conflict, abrogating his

---

14. Translated in Hawkes, 48, lines 23–29. Chinese text from *Chu ci tongshi, juan* 3, 49.

15. In both the *Shang shu*, "Yao dian" (1/3b–4b) and the passage from the *Shi ji* quoted
above (*juan* 2, 50), Yao appointed Shun because Gun was not able to allay the flood.

16. The *Guo yu* (Lu, *shang*) 4/8a states that "Gun was put to death through he dammed
up the waters." The affirmative value of Gun's work may be seen in the parallel with Shun
"dying in the wilds though he diligently pursued the people's affairs" (舜勤民事而野死鯀
鄣水而殛死). In later tradition, Gun stole a "swelling mould" from Yao. He was successful
in allaying the flood, but was punished by Yao for his disobedience. *Guo yu* 14/14b (*Jin*
8) refers to Gun's violation of Yao's orders, but this may be a reference to Gun's rebellion
discussed below.

17. Karlgren, "Legends and Cults," 252, notes this folk theme in the legend that Yu turned
into an animal spirit.

responsibilities to his own father, by his extraordinary piety when faced with his father's attempts to kill him and by his assuming a filial attitude toward Yao as his son-in-law and adopted son before becoming his successor. He could not be the true heir, but his mediatory position in this context was balanced by his mediatory role with respect to the true sages.

Yu, however, became Shun's successor without having mediated the conflict implied by his violation of the hereditary principle. Not only did he not seek revenge for his father's death, he assumed a filial role toward his father's killer. This question is not discussed at any length in the texts, but they do occasionally suggest a conflict of interest. The *Zuo zhuan* quotes an assertion that "Yu did not take [ritual] precedence over Gun."[18] In another passage, the contradiction of "Yu being raised up though Gun was put to death" is explained in terms of Yu's unselfishness and concern for the preservation of the tutelary temple.[19] The reference to the tutelary temple is an attempt to justify Yu's unfilial behavior in terms of a greater filial design, but it also betrays the inherent impropriety of his act of serving Yu. The *Lüshi chunqiu* (19/18a) states more rudely that "Yu coveted the throne" (禹貪位).

Gun's importance as a symbol of heredity is even more apparent in the legends in which he was executed for remonstrating against the transfer of rule from Yao to Shun rather than for his failure to allay the flood. This tradition was evident in the passage from *Hanfeizi* (13/7b–8a) quoted above in which Gun was killed for remonstrating with Yao for bestowing the throne upon a commoner. *Lüshi Chunqiu* includes a variant of the same story:

> Yao ceded all-under-heaven to Shun. Gun was a feudal lord. He was angry with Yao and said, "He who obtains the way of heaven becomes thearch; he who obtains the way of earth becomes [one of the] three dukes. Now I have obtained the way of earth, but you do not make me [one of the] three dukes." He considered that Yao had breached order and wanted to obtain [a position as one of the] three dukes. He incited his wild beasts and wished to make a disturbance with them. He ranged the horns of the animals and made a city wall with them. He raised their tails and made them banners. He did

---

18. 禹不先鯀. *Chunqiu jingzhuan jijie*, Zuo 8/4b (Wen gong 2).

19. 鯀殛而禹興. *Chunqiu jingzhuan jijie*, Zuo 16/13b (Xiang gong 21).

not come when summoned and roamed the fields causing the thearch distress. Thereupon Shun had him put to death at Feather Mountain and cut up with a knife from Wu. Yu did not dare to bear a grievance [against Shun] but on the contrary served him.

堯以天下讓舜鯀為諸侯怒於堯曰得天之道者為帝得地之道者
為三公今我得地之道而不以我為三公以堯為失論欲得三公怒
甚猛獸欲以為亂比獸之角能以為城舉其尾能以為旌召之不來
仿佯於野以患帝舜於是殛之於羽山副之以吳刀禹不敢怨而反
事之[20] (*Lüshi chunqiu* 20/14–15a)

This differs from the *Hanfeizi* account in that Gun remonstrates on his own account rather than against the appointment of Shun and in that Shun, rather than Yao, executes Gun. Nevertheless, the opposition to Shun's succession to the throne is clear: Gun remonstrated at the time of the transfer and refused to recognize the ruler's authority. The author's statement that Yu did not dare to bear a grudge against Shun is further evidence that a grudge against his father's killer would have been expected. For Yu to serve Shun as minister and regent and then to accept the throne from him was surely a violation of his filial obligation to Gun.

Yu, then, violated the principle of heredity in becoming Shun's successor. As a man of worth, he is juxtaposed with Shang Jun, Shun's eldest son and legitimate heir, and his violation of hereditary right is emphasized by the legends concerning his own father Gun. No mediation occurs before Yu accepts the throne from Shun. Instead, the principle of heredity is confirmed and the opposition mediated by the subsequent transfer of rule from the worthy Yu to his son Qi. This projects a bias toward the claims of heredity into the next legend set, but before examining this set, let us examine the extent to which Yu is parallel to Shun as a founding minister and regent.

Yu as Founding Minister

Yu is not the typical founding minister as exemplified by Shun, Yi Yin, and Taigong Wang, but some of the legends concerning him signify the

---

20. *Lüshi chunqiu jiaoshi*, 109 (1.3), gives 其 for 甚 on the basis of "old editions" and *Lun heng* 2/16a. According to *Lüshi chunqiu jiaoshi*, 110 (1.3), 能 should be read as 而.

same concepts. The most important fact about the founding minister is that he is appointed because of his worth and in spite of his birth. Shun was the son of Gu Sou who was both a commoner and a bad person, but Yao still appointed him. Yu's father Gun was of noble birth, but he was also considered a bad person and disgraced his family by his execution. Shun nevertheless appointed Yu as his minister and made him his heir. In the *Zuo zhuan* this contrast is evident when the question of whether the son of a criminal may be appointed is discussed and the precedent of Yu cited:[21]

> With regard to Shun's punishments, he put Gun to death; as to his appointments, he raised up Yu.

> 舜之罪也殛鯀其舉也興禹

So it is clear that Shun appointed Yu because of his worth and despite his parentage.

The low position of the minister before discovery by the ruler or would-be ruler is usually dramatized by the low-status work the minister was performing when he met the ruler. This precise theme does not occur in the case of Yu. Instead, the texts stress the great physical toil and hardship that Yu underwent in dredging the rivers and allaying the flood. Yu devoted himself so much to his task that he refused to enter his own door when he happened to pass by and heard his son crying.[22] By this means he showed that his humility was genuine and that his concern for all-under-heaven was more important to him than family or kin. Like the other founding ministers, his function in this role is to emphasize merit over heredity. In the transformation in which Shun goes out to farm, to make pottery, and to fish in a deliberate attempt to transform the people, Shun's work is paralleled with Yu's labor in allaying the floods.[23]

---

21. *Chunqiu jingzhuan jijie, Zuo* 7/15a (Xi gong 33). The formula 鯀殛而禹與 also appears in *Zuo* 16/13b (Xiang gong 21).

22. The story that Yu passed his door three times without entering is well developed in later sources. In the *Shang shu, Yi ji* (2/11b–12a) Yu states that although he heard his son crying, he did not treat him as a son (予弗子); in the *Shi ji, juan* 2, 80, Yu similarly states that he fathered Qi but, because of his toils allaying the flood, did not treat him as a son (予不子).

23. *Lüshi chunqiu* 22/8b–9a.

Yu as Regent

The function of the founding minister theme is to stress worth rather than heredity. Counter to this is the regency in which the right of heritage is stressed. Yu serves Shun as regent, protecting him in his old age just as Shun did Yao. The *Shi ji* states that Yu was regent for seventeen years before Shun died,[24] and the *Mengzi* that he was presented to heaven seventeen years before Shun's death.[25] Elsewhere there are the references to abdication discussed above and mention of Shun's dying charge,[26] which may imply a period of regency before Shun's death. Nevertheless, neither Yu's role as a founding minister nor his role as a regent is generally stressed.

Legend Set 3: The Foundation of the Xia Dynasty

Yu to Yi: Appointment by Virtue

The rule passes from Yao to Shun and from Shun to Yu, but then it passes not to Yu's minister Yi but to his son Qi. Although Yu is technically the founder of the Xia Dynasty, Qi often is considered the founder,[27] a transfer that includes all of the themes included in the two previous legend sets, not simply those concerned with virtue or with heredity. As stated above, a bias toward heredity in Legend Set 3 was created in the previous set when Yu's violation of heredity in taking the rule from Shun was mediated by Yu's transfer of rule to his son Qi. This hereditary transfer, however, takes place only after an initial period of false or abortive transfer to Yi, which includes the themes of rule by virtue rather than heredity.

Although the rule finally goes to Qi, the texts describe a prior transfer from Yu to Yi in identical terms with the transfers from Yao to Shun and Shun to Yu. In transformations in which Yao passed the throne voluntarily to Shun, the formula is, "Yu bestowed the throne on Yi" (Yu

---

24. *Shi ji, juan* 1, 44.

25. *Mengzi* 9/11a (5A.6).

26. *Lun yu* 10/19a (20.1).

27. See Eberhard, *Local Cultures*, 351–52.

shou Yi).[28] In the *Guben zhushu jinian*, in which Shun imprisoned Yao and took the rule from him, the text states, "Yi transgressed upon Qi's position" (Yi *gan* Qi *wei*);[29] and in the *Mengzi*, where the determination was made by heaven after the ruler had made a recommendation, the text also states that Yu commended Yi to heaven (Yu *jian* Yi *yu tian*).[30]

Yi is parallel to Yu and Shun of the two previous legend sets not only as the recipient of the rule but also as Yu's founding minister and regent, although these roles are not often discussed in the texts. Yi's position as founding minister is evident in a passage from the *Mozi* (3/3a–b) which states that "Yu raised Yi up from the midst of obscurity" (禹舉益 於陰方之中). The line parallels Yao raising up Shun from the fields, Tang raising up Yi Yin from the kitchen, and Wen Wang raising up Hong Yao 閎夭 and Tai Dian 泰顛 from among the hunting and fishing nets, so Yi's role was also that of a founding minister. Yi's role as regent is never directly described, but it is implied in the transformation in the *Mengzi* in which Yi is presented by Yu to heaven seven years before his death. The same passage goes on to parallel him with Yi Yin and Zhougong, regents who did not achieve the rule though their virtue was such that they might expect it according to the principles of the transfer from Yao to Shun or Shun to Yu.[31]

Yi and Bocheng Zigao: The Minister and the Refuser

When Yu accepted the rule from Shun in the previous legend set, he did not subsequently offer the rule to another man of worth but mediated his violation of virtue in accepting a throne which did not belong to him by declining Shun's abdication three times before he accepted. However, Shun did not consider the ministers to whom Yu yielded worthy of the throne and continued to abdicate to Yu. In Legend Set 3, Yi does not actually become ruler, so there is no structural function for a rule-refuser as contrasted to a rule-accepter. However, Yi did serve Yu as minister, and there is a minister-refuser, Bocheng Zigao 伯成子高, whose behavior contrasts with that of Yi in accepting appointment from Yu. The *Zhuangzi* states:

---

28. For 禹授益 see *Zhanguo ce* 9/12b; *Mozi* 2/3b; *Shi ji, juan* 2, 83.

29. For 益干啓位 see *Guben zhushu jinian jixiao dingbu*, 9.

30. For 禹薦益於天 *see* Mengzi 9/11a (5A.6).

31. *Mengzi* 9/12a (5A.6).

When Yao controlled all-under-heaven, Bocheng Zigao was enfeoffed as a feudal lord. Yao bestowed [the throne] on Shun and Shun bestowed it on Yu. Bocheng Zigao excused himself from being a feudal lord and tilled [the land]. Yu went to see him. He was just then tilling land outside the city. Yu hurried towards him, stood in a humble manner, and asked, "Formerly when Yao controlled all-under-heaven, you were enfeoffed as a feudal lord. Yao bestowed the throne on Shun. Shun bestowed it on me. Now you excuse yourself [from serving] as a feudal lord and till the land. May I presume to ask the reason?" Zigao said, "Formerly when Yao controlled all-under-heaven, he did not reward and the people were encouraged; he did not punish and the people were deterred. Now, though you reward and punish, the people are still not humane. From this [time] on, virtue will decline."[32]

堯治天下伯成子高立為諸侯堯授舜舜授禹伯成子高辭為諸侯
而耕禹往見之則耕在野禹趨就下風立而問焉曰昔堯治天下吾
子立為諸侯堯授舜舜授予而吾子辭為諸侯而耕敢問其故何也
子高曰昔堯治天下不賞而民勸不罰而民畏今子賞罰而民不仁
德自此衰 (*Zhuangzi* 5/7b–8a)

Bocheng Zigao appears in this passage as a member of the old aristocracy. He objects to a system of reward and punishment and will not violate his principles by serving in a system that would allow appointment according to worth in violation of hereditary right. In order to maintain his purity and personal virtue, he declines office. Bocheng Zigao is never directly juxtaposed with Yi. Yi, however, is raised up by Yu and made his founding minister. He is willing to serve Yu and to accept his appointment. As such, he accepts office when Bocheng Zigao refuses to sully himself, and his acceptance may be implicitly contrasted with Zigao's superior virtue. More generally, Bocheng Zigao may be contrasted with two figures, Yu acting in concert with Yi—that is, to the system of government in which ministers are appointed and dismissed, rewards are offered, and punishments are imposed.

---

32. A similar passage occurs in *Lüshi chunqiu* 20/4a–b.

Yi to Qi: From Virtue to Heredity

With respect to Yu's relationship to Yi, Legend Set 3 follows the pattern established in Legend Sets 1 and 2 without deviation. The only indication of a change from rule by worth to rule by heredity lies in the replacement of a rule-refuser by a minister-refuser. According to the established pattern, Yi should now become ruler and Qi should be juxtaposed with him as the legitimate son whose hereditary right has been violated. Qi, however, takes the rule from Yi and is juxtaposed in turn with his rebellious son, or sons—the Wu Guan. Thus, the graph:

The transfer of rule from Yu to Yi follows the pattern of nonhereditary transfer established in the first two legend sets and includes a mediation of the principle of rule by virtue. The transfer from Yi to Qi follows that of dynastic continuation which will be established in Legend Sets 4 and 5 and includes a mediation of the principles of hereditary right.

The manner in which rule passes from Yi to Qi undergoes a set of transformations similar to those in which the first rulers of the Shang and Zhou take the rule from the last kings of Xia and Shang. These will be discussed in greater detail with respect to those sets, but there are three general categories. The new ruler may be regarded as a subject who attacks the legitimate ruler and usurps his position, he may be regarded as the legitimate ruler by virtue who chastises a subject, or he may be the recipient of heaven's mandate. These transformations occur in direct parallel to the transformations of the transfer from Yu to Yi, so the principle of worth is always opposed by that of heredity, and structural balance is maintained.

If a writer regards the transfer from Yu to Yi as a voluntary bestowal parallel to the "abdications" of Yao and Shun, then the rule should rightfully have gone to Yi, and Qi is regarded as a usurper. This interpretation is clearly described in the *Zhanguo ce*:

Yu bestowed the rule on Yi and made Qi's men his officers. When he was old, he considered Qi unsuitable to entrust with all-under-heaven and transmitted the rule upon Yi. Qi and his party of friends attacked Yi and snatched [the rule] from him.

禹授益而以啓人為吏及老而以啓為不足任天下傳之益也啓與友黨攻益而奪之 (*Zhanguo ce* 9/12b)

In a similar vein, "Tian wen" states that "Qi supplanted Yi and made himself lord."[33]

If, however, the recipients of the rule in the first two legend sets are regarded as usurpers, and if Yi tried to force the rule from Qi, then Qi acts as a ruler chastising a subject. This transformation occurs in the *Guben zhushu jinian*, which states that Shun imprisoned Yao and took the rule from him. Similarly, "Yi transgressed upon Qi's position and Qi killed Yi."[34]

In the *Mengzi*, heaven transfers the mandate and expresses its transfer in shifts in the loyalties of the people. This is true both in pre-dynastic and the dynastic times, though in the earlier period the ruler must present his successor to heaven, and in the later be so evil that he deserves punishment. In this case, Yi is presented to heaven by Yu, but the people go to Qi. Thus, just as Yi could be considered legitimate ruler (as recipient of an abdication), usurper, or subject presented to heaven, so Qi may be considered usurper, legitimate heir, or recipient of heaven's mandate.

When Mencius was asked why Yu was succeeded by his son rather than by a sage, he gave two reasons. The first was that Yi had only assisted Yu for a few years, and so "the people had not enjoyed his bounty for a long period of time." The second was that Qi was a man of worth, capable, and "able to follow in the footsteps of Yu."[35] The first argument is obviously weak and contradicts Mencius's own philosophy that the action of the people is only a manifestation of heaven's will, not a conscious force in itself. If heaven mandated Yi, then the people should have gone to him. As demonstrated above, the relationship between Yu

---

33. 啓代益作后. Hawkes, trans., p. 49, line 61 (*Chu ci* 3/14a).

34. For 益干啓位, 啓殺之, see *Guben zhushu jinian jijiao dingbu*, 9.

35. . . . . . . 啟賢能敬承繼禹之道. Lau, trans., 145 (*Mengzi* 9/11b, 5A.6). See also *Shi ji*, *juan* 2, 83.

and Yi is always described in identical terms with that between Yao and Shun or Shun and Yu. Mencius does not dispute this and argues only in terms of length of time. If there were a cause-and-effect relationship, we would have to find it in terms of the character of Qi.

Though Mencius argues that Qi was a man of worth and contrasts him with the depraved sons of Yao and Shun, this stereotype is not generally accepted. The *Mozi*, for example, states that Qi was "lascivious and played music in the wilds."[36] In the passage from the *Zhanguo ce* just quoted, Qi was depicted as a usurper who schemed with his friends to grab the rule from Yi. Though there are not enough references for definite proof, Qi's character seems to be subject to transformations corresponding to the manner in which he won the throne. In the *Mengzi*, the ruler is by definition virtuous; otherwise he cannot obtain the rule. However, Qi's character is not constant and therefore cannot provide justification for the change in pattern of the transfer of rule. There is, in fact, no "reason" per se, for the legends are not logical projections of rational thought. There is instead a pattern of structural opposition and mediation which functions, in the final analysis, to balance the internally conflicting demands of heredity and merit.

Qi and the Wu Guan: The Ruler and the Rebel

The "Tian wen" also asks why Yu was succeeded by his son rather than his minister. The intended answer is not clear (though the reason is certainly not Qi's virtuous character), but the question provides the final figure of opposition and the mediation that restores, once more, structural balance:

> How is it that though Yi made rebellion, Yu's seed was still continued? Qi was often the guest in heaven and obtained the Nine Bian and Nine Songs. Why then did he kill his son and slay his mother and have his lands divided up?"[37]

何后益作革而禹播降
啟棘賓商九辨九歌
何勤子屠母而死分竟地 (*Chu ci* 3/14b–15a)

---

36. 啓乃淫溢康樂野于, *Mozi* 8/19a. Here I have taken 野于 as 于野.

37. Hawkes, 49–50, lines 64–66, emended translation.

Here Qi is shown to have breached heredity just as Yao and Shun did. The reference to slaying his mother is usually interpreted as a reference to his supernatural birth, in which his mother turned into a stone. It may be somewhat facetious. His son or sons, however, are the Wu Guan 五觀, whom he killed when they rebelled. In the previous chapter, I noted that they were contrasted with Qi and paralleled with other rebel members of ruling families—Dan Zhu, Shang Jun, Tai Jia, and Guan and Cai.[38] Qi, then, in his opposition to Yi, represents heredity as opposed to worth. Here, however, he is juxtaposed with another figure of heredity, and it is shown that he breaches hereditary obligations himself. The juxtaposition of Qi with the Wu Guan shows that he is a mediatory figure just as Yi was a mediatory figure with respect to Bocheng Zigao.

In both Legend Sets 1 and 2, the recipient of the throne was juxtaposed on one side with a sage and on the other with an heir and shown in both respects to be a figure of mediation. Legend Set 3 is crucial because it represents the change from a system of nonhereditary transfer to one based on heredity. Nevertheless, the same themes occur and the same opposition is mediated. An initial abortive transfer from Yu to Yi includes all of the themes of rule by virtue included in the nonhereditary transfers of Legend Sets 1 and 2. Yi is juxtaposed with a symbol of greater purity in his service to Yu, but not to a symbol of heredity. Instead, the son follows the initial, usually described as peaceful, transfer by taking the rule from the man of worth. He is himself then juxtaposed with another figure representing hereditary interests.

In each set, both principles are equally weighted, opposed, and mediated. The form of one set, however, influences the next and creates a bias toward rule by heredity or rule by virtue. In this way, the form of the mediation of the principle of virtue in Legend Set 1 influences the second legend set and creates a bias toward rule by virtue. In Legend Set 2, Yu breaches the hereditary principle with respect to his father, and this is only mediated by the transfer of rule from Yu to Qi. This, then, is the structural motivation for the change in the system of transferring rule.

---

38. *Hanfeizi* 17/7b–8a, *Guo yu* (*Chu, shang*) 17/1a. The precise identity of the Wu Guan is quite uncertain, though the term clearly refers to a member or members of the ruling family. They do not, however, seem to have been the first son or sons of Qi and are not regarded as his legitimate heirs. They are thus much weaker figures than Dan Zhu and Shang Jun, but in this they balance Bocheng Zigao, who was a minister rather than a rule-refuser.

4

Legend Set 4:
The Foundation of the Shang Dynasty

In discussing the relationship between Yao and Shun in chapter 2, I pointed out that with respect to the theme of breach of heredity, a parallel series could be established:

Shun : Yao :: Yu : Shun :: Jie : Tang :: Zhòu : Wu Wang

This parallel was validated by the transformation in which all of the new rulers were thought to have achieved their position through force. In the words of *Hanfeizi* (17/8b): "Shun forced Yao; Yu forced Shun; Tang banished Jie; and Wu Wang smote Zhòu. These four kings were all subjects who committed regicide on their rulers." *Hanfeizi* not only associates the new kings by their use of force, but also points out that they have violated their status relationships and, by implication, the right of the former ruler to his position.

However, in transformations in which the transfers in the predynastic era are considered abdications from the former ruler to his successor, there can no longer be a grammatical parallel. This distinction was graphed as follows:

Yao → Shun, Shun → Yu
Jie ← Tang, Zhòu ← Wu Wang

Yao, Shun, Tang, and Wu Wang are the actors or grammatical subjects, and Shun, Yu, Jie, and Zhòu are the recipients or objects of the action.

This contrast, marked by the intervention of violence and its recognition as a necessary part of a nonhereditary transfer of rule, points up the change from the purely legendary era to one in which legend is tempered with historical reality. Yao, Shun, and Yu have long been recognized as legendary figures, and noneuhemerized forms of these figures continue to exist even in the texts under discussion.[1] Whereas the historicity of the Shang Dynasty has been beyond question since the discovery of inscribed oracle bones at the turn of the century and the excavation of the Xiaotun site in the 1920s and '30s, the absence of archeological evidence that can be definitely tied to the Xia Dynasty (and especially writing predating the last Shang capital) means that the historicity of the Xia Dynasty after Yu is still hotly debated. The arguments perhaps reflect the structural ambiguity of its foundation—peaceful abdication (Yu-Yi) and then overthrow and hereditary continuation (Yi-Qi)—the former leading our pragmatic minds to doubt, the latter, to suspect the historicity of the data.

The relationship of history to legend is an intriguing, if largely insoluble, problem, especially with regard to the foundation of the Shang. There are no contemporary texts for this period—inscribed oracle bones do not occur in quantity until the capital is moved to Yin, traditionally dated some three or four hundred years later. In these bones, however, Yi Yin, the founding minister of Tang and the regent of Tang's grandson Tai Jia according to the traditional texts, receives sacrifices and influences natural phenomena in the same manner as the ancestors of the Shang kings, though he has no cyclical name and was clearly not an ancestor.[2] The bones, written so much after the fact, cannot be taken as evidence

---

1. For early studies of these figures as legendary, see *Gu shi bian*, esp. v. 1. The term *euhemerized* (introduced by Maspero) is somewhat misleading because it implies a historical process by which the mythical figures of Yao, Shun, and Yu came to be regarded as emperors. I would prefer to think of the legend transformations as generated by the virtue-heredity conflict and associated with the folk myths, but not necessarily developed from them. The "noneuhemerized" myths thus continued to exist as long as they were relevant to those conflicts which generated them; they did not become (or develop into) the euhemerized forms. On the other hand, it is interesting to differentiate between those legends with a purely mythological base and no restrictions according to historical reality and those subject to the exigencies of historical times in order to demonstrate the continuity of the structure.

2. Chang, 79, 143. For a discussion of Shang sacrifices to Yi Yin, see also Chen, *Yinxu*, 361–64; and Shima, 247–52.

of a historical Yi Yin, but the status given to the minister at this early date is significant with respect to the origin of the structural conflict between heir and sage or, alternatively, king and minister.[3] This suggests that the peculiar position of the minister in early Chinese thought predates not only the fifth to first centuries, when the texts under consideration were written, but also the regency of Zhougong at the beginning of the Zhou Dynasty, which became in later historiography the chief symbol of the minister-ruler relationship.

Zhang Guangzhi has suggested that the Shang ruling clan was divided into two sections, and that the rule alternated between the two when it passed from one generation to the next, the head of the second section acting as chief minister to a ruler from the first section, and vice versa. According to his calculations, based on the cyclical *gan* 干 names and the days of sacrifice, Tang belonged to one group and Yi Yin to the other. This is supported by the days on which sacrifices were offered to Yi Yin, since he has no cyclical name.[4] If Zhang is correct, in Shang times the opposition between king and minister corresponded to the opposition between the two sections of the ruling clan, and the need to cede the interests of one's own kinship group to those of the larger community corresponded to the need for one section of the ruling clan to cede to the other. This may well be the origin of the structural opposition under discussion, although the Zhou writers, acquainted only with an agnatic stem dynasty, had no knowledge of it.

In chapter 2, I noted that in the legends of the dynastic era the parallels to the abdications of Yao and Shun and the related regencies of Shun and Yu are found in the relationships of the regents Yi Yin and Zhougong Dan to the heirs of the Shang and Zhou kings, Tai Jia and Cheng Wang, rather than in the relationships of the last kings Jie and Zhòu Xin to Tang and Wu Wang. Likewise, the precedent for the violence used by Tang and Wu Wang toward Jie and Zhòu may be found not in the relationship of Shun and Yu to Yao and Shun, but in that of Yao and Shun to the miscreants, the Huan Dou 驩兜 and the San Miao 三苗. For example, *Xunzi* states:

---

3. The importance and power of deceased ministers in Shang sacrifices is also mentioned in Creel, *Statecraft*, 27. For sacrifices to other ministers besides Yi Yin, see also Chen, *Yinxu*, 364–66; Shima, 252–57.

4. Zhang, 111–27.

Yao smote Huan Dou; Shun smote the Miao ruler; Yu smote
Gong Gong; Tang smote the Xia ruler; King Wen smote
Chong; and King Wu smote Zhòu.[5]

堯伐驩兜舜伐有苗禹伐共工湯伐有夏文王伐崇武王伐紂 (*Xunzi*
10/14a)

In this chapter and the next, I will examine the manner in which the
themes of transfer of rule in the predynastic era have been transformed
into those of the dynastic era. This chapter will be particularly concerned
with the transfer from Jie to Tang, the following with that from Zhòu
to Wu Wang. I will attempt to show how the themes that occurred in
the first legend sets in the transfer of rule from king to new king are
restructured in the legend sets of the dynastic era. Except for the actual
breach of hereditary succession, these themes are repeated in terms of
new kings and their ministers rather than in terms of last kings and new
kings. The transfer-of-rule legends are separated into two groups, overthrow and regency, but the same themes of breach of virtue and breach
of heredity are opposed and mediated in each. The new rulers of the
dynastic era assume the roles that both the old king and his successor
played in the predynastic transfers and thus assume the same legitimacy;
the new rulers' predecessors, the last rulers of Xia and Shang, come to be
regarded as subjects rather than as rulers, chastised but not overthrown.

This transference of themes sheds much light on the function of the
legends. As stated above, legend—and, indeed, myth in general—serves
to express inherent social conflict, to explore by its numerous variations
and transformations the depths and extent of the conflict, and to provide
a model to overcome it. In this case, the legends of the dynastic era that
have a historical basis include violence as a necessary part of nonhereditary transfer of rule. They appear more realistic than the euhemerized
myth of the predynastic era, but their structure is less apparent. When
viewed in the light of the earlier era, however, the structure and meaning of the themes become clear. Furthermore, the legends of the earlier
period that may be considered violence-free lend an aura of legitimacy

---

5. A similar passage, but with the list of rebels slightly expanded, occurs in *Zhanguo ce*
3/3a. Yu rather than Shun is often given as the subjugator of the San Miao, as in *Zhanguo
ce* 7/4a and *Mozi* 5/11a. These passages also include parallels to the subjugation of Jie and
Zh ò u by Tang and Wu.

to the more realistic transformations of the same structural conflict in historic times.

Jie to Tang: The Transfer of Rule

Jie, the last king of the Xia Dynasty, represents the earliest expression of the theme Arthur Wright called the "bad last king."[6] The only other "bad last king" in the period under consideration, and the only perfect parallel to Jie, is Zhòu Xin 紂辛, the last king of the Shang Dynasty, who will be discussed in more detail in the following chapter. The character of Jie is much less developed than that of Zhòu Xin, or at least the references in our texts, which were written for the most part during the Warring States period, are much sketchier with respect to Jie than to Zhòu Xin. Nevertheless, if we examine the relationship of Jie to his contemporaries and the system of parallels and contrasts with figures of other periods, the major features of the theme of the bad last king become evident.

As stated above, Jie as the object of Tang's attack is more like the miscreant subjects of Yao, Shun, and Yu than a preceding king. The term used to describe Tang's attack on Jie was *fa* 伐, which I have translated as "to smite." The other terms commonly used to describe the relation between Tang and Jie are *fang* 放 "to banish" and *zhu* 誅 "to punish." All three of these terms are normally used with reference to an action by a superior or legitimate authority toward an inferior, usually a rebel or barbarian power. However, *fa* and *fang* are also used in the transformation in which the authority is illegitimately usurped. This transformation may be designated by the more general term *shi* 弒, "to commit regicide," as in the passage from the *Hanfeizi* (17/8b) quoted above.

At the level of deep structure, Tang banished Jie. To my knowledge, no text ever states that Tang or his officers killed Jie, though there is general agreement that Wu Wang or his minister Taigong killed Zhòu Xin at the beginning of the Zhou Dynasty. *Fang* is normally used to describe the action of a ruler toward his subject, but when *qi zhu* 其主, "his ruler," is substituted for Jie (as in *Zhuangzi* 9/37a, pian 28, in which *Tang fang qi zhu* is paralleled with *Wu Wang sha Zhòu* 武王殺紂 "Wu Wang killed Zhòu"), the texts imply that Tang has usurped rights that did not properly belong to him, a moral breach.

---

6. Wright, "Sui Yang-ti: Personality and Stereotype."

Fa is a more general military term, whereas *fang* and *zhu* refer specifically to the relations between the two contending rulers. Since *zhu* refers to the punishment of an individual, it may be used in transformations in which larger military action is denied and the transfer is attributed to a shift in the loyalty of the people or to the transfer of the heavenly mandate. Mencius, for example, is asked by Xuan Wang of Qi if it is true that "Tang banished Jie and Wu Wang smote Zhòu." Mencius accepts the veracity of the record, but denies the interpretation that "a subject may commit regicide on his ruler" and states that Zhòu Xin was an outcast, not a prince. "I have heard of the punishment (*zhu*) of one fellow Zhòu, but not that regicide was committed" (*Mengzi* 2/12a, 1B.8). Elsewhere he denies that there could have been great bloodshed when "the most benevolent waged war against the most cruel."[7]

The *Xunzi* (12/2b–6b) also includes a long argument in refutation of the saying "Jie and Zhòu had all-under-heaven; Tang and Wu snatched it and usurped the rule." It argues that this is a case of punishment (*zhu* 誅) rather than regicide (*shi* 弒), because although Jie and Zhòu Xin had the accoutrements of rule, Tang and Wu were the rulers who commanded the loyalty of the people. A similar argument is said to have taken place between Yuan Gusheng 轅固生 and Huang Sheng 黃生 before Emperor Jing 景帝 of the Han Dynasty (*Shi ji, juan* 121, 3122–23). The question again is what constitutes a ruler. Here the argument is won by the observation that if the overthrow of Jie and Zhòu Xin was regicide, then so was the overthrow of the Qin by the founder of the Han Dynasty. This brings us back to the paradox mentioned in chapter 1: if it is by definition regicide to overthrow a hereditary ruler, then the founder of a new dynasty has committed a crime, but if it is not, then the successor must guard against usurpation under the name of "punishment." This paradox is contained in the possible transformations from regicide to punishment and is also reflected in the arguments recorded in the texts.

Both the paralleling of Jie with the punished subjects of the predynastic era and the terminology used for Tang's overthrow of Jie indicate that, except in the transformation in which Tang has committed regicide, he has been transformed into the legitimate authority *before* he exercises any force on Jie. This is further reflected in the terminology that is used to contrast Jie and Zhòu, not only with Tang and Wu, who

---

7. *Mengzi* 14/2b (7B.3); Lau, 194. This refers specifically to Wu and Zhou rather than Tang and Jie, but presumably the transformation would be the same in both cases.

overthrew them, but also with Yao, Shun, and Yu. The *luan* 亂 "disorder" or "chaos" of the reigns of Jie and Zhòu Xin is compared to the *zhi* 治 "control" or "good order" of the reigns of the legitimate rulers.

The *Huainanzi*, for example, speaks of *zhi* and *luan* as resulting from the authority of the ruler:

> Shun had not come down from the mat, and all-under-heaven was well-governed; Jie had not descended the steps, and all-under-heaven was in chaos.

> 舜不降席而天下治桀不下陛而天下亂 (*Huainanzi* 10/3b)

The *Xunzi*, on the other hand, stresses the techniques of *zhi* and *luan*:

> The movement of heaven is constant. It is not preserved by a Yao nor destroyed by a Jie. If it is met by government, then it is auspicious; if it is met by misrule, then it is inauspicious. . . .

> Yu used government; Jie used disorder.[8]

> 天行有常不為堯存不為桀亡應之以治則吉應之以亂則凶

> 禹以治桀以亂 (*Xunzi* 11/15b, 19a)

And the *Mozi* speaks of the ascendance of *zhi* over *luan*:

> What Jie had disordered (*luan*), Tang put in order (*zhi*); what Zhòu had disordered, Wu Wang put in order.[9]

> 桀之所亂湯治之紂之所亂武王治之 (*Mozi* 9/11a)

Whatever the political point, the texts juxtapose, apparently randomly, the misrule of Jie and Zhòu Xin with the order of Yao, Shun, Yu, Tang, or Wu.

---

8. The *Sibu congkan* edition gives *li* 理 for the *zhi* 治 in this passage (*li* is the *ming* 名 of Tang Gaozong 唐高宗), but I have followed *Xunzi jijie* and *Xunzi jianshi*, 220, in restoring the *zhi*.

9. Almost identical passages occur in *Mozi* 9/2a–b, 8a.

Jie and Zhòu Xin are not only creators of *luan*. The texts also describe their characters in negative terms. Specific charges that are leveled against them in the *Shang shu* and the *Shi ji*—drunkenness, indulgence in music, and excessive (particularly licentious) behavior— are not so evident in the Warring States texts, but their bad character is frequently described in general terms, such as *bao* 暴 "violent," *nüe* 虐 "cruel," and *yin* 淫 "inclined to excess," "licentious." These are the same terms used to describe Dan Zhu, Shang Jun, and Qi, the bad sons of Yao, Shun, and Yu.

More important in the texts under consideration even than personal immorality or oppression of the people are violations of the ministerial relation by a bad last king. It is this violation, I believe, that irretrievably destroys the balance between rule by worth and rule by heredity at the end of the Xia and Shang and places the last rulers outside the pale of legitimate government. There are innumerable minister figures associated with Zhòu Xin at the end of the Shang Dynasty, each illustrating various aspects of the moral dilemma that may arise for the minister who faces the overlordship of a bad king—that is, when the obligations of virtue are no longer compatible with those of respect for hereditary rule. The ministers of Jie, the last king of the Shang, are less numerous and well developed than the ministers of Zhòu Xin, but when the parallels are examined, three general categories may be discerned.

The first is that of the evil minister. These include such figures as Tuiyi Daxi 推哆(移)大戲 and Si Guan 斯觀 at the end of the Xia, and Fei Lian 飛廉, E Lai 惡來, Chong Hou Hu 崇候虎, and Zuo Qiang 左彊 at the end of the Shang. Jie and Zhòu Xin appoint and rely on these ministers just as their successors appoint and rely on their founding ministers, but rather than remonstrating with their rulers and offering them sage advice about governing the people, they encourage them in their oppression and evil deeds. Their importance in misleading the heir to the throne is such that Tuiyi and Fei Lian are personally executed by Tang and Wu Wang, respectively, when they defeat the forces of Xia and Shang.

A second, and perhaps even more important, category is that of the loyal minister who remonstrates with his ruler and is killed or imprisoned as a result. These ministers are similar in their purity and loyalty to principle to those who refuse to serve under a king when they consider him to be illegitimate, such as Wu Guang, Bian Sui, Bo Yi, and Shu Qi. The principle to which they adhere, however, is that of the virtue of the king. They therefore remonstrate with him and lose their lives. The minister-refusers, on the other hand, adhere to the principle of hereditary rule and cannot serve or live in the realm of a man who has committed regicide. They therefore must leave all-under-heaven or commit suicide. The remonstrating ministers are contrasted with the evil ministers who aid the king in his breach of virtue, just as the minister-refusers are with the founding ministers who aid the new king in the overthrow of his hereditary lord. In this respect, the end of a dynasty presents a mirror image of the foundation of the next one.

There are a number of variations on the theme of the remonstrating minister at the end of the Shang Dynasty. Two famous examples are Bi Gan 比干 and Ji Zi 箕子, who represent both the minister who is killed because he insists on maintaining his integrity and the minister who feigns madness in order to escape the consequences of his opposition to the evil king. I have not found a parallel among the ministers of Jie for Ji Zi, who feigned madness, but Guan Longfeng 關龍逢 matches Bi Gan.[10]

The new king, who was formerly a feudal lord, has also been wrongfully treated by the bad last king. Both Cheng Tang and Wen Wang (Wu Wang's father, usually revered as the founder of the dynasty) were imprisoned by their former rulers. Cheng Tang was imprisoned in the "numinous tower" (*ling tai* 靈臺), Wen Wang at You Li 羑里.[11] Imprisonment serves to release the new king from his obligation to the former king, whom he can no longer serve as a feudal lord. He then takes as his ministers the men who have fled from the former king or whose merit was unrecognized. This theme of turning from the oppression of the former ruler to the virtue of the new ruler may be developed and expanded so that it becomes the transformation in which all of the people turn from one ruler to the other, but even where some degree of military force is admitted, the impending doom of the old dynasty is evident in the flight of its ministers. The flight of the Grand Scribes (*tai shi* 太史) is specifically cited as evidence of the decline of the old dynasty and rise of the new.[12]

Yi Yin and Taigong Wang, the founding ministers of the Shang and Zhou Dynasties, may even be placed in the category of fleeing ministers. In some texts they are said to have served Jie and Zhòu Xin before turning to the would-be rulers Tang and Wen Wang. They are both recluses,

---

10. *Shi ji, juan* 88, 2569.

11. *Shi ji, juan* 2, 88; *juan* 3, 106.

12. *Lüshi chunqiu* 16/1a–b; *Huainanzi* 13/9a–b.

and their reclusion is due to a desire to avoid the rule of the old king. Even in their pursuit of low occupations they are playing out the role of waiting in obscurity for a true king who will recognize them and whom they can serve. The new king, then, does not only reverse the pattern of the old by mourning those the old king has executed and executing those the old king has relied upon; he builds his government by employing those men of virtue who were unable to serve the former king.

The texts include one further relationship to the bad last king, though it is not nearly as important in the texts under consideration as in later accounts—the relationship of the bad last king to his wives and concubines. Both Jie and Zhòu Xin are infatuated with their concubines to the extent of ignoring the advice of their ministers and following that of their concubines. This is an extreme violation of the king-minister relation, since the words of the minister are regarded as of even less account than those of a woman, and may also imply a violation of kinship, since the concubine is placed over the proper wife. At the end of the Xia Dynasty, Jie is infatuated with the two women of Min Shan 岷 山 and, according to the *Guben zhushu jinian*, therefore expels his wife Mo Xi 末喜, who then plots with Yi Yin to overthrow the Xia Dynasty.[13]

The Period of Foundation

In the discussion above, I have shown that although the breach of heredity in the transfer of rule from Jie to Tang finds precedent in that from Yao to Shun, Jie is contrasted with Tang as a miscreant rather than as the legitimate ruler and as a representative of disorder as opposed to order. In this comparison Tang takes on the authority of a Yao as well as of a Shun—that is, he is like the preceding as well as the succeeding king of the predynastic era. I found the reason for the loss of authority by Jie and Zhòu Xin to be their total negation of the principles of virtue. This negation released their followers and ministers from their obligation of loyalty and caused a movement toward the new dynasty. In the following I will show the manner in which the themes of virtue from the predynastic era are transformed into those of the period of foundation of the Shang. In this period, the principles of virtue negated by Jie

---

13. *Guben zhushu jinian*, 15–16; *Guo yu* 7/2a Jin 1. Min Shan sometimes occurs as Meng 蒙 Shan.

are affirmed by Tang. Tang's affirmation of these principles parallels Yao, who appointed Shun—which explains how Jie can be regarded as an outcast punished by the ruler and contrasted with Yao, Shun, and Yu, as well as with Tang.

In order to explain the transformation of the themes of rule by virtue, I take Legend Set 1 as a model:

Xu You   Wu Guang, Bian Sui
| |
Yao → Shun   Jie ← Tang

Yao abdicates to Shun, who is juxtaposed with the more virtuous Xu You. Tang and his minister Yi Yin take the rule from Jie, and they are in turn juxtaposed with the more virtuous Wu Guang and Bian Sui. This transformation may be further analyzed into two levels. The first is that of nonhereditary transfer. Yao and Jie are the preceding rulers; Shun and Tang are the succeeding rulers, not of the same family; and Xu You, Wu Guang, and Bian Sui are rule-refusers:

Xu You   Wu Guang, Bian Sui
| |
Yao → Shun   Jie ← Tang + Yi Yin

The second level is that of appointment by virtue. At this level, Tang becomes equivalent to Yao; Shun and Yi Yin are "founding ministers"; and Xu You, Wu Guang, and Bian Sui are minister-refusers who will not serve the king:

Xu You   Wu Guang, Bian Sui
| |
Yao + Shun   Tang + Yi Yin

Tang and Wu Guang: The Ruler and the Refuser

In Legend Set 1, Shun's acceptance of the throne from Yao was contrasted with Xu You's refusal. Compared with Dan Zhu, Shun was a sage rather than an heir, but compared with Xu You, Shun's virtue was not, after all, perfect. In the following passage from the *Hanfeizi*, Tang's character in overthrowing Jie is contrasted implicitly with the pure virtue of Wu Guang:

Tang was afraid all-under-heaven would call him covetous for attacking Jie, so he yielded all-under-heaven to Wu Guang. But he was afraid Wu Guang would accept it, so he sent someone to persuade Wu Guang, "Tang killed his ruler and wishes to transmit the taint to you, so he yielded all-under-heaven to you." Wu Guang consequently threw himself into the river.

湯以伐桀而恐天下言己為貪也因乃讓天下於務光而恐務光之
受之也乃使人說務光曰湯殺君而欲傳惡聲于子故讓天下於子
務光因自投於河 (*Hanfeizi* 7/5a)

Thus, Tang is the sage as opposed to the heir when compared to Jie but lacks pure virtue when compared to a true sage such as Wu Guang. The rule-refusers Wu Guang and Bian Sui serve to emphasize the breach of heredity, but since Tang offers the rule to them, he is able to rid himself to some extent of the stigma associated with the overthrow as well. This is clear even from the above transformation, in which Tang's offer is regarded as a deliberate plot. There are not nearly as many references to Wu Guang and Bian Sui as to Xu You, though Sima Qian parallels the three as refusers.[14] A passage from the *Zhuangzi* discusses Tang's abdication to Bian Sui and then to Wu Guang at some length:

> Tang planned with Yi Yin to attack Jie. Having conquered [Jie], he yielded [the throne] to Bian Sui. Bian Sui refused, saying, "When your lordship attacked Jie, you [wished to] plot with me, so you must consider me a rebel. Having vanquished Jie, you now wish to yield to me, so you must consider me covetous. I was born into a generation of disorder, and now a man who is without the Way comes twice to taint me with his disgraceful conduct.[15] How can I bear to hear of this over

---

14. *Shi ji, juan* 61, 2121. (The *Lüshi chunqiu* 19/2b parallels Wu Guang and Bian Sui with the Farmer of the Stone Door and the Northerner Wu Ze, other rule-refusers during Yao's reign.

15. The phrase *man* 漫我以其辱行 appears in the almost identical passage in the *Lüshi chunqiu* (19/2a) simply as 詢我 "shame me" (though the *Lüshi chunqiu jiaoshi* revises this on the basis of the *Zhuangzi* to 詢我以其辱行). This use of *man* 漫, which I have translated as "taint" (glossed as *wu* 汙), seems unusual, but it is used in the same sense in a previous passage, *Zhuangzi* 9/29a and *Lüshi chunqiu* 19/2b, for the Northerner Wu Ze (see chapter 2).

and over again." Thereupon he threw himself in the Zhou River[16] and died.

Tang yielded the throne once more, [this time to] Wu Guang, and said, "For the wise man to plot [the overthrow], the military man to follow it up, and the humane man to enjoy the fruits—this was the way of the ancients. Why do you not take the position [of ruler]?" Wu Guang refused saying, "To cast aside one's superior is not right. To kill the people is not humane. For me to enjoy the profit when others take the risks is not purity. I have heard it said, 'Do not accept the pay of a man you believe to be unrighteous; do not set foot in a land when it is without the Way.' How much more is this so when I am offered the highest honor of all! I cannot bear to see you again." Thereupon he put a stone on his back and sank himself in the Lu river.[17]

湯遂與伊尹謀伐桀剋之以讓卞隨卞隨辭曰后之伐桀也謀乎我必以我為賊也勝桀而讓我必以我為貪也吾生乎亂世而無道之人再來漫我以其辱行吾不忍數聞也乃自投椆水而死

湯又讓瞀光曰知者謀之武者遂之仁者居之古之道也吾子胡不立乎瞀光辭曰廢上非義也殺民非仁也人犯其難我享其利非廉也吾聞之曰非其義者不受其祿無道之世不踐其土況尊我乎吾不忍久見也乃負石而自沈於廬水 (*Zhuangzi* 9/29b–30b)

Here Tang is contrasted implicitly with both Bian Sui and Wu Guang. The suggestion is clearly that he is himself a thief, covetous of all-under-heaven, a man who has usurped the rule and caused others misfortune and death. There is a stigma associated with the violent overthrow of his hereditary lord before which Bian Sui and Wu Guang,

---

16. The site of the Zhou River is never identified, and in the *Lüshi chunqiu* (19/2a) the Ying River 潁水, a tributary of the Huai which enters it in Anhui Province, is substituted. (I suspect 椆 may be a mistake for *tong* 桐, and another name for the Zhe 浙, and the name of the place where Yi Yin was banished.)

17. Anhui Province. The *Lüshi chunqiu* (19/2b) gives it as the Mu River 募 (unidentified as to place).

men of pure virtue, cringe and commit suicide. The stigma is lessened by Tang's abdication to the refusers, but his virtue, established with relation to Jie, can no longer be considered pure, just as Shun's virtue, established with relation to Dan Zhu, appeared mediatory when compared with that of Xu You.

Tang and Yi Yin: The Ruler and the Founding Minister

In the above, Bian Sui compared himself not only with Tang, who overthrew his ruler, but also with Tang's minister Yi Yin, who aided him in the overthrow. Once again Yi Yin is appointed by Tang because of his worth, but his virtue appears as a mediation in contrast with that of the true sage. Tang's affirmation of rule by virtue in appointing Yi Yin is emphasized by Yi Yin's low initial status. Most texts describe Yi Yin as a simple kitchen worker in the retinue of the Lady of You Shen (You Shen Shi 有辛氏) before she became betrothed to Tang. Yi Yin carried the sacrificial vessels and by this means gained access to Tang. He lectured him on the five flavors (a simile for the art of government) and so became his minister. The texts often refer to this legend by epithets that emphasize Yi Yin's low initial status. He is frequently called a "cook," or even "preparer of meat" (pao 庖 or zai ren 宰人), and "carrier of the ding-tripod and sacrificial stand" (fu ding zu 負鼎俎) before he meets Cheng Tang.[18] This role parallels that of Shun, who was a poor farmer before he met Yao.[19]

In some transformations, Yi Yin's low status is muted. The Shi ji, for example, describes him as a persuader who deliberately became a cook in order to meet Cheng Tang:

> Yi Yin's personal name was E Heng. E Heng wished to importune Tang, but had no means. Therefore he became a servant of the Lady of the You Shen clan. He carried the ding-tripod and sacrificial stand on his back and persuaded Tang to go the kingly way by [discussing] flavors.

---

18. For reference to Yi Yin's kitchen work see Hanfeizi 1/7a, 15/9a, 4/5b; Lüshi chunqiu 18/19b; Mozi 2/9b, 15a; Shi ji, juan 63, 2153; and Zhuangzi 8/18a. For carrying the ding see Zhanguo ce 6/80a; Huainanzi 19/2b, 13/15a; and Shi ji, juan 124, 3182.

19. Mozi 2/9b, 15a–b. Other frequent parallels with Yi Yin as founding minister include Taigong Wang; Boli Xi, "who sold himself for five sheepskins" to Duke Mu of Qin; and Fu Yüe, discovered by Wu Ding of the Shang Dynasty while doing forced labor at Fu Yan.

伊尹名阿衡, 阿衡欲奸湯而無由, 乃為有莘氏媵臣負鼎俎, 以滋
味說湯致于王道 (*Shi ji, juan* 3, 94)

This passage parallels the account in which Shun became a farmer, pot-
ter, and fisherman in order to transform the people. Though the low
position of Shun and Yi Yin is less emphatic in this transformation, they
are still raised up from obscurity and appointed according to their worth.
Yao and Tang also show their virtue in their ability to attract such sages
into their service.

In a further transformation, Yi Yin is regarded as having been a
recluse rather than a cook when he met Cheng Tang. The *Mengzi* specifically denies that Yi Yin would have degraded himself by becoming a
cook or that a later founding minister, Boli Xi 百里奚, would have sold
himself for five sheepskins and tended cattle to attract Duke Mu of
Qin. Instead, Yi Yin was "plowing the fields in the outskirts of You Shen,
delighting in the way of Yao and Shun" when Tang sent for him.[20] This
transformation is also included in the *Shiji* immediately following the
passage quoted above:

> Some say that Yi Yin was an eremitic gentleman. Tang sent
> someone to invite him to take office, but he turned him away
> five times before he was willing to go and serve Tang. . . . Tang
> raised [Yi Yin] up and entrusted him with the government of
> the state.
>
> 或曰伊尹處士, 湯使人聘迎之, 五反然後肯往從湯⋯⋯湯舉任
> 以國政。 (*Shi ji, juan* 3, 94)

The view that Yi Yin was a recluse before he met Tang corresponds to that
in which Shun was a man who "hid himself among the people" until Yao,
hearing of his virtue, summoned him. The recluse theme further softens
the emphasis on the low social status of the founding minister, but this
is compensated for by the ruler's willingness to lower himself in seeking
the advice of the recluse and by his determination to promote a man of
virtue, regardless of the number of times he has to make the request.

Tang in appointing Yi Yin affirms the principle of rule by worth and
repeats the action of Yao in appointing Shun. He is also able by this

---

20. *Mengzi* 9/12b (5A.7). For Boli Xi, see 9/16a–b (5A.9).

appointment to shift some of the responsibility for the overthrow of his hereditary lord from himself to his minister. Yi Yin, like Taigong Wang of the Zhou Dynasty, is particularly associated with the military aspects of the overthrow and is especially known for his craft and strategy. The following formula is frequently used for obtaining a founding minister:

A *de* X *er bawang*   A 得 X 而霸王

A (founding king) got X (founding minister) and attained hegemony or kingship.

It refers as much to the military ability of the founding minister as to his knowledge of the kingly way.

Yi Yin and Wu Guang and Bian Sui: The Minister and the Refusers

As a founding minister, Yi Yin is contrasted with Wu Guang and Bian Sui, who refused to aid Tang in his overthrow of Jie. The following passage from the *Zhuangzi* stresses Yi Yin's military role:

> When Tang was about to attack Jie, he solicited plots from Bian Sui. Bian Sui said, "This is not my [kind of] affair." Tang said, "Who can do it?" "I do not know." Tang further solicited plots from Wu Guang. Wu Guang said, "It's not my [kind of] affair." Tang said, "Who can do it?" "I do not know." Tang said, "What about Yi Yin?" [Wu Guang] said, "He is a man who promotes power and does not mind a sullied reputation.[21] I know nothing else of him."
>
> 湯將伐桀因卞隨而謀卞隨曰非吾事也湯曰孰可曰吾不知湯又因務光而謀務光曰非吾事也湯曰孰可曰吾不知也湯曰伊尹何如曰強力忍垢吾不知其他也 (*Zhuangzi* 9/29b–30a, pian 28)

---

21. 忍垢 appears in the otherwise almost identical *Lüshi chunqiu* (19/1b–2a) as 忍訽, "to endure shame." A similar use of 垢 occurs in the *Laozi, zhang* 78—忍國之垢—and is translated by D. C. Lau (*Lao Tzu*, Penguin, 1970, 140) as "one who takes on himself the humiliation of the state."

In this passage Yi Yin is seen as Tang's minister. His juxtaposition with Wu Guang and Bian Sui, who refuse to aid Tang in the overthrow of his hereditary lord, emphasized his shortcomings. Xu You was similarly juxtaposed with Shun, who, though virtuous, was willing to breach the principle of hereditary right.

Period of Regency: Hereditary Continuation

Since Yi Yin is raised up by Tang just as Shun was raised up by Yao, and since he is also compared to a recluse who maintains a more perfect purity of principle, we might expect him to succeed Tang just as Shun succeeded Yao. This is particularly true since Tang's grandson Tai Jia, whom Yi Yin temporarily replaces, is considered bad and, as mentioned in chapter 2, is paralleled to Yao's son Dan Zhu as a rebellious member of the royal family. Even graphically the parallel would seem to be perfect:

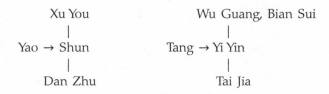

Yi Yin and Tai Jia: The Ruler and the Rebel

In one respect the graph is an accurate representation of the legends. According to all accounts, Yi Yin does replace Tai Jia, who is described in the following passage from the *Shi ji*, in terms remarkably similar to those used for Dan Zhu:

> When Di Tai Jia had been on the throne for three years, he was unenlightened, violent, and tyrannical, did not respect the laws of Tang, and disordered virtue. Thereupon Yi Yin banished him to Tong Gong. For three years Yi Yin carried out the government of the country in his stead, holding audience with the feudal lords.
>
> 帝太甲既立三年, 不明, 暴虐, 不遵湯法, 亂德, 於是伊尹放之於桐宮。三年, 伊尹攝行致當國, 以朝諸侯。 (*Shi ji, juan 3, 99*)

In another respect, however, the graph is not accurate. Tang did not abdicate to Yi Yin as Yao abdicated to Shun, nor did Yi Yin serve Tang as his regent. Structurally, this means that there is no mediation of the principle of heredity. Tang has already breached the right of heredity in his overthrow of Jie, so Yi Yin is appointed according to his virtue, just as Shun was appointed by Yao, and both Tang and Yi Yin are juxtaposed with sages of pure virtue, just as Shun was juxtaposed with Xu You. Shun is also juxtaposed with Dan Zhu and Yi Yin with Tai Jia. However, the contrast between Shun and Dan Zhu is mediated by Shun's position as Yao's son-in-law and adopted son. He further served Yao as his regent and protected his right of rule in his old age. Up to this point there is no similar mediation of heredity in Yi Yin's juxtaposition with Tai Jia: Yi Yin is neither Tang's regent nor in any manner kin to him. Yi Yin's replacement of Tai Jia is a confirmation of the right of virtue over heredity, as was Tang's replacement of Jie, but it does not include any corresponding confirmation of the right of heredity over virtue.

Yi Yin and Tai Jia: The Regent and the Ruler

The legend, however, does not end with Yi Yin's replacement of Tai Jia. After a period of three years Yi Yin returns the rule to Tai Jia—or Tai Jia takes it from him, according to the transformation—and symmetry is thus restored. The full graph of Legend Set 3 is therefore modified:

a) *Period of foundation:*
$$\text{Wu Guang, Bian Sui}$$
$$|$$
$$\text{Jie} \leftarrow \text{Tang} + \text{Yi Yin}$$

b) *Period of Regency:*
$$\text{Yi Yin} \Rightarrow \text{Tai Jia}$$
$$|$$
$$\text{Tai Jia}$$

Tang's overthrow of Jie, in which the right of heredity is breached, is now balanced by the return of the rule from Yi Yin to Tai Jia, in which the right of heredity is restored. Tang appointed Yi Yin as his founding minister and was himself juxtaposed with Wu Guang and Bian Sui. Yi Yin temporarily replaced Tai Jia as ruler and then was opposed by Tai Jia.

Between the two periods, Wai Bing 外丙 and Zhong Ren 中壬 ruled briefly, but their reigns are never given any legendary significance and are not usually mentioned. Tang's eldest son and heir-apparent Tai Ding 太丁 did not assume the throne, Wai Bing and Zhong Ren were Tai Ding's younger brothers. Thus, the texts virtually ignore the fraternal succession and build the legends of hereditary succession around the descendant in the main line (*da zong* 大宗), Tai Jia 太甲.[22]

The transfer of rule from Yi Yin to Tai Jia follows from the predynastic transfer from ruler to successors. In the texts in which the predynastic rulers are said to abdicate, Yin Yin is described as voluntarily returning the rule to Tai Jia. The *Shi ji* gives one such account:

> Di Tai Jia lived at Tong Gong for three years. He regretted the past, reproved himself, and returned to goodness. Yi Yin therefore went to meet Tai Jia and bestowed the government on him.

> 帝太甲居桐宮三年, 悔過自責, 反善, 於是伊尹迺迎帝太甲而授之政 (*Shi ji, juan* 4, 99)

The term *shou* "bestowed," used here for Yi Yin's return of the rule to Tai Jia, was seen above as a term signifying abdication in the predynastic era. This theme is repeated in the dynastic era, but the structural realignment is such that it now serves to confirm the right of hereditary rule. Yao and Shun voluntarily gave the rule to outsiders rather than to their own sons. By this action the right of their posterity was subordinated to that of men of worth. This same freedom of choice is exercised here, but it is the man of worth who subordinates his own right of rule to that of the heir, thus legitimating the hereditary pattern.

---

22. I have found references to Wai Bing and Zhong Ren in the *Shi ji* (*juan* 3, 98); *Guben zhushu jinian jijiao dingbu*, 17; and *Mengzi* 9/12a (5A.6). All of these record the brevity of their reigns, two and four years respectively, but give no further information about them. Zhang Guangzhi (126) has suggested on the basis of their stem names that Tai Ding was the heir-apparent of the B group when Tang was king and Yi Yin minister, but died before assuming the rule. Wai Bing and Zhong Ren, B members of the same generation as Tai Ding, then ruled briefly, the rule reverting to A with the ascendancy of Tang's grandson Tai Jia. This seems plausible, though I do not see why the account of Yi Yin and Tai Jia's struggle in the *Guben zhushu jinian* need therefore be taken as more historical than other early accounts.

It is noteworthy that in the same transformation in which Shun forced the rule from Yao, Yi Yin did not "bestow" the rule on Tai Jia; Tai Jia killed Yi Yin. The *Guben zhushu jinian* gives this account:

> Yi Yin banished Tai Jia to Tong and then established himself. After Yi Yin occupied the throne, he banished Tai Jia for seven years. Tai Jia secretly left Gong and killed Yi Yin.

> 伊尹放太甲于桐, 乃自立。伊尹既位, 放太甲七年, 太甲潛出自桐殺伊尹。(*Guben zhushu jinian*, 17–18)

Yi Yin's intention was clearly usurpation. He did not voluntarily return the rule to Tai Jia. Instead, Tai Jia returned from Tong, killed Yi Yin, and retook his rightful position as the heir of Tang.

In the transformation in which the people go from one predynastic ruler to another, Yi Yin did not take or return the rule except in accordance with the people's wishes. The *Mengzi* states:

> Gongsun Chou said, "Yi Yin banished Tai Jia to Tong, saying, 'I do not wish to be close to one who is intractable,' and the people were greatly pleased. When Tai Jia became worthy, Yi Yin restored him to the throne, and the people, once again, were pleased. When a prince is not worthy, is it permissible for a good and wise man who is his subject to banish him?"

> "It is permissible," said Mencius, "only if he had the motive of a Yi Yin; otherwise, it would be usurpation."[23]

> 公孫醜曰伊尹曰予不狎于不順放太甲于桐民大悅太甲賢又反之民大悅賢者之爲人臣也其君不賢則固可放與孟子曰有伊尹之志則可無伊尹之志則簒也 (*Mengzi* 13/12b, 7A.31)

Legitimacy, as before, is defined by the people's loyalty. Yi Yin could not have "abdicated" the rule unless the people had turned back to the heir.

In the passage quoted above, the *Mengzi* poses the question of usurpation. Yi Yin's replacement of Tai Jia may be regarded as either

---

23. Translated in Lau, 188–89.

regency or usurpation. The former corresponds to the transformation in which Yi Yin voluntarily gave the rule to Tai Jia, the latter to that in which Tai Jia killed him. Yi Yin's replacement of Tai Jia parallels the regencies of Shun, Yu, Yi, and the Duke of Zhou on behalf of Yao, Shun, Yu, and King Cheng of the Zhou Dynasty. The role of the regent is to protect the hereditary interests of the ruling house, and it balances the role of "founding minister" in which the right of worth is placed over that of heredity. Shun, Yu, and Yi served as regents for the king who had appointed them "founding minister." In the dynastic era, however, the regent serves not the king himself but the posterity of the king he has served as founding minister. The dynastic king is weak because of his youth rather than his old age, but the same terminology is used in both cases—*dai* 代, *she* 攝, and *jia* 假 or *jia wei* 假位.

Yi Yin's regency for Tai Jia is paralleled in the texts with the regency of the Duke of Zhou for the young king of the Zhou Dynasty, Cheng Wang.[24] The legends of the two dynasties are thematically similar, but they are not identical. Yi Yin temporarily banished the young heir because he breached the principles of his father. In so doing, Yi Yin acted to protect the principles of the Shang founder, if not the actual fact of the Shang succession, and he returned the rule to Tai Jia when Tai Jia had reformed. Thus, Yi Yin is considered Tai Jia's regent, but at the point at which Tai Jia was banished, Tai Jia parallels the bad son of Yao, Dan Zhu. In the Zhou Dynasty, Zhougong ruled for Cheng Wang only because he was still a child. The role of rebellious member of the royal family in Legend Set 5 is played by the two uncles of Cheng, Guan and Cai.

A defining factor of the regent, whether he be Shun, Yu, Yi, Yi Yin, or Zhougong, is that he has the potential of usurpation but does not take advantage of his power, though to his wary contemporaries he may appear to be acting illegally. Zhougong was accused of usurpation by the Duke of Shao 召, but he cited the precedent of Yi Yin to justify his actions:

> When Cheng Wang was young, Zhougong took over the reins
> of government, managed the affairs of state, and offered the
> imperial sacrifices. This aroused the suspicion of Shao Gong,
> and he wrote the *Jun Shi*. The *Jun Shi* showed his displeasure

---

24. *Zhanguo ce* 5/46b, *Mengzi* 9/12a–b.

with Zhougong, so Zhougong stated, "At the time of Tang, there was Yi Yin who assumed the throne before the august heaven."[25]

成王既幼, 周公攝政, 當國踐祚, 召公疑之, 作君奭, 君奭不說周公。周公乃稱「湯時有伊尹, 假于皇天」 (*Shi ji, juan* 34, 1549)

The regent of the dynastic era assumes the power of government from the heir but voluntarily returns it to him. The regent of the predynastic era, on the other hand, assumes the power of rule during the king's old age but does not take advantage of his position to overthrow him. In both cases, however, he voluntarily subordinates his power and right to rule by virtue to the heir's hereditary right to the throne. Yi Yin, so regarded, banished Tai Jia because he did not follow the laws of his father, but his purpose was instruction, not usurpation, and he returned the rule when Tai Jia reformed.

In returning the rule to Tai Jia, Yi Yin abdicated his right of rule by virtue to Tai Jia's right by heredity. Thus, all of the themes of virtue and heredity that occurred in the previous sets recur in Legend Set 4, but the final impulse of the legend set lies with rule by heredity. Tang raised up Yi Yin, just as Yao raised up Shun. His appointment by virtue and the overthrow of Jie represent the themes of rule by virtue, but he and Yi Yin are also juxtaposed with the pure sages Wu Guang and Bian Sui. Wu Guang and Bian Sui refused to take the rule from Tang or to aid him in his overthrow of Jie. In so doing they pointed up the breach of hereditary right, and showed that Tang and Yi Yin are in reality mediatory rather than pure examples of virtue. Following Tang's death, the themes of rule by heredity are exposed and mediated. Yi Yin assumed the rule in place of Tai Jia, just as Shun replaced Dan Zhu, but Tang did not yield to Yi Yin, nor did Yi Yin serve him as regent or son-in-law. Instead, Yi Yin became Tai Jia's regent and, by finally yielding the throne to him, confirmed Tai Jia's right to rule by heredity.

---

25. This phrase as it appears in the *Shang shu, Jun shi*, is 格于皇天. The traditional gloss for 格 (frequently interchangeable with 假 in early texts) is 至 and it has been translated by Karlgren in *Documents*, 61, as "Yi Yin attained to august Heaven." However, *jia* 假 appears in the texts under consideration as a technical term for regency, as discussed in chapter 2, note 46. Thus, my translation "assumed the throne before the august Heaven."

5

Legend Set 5:
The Foundation of the Zhou Dynasty

Legend set 5, so much closer in time to the fifth to first centuries when the texts were written, is recorded in much greater detail than Legend Set 4, and includes more legendary figures representing more specific aspects of the legend themes. This proliferation of legendary figures may be seen in the accompanying diagram:

Legend Set 4	*Legend Set 5*
Wu Guang, Bian Sui	Bo Yi, Shu Qi
|	|
Jie ← Tang + Yi Yin	Zhòu ← Wen, Wu + Taigong
Yi Yin ⇒ Tai Jia	Zhougong ⇒ Cheng
|	|
Tai Jia	Guan, Cai

In Legend Set 5, Wen Wang 文王 and his son Wu Wang 武王 together take the place of Tang, the dynastic founder of Legend Set 4. Taigong Wang 太公望 likewise parallels Yi Yin as founding minister, and Zhougong Dan 周公旦 parallels him as regent. Wu Wang's two brothers, Guan 管 and Cai 蔡, parallel Tai Jia in their rebellion against Zhougong's regency, but Cheng Wang 成王 parallels Tai Jia as heir to the throne.

With the foundation of the Zhou Dynasty, we are for the first time in an era in which there is contemporaneous historical evidence of the period under consideration. This evidence is in the form of Western Zhou bronze inscriptions cast to memorialize certain events or rewards received from the king for certain achievements. Unlike the texts under consideration, the inscriptions do not mythologize or attempt to extract principles from history. They confirm the existence of many of the figures and events with which I will be concerned, but the facts recorded in the inscriptions do not entirely accord with any of the transformations that appear in the later texts. Wen Wang, Wu Wang, Cheng Wang, and Zhougong are mentioned in bronze inscriptions. However, Zhougong probably did not replace Cheng Wang because of his youth. Zhougong did conduct campaigns in the east, but the inscriptions make no mention of the rebel brothers Guan and Cai. Similarly, the inscriptions indicate that Taigong may have been a relative by marriage of the Zhou rulers rather than a poor man raised up by Wen Wang.[1] Although there was a historical basis for the legends recorded in the corpus of texts under consideration, it is clear that mythic structure rather than historical fact determined the manner in which later writers perceived that history, and that this structure was the same as that in terms of which they perceived all history, whether euhemerized from folk myth or based on historical fact.

Wen Wang and Wu Wang:
The Founders of the Zhou Dynasty

Wen Wang, known as Xi Bo Chang 西伯昌, the "Western Lord Chang," before the Shang was overthrown, was a feudal lord during the reign of the infamous Zhòu Xin 紂辛, the bad last ruler of Shang. When Zhòu Xin executed the Lord of E 鄂候, who had remonstrated with him for his cruelty, Wen Wang sighed secretly, but Zhòu Xin heard of it and had him imprisoned at You Li 羑里. This imprisonment parallels that of Tang in the Ling Tai ('numinous tower'). According to the *Huainanzi* (13/10a):

> Formerly Jie was imprisoned at Jiao Men, but he was unable to see the error of his ways and only regretted that he did not kill Tang in the tower of Xia. Zhòu dwelt at Xuan Shi but did not repent his trespasses and only regretted that he did not execute King Wen at You Li.

---

1. For a summary of the historical facts in W. Zhou bronze inscriptions, see Chen, "Xi Zhou," 137–50. For a discussion of inscriptions that may relate to a historical Taigong Wang, see "Identities of Taigong Wang," Appendix 2, 149–90.

故桀囚於焦門而不能自非其所行而悔不殺湯於夏臺紂居於宣
室而不反其過而悔不誅文王於羑里

Jie's and Zhòu Xin's misdeeds and their victimization of those who
remonstrated with them meant that their ministers and feudal lords
could no longer fulfill their appropriate functions.

Tang after his imprisonment made an attack on Jie. Wen Wang,
however, declined to attack his ruler. Zhòu Xin's ministers fled to him,
and he attracted sages such as Taigong Wang into his service, but rather
than commit regicide, he offered Zhòu Xin one thousand li of land in
return for the abolition of the roasting pillar on which he burnt his vic-
tims. By his restraint Wen Wang demonstrated his loyalty, benevolence,
and lack of greed. Only after Wen Wang's death did his son, Wu Wang,
take up arms and redress his wrong.

This division of the theme of the founding king affects the structure
of the legend set. Wen Wang, the "cultured king," established the virtue
of the dynasty and the right of the Zhou to rule, but he did not actually
overthrow his ruler. Wu Wang, the "military king," performed the act of
regicide, but in so doing he also acted to avenge his father and carry on
his work. His breach of heredity in overthrowing Zhòu Xin was mediated
by his affirmation of heredity toward Wen Wang. Wen Wang had further
shown his lack of greed in not attacking Zhòu Xin. In his restraint he is
similar to a recluse. Therefore, there is no need for the further mediation of subsequently offering the throne to a recluse. Indeed, since Wu
Wang carried on his father's work, to do so would have been a further
breach of heredity.

Zhòu Xin to Wu Wang: The Transfer of Rule

The transformations concerning transfer of rule from Zhòu Xin to Wu
Wang follow the pattern discussed with respect to Legend Set 4, although
the legends are not identical.[2] The most common terms for the transfer

---

2. Various historians have hypothesized that the legends surrounding the foundation of the
Shang Dynasty are simply a projection backward of those surrounding the later and more
"historic" Zhou Dynasty. However, as the following discussion should make clear, the legends are similar only in their structural form; the content and details of the legends are not
simply copies of one another. That is, the transformations derive from the same structure,
and the themes repeat, but the legends of the different sets are never precisely the same.

of rule include *fa* 伐 "to smite," *zhu* 誅 "to punish," and *sha* 殺 "to kill" (as opposed to *fang* 放 "to banish" in Legend Set 4). All of the transformations are based on Wu Wang's execution of Zhòu Xin, but the range of interpretation, like that in Legend Set 4, is from regicide to the punishment of an individual and most often includes the chastisement of the Shang army.

The texts frequently state that Wu Wang carried his father's memorial tablet (*mu zhu* 木主) into battle with him. The *Chu ci* (3/31a), however, says it was the actual corpse (*shi* 尸):

> When Wu set out to kill Yin, why was he so grieved? He went into the battle carrying the corpse. Why was he in such haste?[3]

武發殺殷何所悒
載屍集成何所急

In one case, the *Shi ji* also states that after Wen Wang had died of illness, Wu Wang advanced on Yin (i.e., the Shang capital) carrying the corpse.[4] The lack of mourning and seemingly casual treatment of the corpse (or even the ancestral tablet) are an obvious violation of filial piety. Although there is no textual connection, this transformation may be associated with those in which Wu Wang committed regicide. On the other hand, in the transformations in which the people went from one ruler to the other, there may have been almost no bloodshed. In the *Mengzi* the people are said to have grieved until Wu Wang came to them, when they knocked their heads on the ground in greeting, refusing to fight for Zhòu Xin. In the *Xunzi*, the Yin officers fled rather than fight against Wu Wang.[5]

Zhòu Xin, like Jie, appointed evil ministers and killed those who remonstrated with him. Particularly atrocious was his murder of Jiu Hou

---

3. Translated in Hawkes, 55 ("Tianwen" 162).

4. *Shi ji, juan* 128, 3234. The commentators explain both the *Shi ji* and the *Chu ci* references to *shi* 尸 as *mu zhu* 木主. However, the commentaries must derive from other transformations of the legend, which speak of Wu Wang carrying the ancestral tablet, rather than any ordinary usage of *shi*, which refers specifically to an unburied corpse. See, for example, the *Zuo zhuan* 1/3b (Yin gong 1), 贈死不及尸 (and Du Yu's 杜預 commentary, 尸未葬之通稱) and the *Zuan tu hu zhu Li ji* 纂圖互註禮齊 (Qu li 曲禮) 1/25a, 在牀曰尸在棺曰柩.

5. *Mengzi* 14/2b, 7B.4. *Xunzi* 18/2a.

九侯 and/or Mei Bo 梅伯 whom he pickled and distributed in pieces to the feudal lords. Wen Wang received the pieces but gave them to heaven as a ritual offering, testimony of Zhòu Xin's evil deeds. When Bi Gan 比干 remonstrated with Zhòu Xin, Zhòu Xin killed him, saying, "I have heard the heart of a sage has seven apertures," but Ji Zi 箕子 feigned madness and escaped. The ministers who received death at Zhòu Xin's hands were many. Zhòu Xin was also infatuated with his concubine Da Ji 妲己 and killed the pure daughters of Jiu Hou and Mei Bo, but there is no mention of a wife in this legend set equivalent to Mo Xi of the previous one.

As Zhòu Xin's evil deeds multiplied, the sages of all-under-heaven began to turn to Wen Wang. When Zhòu Xin imprisoned Wen Wang at You Li, Hong Yao 閎夭 and Sanyi Sheng 散宜生 gathered gifts of precious objects and beautiful women to ransom him. Later Wu Wang made use of the virtuous men whom his father had gathered to attack the Shang. He personally executed the evil minister Fei Lian 飛廉, built a mound on Bi Gan's tomb, and released Ji Zi from captivity. Zhòu Xin negated the principles of virtue and repressed or executed those who would serve him with virtue. By his contrasting acts, Wu Wang showed his affirmation of these principles.[6]

Taigong Wang: The Founding Minister

The Shang lost their right to rule through Zhòu Xin's maltreatment of his subjects and negation of the principles of virtue. For Wu Wang to punish him, however, the Zhou had to establish their own right of rule. Structurally, Wen and Wu Wang's reliance on the virtuous minister Taigong Wang and the opposition of Bo Yi 伯夷 and Shu Qi 叔齊, who remonstrated against the breach of heredity, is the obverse of Zhòu Xin's reliance on the evil minister Fei Lian 飛廉 and the opposition of Bi Gan and Ji Zi, who remonstrated against the breach of virtue. The case also parallels Yao's appointment of Shun and the opposition of Xu You. Wu Wang, then, acts as a man of virtue against the negation of virtue.

---

6. For extensive accounts of Zhou's evil deeds and his overthrow by the Zhou rulers, see the *Shi ji, juan* 3, 105–109, *juan* 4, 116–24; *Lüshi chunqiu* 17/11b, 20/15a, 23/7b include references to Mei Bo. Jiu Hou is sometimes written as Gui 鬼 Hou.

Wen Wang discovered Taigong Wang and raised him up out of obscurity. Wu Wang used him to defeat the Shang. Both Wen Wang's appointment of Taigong and Wu Wang's use of him parallel Tang's relation to Yi Yin in Legend Set 4, but the division of roles reflects the distinction in the Zhou Dynasty between Wen Wang, who established the virtue of the dynasty, and Wu Wang, who actually overthrew Zhòu Xin. The texts most frequently parallel Tang's raising up Yi Yin from the kitchen or from carrying the *ding*-tripod to Wen Wang's raising up Taigong Wang from fishing on the banks of the river Wei. In other texts, Taigong was a butcher or a boatman when Wen Wang met him and made him his minister. I discuss these variants in "The Identities of Taigong Wang in Zhou and Han literature," and argue that they are regional illustrations of a similar theme.[7] The structure requires such a sign at this point in the set, and the legends grew up independently to accord with the requirement, although eventually the fishing legend became dominant. The *Mozi* also speaks of Hong Yao and Tai Dian "raised up from the fishing nets." Since the text never mentions Taigong in his role as founding minister, this may be a further variant of the same theme.[8]

In two further variants, Taigong Wang was not a poor man when he met Wen Wang but a recluse or a persuader. According to the *Mengzi*, Taigong Wang was a recluse by the Eastern Sea when he heard of Wen Wang's virtue and turned to him.[9] This presumably reflects a transformation of the theme of the founding minister to one that stresses the attracting virtue of the new king rather than the poverty or obscurity of the founding minister. As such, it accords with the denial of the poverty of Yi Yin and Boli Xi that occurs elsewhere in the *Mengzi*, as stated above, and the transformation in which the people turned from Zhòu Xin to Wu Wang. However, the transformation is not simply thematic, since the basic elements of the Taigong legends in other texts could not serve as the deep structure for this account (except perhaps for the

---

7. See Appendix 2.

8. *Mozi* 2/3b. I do not mention this in "Identities of Taigong Wang." Aside from the exclusive mention of Hong Yao and Tai Dian in this role in the *Mozi*, there is evidence that the legends of Hong Yao and Tai Dian have been combined with that of Taigong Wang in the *Shi ji* account of the bribery of Zhòu Xin to obtain the release of Wen Wang, in *juan* 32, 1478 (*Qi Taigong shijia*); Taigong is not mentioned in this legend in the *Ben ji* section of the *Shi ji* (*juan* 3, 106, *juan* 4, 116) or in any other ancient text.

9. *Mengzi* 7/10a–b, 4A.13; 13/9a, 7A.22.

accounts of Taigong Wang as a fisherman, but these usually have the Wei River rather than the Eastern Sea as their location and include different nomenclature). It seems rather to reflect both a regional variant and a thematic transformation.

The *Shi ji* records another variant in which Taigong Wang was a persuader formerly in the service of Zhòu Xin. This is a further step away from the theme of Taigong's poverty, but there are too few references to associate it with a pattern of transformation.[10] It possibly accords with Wu Wang's usurpation of the throne—Taigong would in that case simply have been a persuader who aided Wu Wang in his regicide.

Although Wen Wang raised up Taigong, Wu Wang employed his talents. Wen Wang *yu* 遇 "met," *ju* 舉 "raised up," and *de* 得 "obtained" Taigong. Wu Wang, on the other hand, *yong* 用 "employed" him. Taigong, like Yi Yin before him, was famous for his military craft and *mou* 謀 "strategy," with which he assisted the king in founding his rule. As Shi Shangfu 師尚父, another name identified with Taigong Wang, he was the primary general in Wu Wang's overthrow of the Shang Dynasty.[11]

So Wu Wang, with the aid of Taigong Wang, overthrew the Shang Dynasty and established the Zhou, venerating his father, Wen Wang, as its founder. Wen and Wu Wang together manifest the same themes of virtue and breach of heredity exhibited by Tang alone in his role as founder of the Shang. Taigong Wang parallels Yi Yin in his role of founding minister appointed because of his virtue and assisting the new king in overthrowing the old. Opposed to the founding kings and their minister are Bo Yi and Shu Qi, two brothers whose virtue was so pure that they would rather starve to death than acquiesce in a breach of hereditary position.

Bo Yi and Shu Qi refuse both rule and office. Sima Qian parallels them to Xu You, Bian Sui, and Wu Guang.[12] However, Bo Yi and Shu Qi in most transformations do not refuse to rule all-under-heaven but only the state of Gu Zhu 孤竹. The *Shi ji* (*juan* 61, 2123) gives this account:

---

10. *Shi ji, juan* 32, 1478.

11. As I show in "Identities of Taigong Wang," Appendix 2, this name is associated with the historical accounts of the overthrow of the Shang by the Zhou. It does not occur in parallel form with Yi Yin or any of the other figures with a role in "legend," but the combination of the accounts of Shi Shangfu's military role with the role of the founding minister, Taigong Wang, was thematically suitable.

12. *Shi ji, juan* 61, 2121.

Bo Yi and Shu Qi were two sons of the Prince of Gu Zhu.
Their father wished to set Shu Qi [on the throne]. When the
father died Shu Qi yielded place to Bo Yi, but Bo Yi said "It
is a paternal order" and then fled. Shu Qi was also unwilling
to take the throne and fled. The people of the state set the
middle son [on the throne].

伯夷, 叔齊, 孤竹君之二子也, 父欲立叔齊, 及父卒, 叔齊讓伯
夷, 伯夷曰: 「父命也」 遂逃去, 叔齊亦不肯立而逃之, 國人
立其中子。

This story differs from the accounts of rule-refusal in previous
dynasties, but it serves as an appropriate counter to the division of the
founder theme into two figures, Wen Wang and Wu Wang. For Wu Wang
to have offered the throne to a sage would have been inappropriate. He
did breach the hereditary position of Zhòu Xin, but in so doing he was
acting as a filial son toward his own father. Wen Wang, on the other
hand, restrained himself from assuming the rule, though his virtue and
power were sufficient to enable him to attain it. Wu Wang's veneration
of his father as the founder of the dynasty thus removes the stigma
from his breach of heredity, and he has no need to offer the throne to
a sage. However, the story of Bo Yi and Shu Qi's refusal of the rule of
Gu Zhu may be compared with the accounts of the manner in which
both Wen Wang and Wu Wang succeeded to the rule of the state of
Zhou before the overthrow of the Shang. The comparison shows that
both Wen Wang's virtue and Wu Wang's hereditary right are mediations
rather than unqualified examples of virtue and heredity.

Wen Wang's father, Wang Ji 王季, was the second son of Tai Wang
太王. Wang Ji's brother, Tai Bo 太伯, was the eldest son and heir apparent, but Tai Wang wished to set Wen Wang on the throne. Knowing
this, Tai Bo yielded the throne to Wang Ji, who accepted so that the rule
would pass to Wen Wang. When this story is set beside that of Bo Yi
and Shu Qi, Bo Yi parallels Tai Bo.[13] Wang Ji's acceptance of the throne
for Wen Wang is therefore implicitly contrasted to Shu Qi's refusal in
a similar circumstance. Thus, Wen Wang's right of rule by virtue, which
appeared perfect when contrasted to the evil of Zhòu Xin, now appears
to be only a mediation—just as Shun's virtue appeared perfect in contrast

---

13. Ibid.

with Dan Zhu but a mediation in contrast to the pure virtue of Xu You. Similarly, Wu Wang achieved the rule when his elder brother Bo Yi Kao 伯邑考 was set aside. Thus, although he fulfilled a duty to his father in overthrowing the Shang, he breached the hereditary position of his brother—once again an affirmation of hereditary right is mediated by a breach of the right.[14]

Bo Yi and Shu Qi not only refused the rule of the state of Gu Zhu, they also refused to serve or even to live under the rule of the new dynastic founder, Wu Wang. Their refusal serves to highlight the fact that the new dynasty, though founded on the principle of rule by virtue, had nevertheless compromised that virtue by regicide. And it shows that the founding minister, though a symbol of worth, had compromised his integrity by his complicity in that regicide. The *Shi ji* (*juan* 61, 2123) gives the following account of Bo Yi and Shu Qi's refusal to serve the Zhou:

> Bo Yi and Shu Qi then heard that the Western Lord, Chang, liked to care for the elderly and said, "Let us turn to him." When they arrived, the Western Lord had died. Wu Wang, carrying [his father's] wooden memorial tablet and calling him Wen Wang, attacked Zhòu [Xin] to the East. Bo Yi and Shu Qi whipped their horses and went to remonstrate with him, saying, "Your father has died, and you do not bury him but go so far as to take up sword and shield. Can this be called filial piety? For a minister to commit regicide on his ruler, can this be called humaneness?" The aides of Wu Wang wished to cut them down, but Taigong said, "These are men of integrity," and supported them on their way out. When Wu Wang had already pacified the disorder of Yin and all-under-heaven reverenced Zhou, Bo Yi and Shu Qi were ashamed of it and to maintain their integrity did not eat the grain of Zhou. They secluded themselves on Shouyang mountain and gathered wild ferns for food. On the point of starvation, they composed a song which went: "We climb the Western Mountain and gather its ferns. . . ." And so they starved to death on Shouyang Mountain.

---

14. Textual references to Wu Wang as Taizi Fa 太子發, the "Heir-apparent *Fa*," may imply the death of Bo Yi Kao before Wu Wang succeeded his father, but other references explicitly state that Wen Wang "set aside" (*she* 舍) Bo Yi Kao—e.g., *Shi ji, juan* 35, 1563; *Huainanzi* 13/2a (parallel to Shun marrying without his father's consent); *Zuan tu hu zhu li ji* (*Tan gong* 檀弓) 2/1a.

於是伯夷, 叔齊聞西伯昌善養老, 盍往歸焉, 及至, 西伯卒, 武
王載木主, 號為文王, 東伐紂, 伯夷, 叔齊叩馬而諫曰: 「父死
不葬, 爰及干戈, 可謂孝乎? 以臣弒君可謂仁乎? 」左右欲兵
之, 太公曰: 「此義人也」扶而去之, 武王已平殷亂, 天下宗
周, 而伯夷, 叔齊恥之, 義不食周粟, 隱於首陽山, 采薇而食之,
及餓且死, 作歌, 其辭曰: 「登彼西山方, 采其薇矣……」遂餓
死於首陽山

As righteous men, Bo Yi and Shu Qi could not serve in or enjoy
benefits from a state founded on a breach of heredity. That objection
is clearly pointed out in their remonstrance to Wu Wang, first for not
mourning his father properly, and second for committing regicide. They
are unable to remove themselves totally from the state; therefore, like Xu
You, Shan Juan, Wu Guang, and Bian Sui before them, they must commit suicide. In this passage from the *Shi ji* they appear to have starved
to death on their diet of wild ferns. In later accounts they realized that
even these were the property of Zhou and refused to eat them.

Here Bo Yi and Shu Qi are protected by Taigong Wang, who recognizes their integrity. Taigong, like Bo Yi and Shu Qi, was a "worthy." He
too was attracted by the virtue of Wen Wang, who recognized his merit
and appointed him as his minister (in the *Mengzi*, Bo Yi and Taigong travel
together from the Eastern Sea to serve Wen Wang).[15] Far from refusing
to serve Wu Wang, however, Taigong Wang helped him to plot the overthrow of the Shang. His willingness to serve may be contrasted with the
refusal of Bo Yi and Shu Qi, just as the service of Yi Yin may be contrasted
with the refusals of Wu Guang and Bian Sui. In the *Shi ji* account Bo Yi
and Shu Qi are not actually offered office by Wu Wang, though in other
accounts, hearing of their arrival, he offers them both rank and wealth,
which they refuse.[16] However, whether they refuse to serve the state as
citizens or as officials, the principle is essentially the same.

The juxtaposition in the texts of refuser and founding minister often
crosses dynastic bounds, a characteristic that shows the symbolism of the
theme to be more significant than the individual story. The *Huainanzi*
(20/7a), for example, states:

Yi Yin and Bo Yi followed different ways but were both humane.

伊尹伯夷異道而皆仁

---

15. *Mengzi* 7/10a–b (4A.13), 13/9a (7A.22).

16. *Zhuangzi* 9/30a–b (*pian* 28), *Lüshi chunqiu* 12/6b. The emissary is Zhougong.

The *Mengzi* frequently juxtaposes the purity of Bo Yi with the responsibility of Yi Yin.[17] It also includes a third figure from a later period, Liu Xiahui
柳下惠, a man willing to serve any prince, but since little is known of him
from other texts, it is difficult to know what his parallel in these legend
sets would be—perhaps the good ministers of Jie and Zhòu Xin. The
Zhanguo ce (3/83a–84a) similarly contrasts a series of founding ministers,
beginning with Taigong Wang and including those of the hegemons, with
Wu Guang, Bian Sui, and Shentu Di 申屠狄, another refuser from the
beginnings of the Zhou Dynasty.

The structural function of Bo Yi and Shu Qi, like that of the other
refusers, is to stand as exemplars of pure virtue in contrast to the new
nonhereditary rulers—and, in the dynastic period, their ministers. These
rulers first establish their right to rule by their virtue. When compared
with the refusers, however, their virtue is shown to be a mediation of the
breach of hereditary right. On the one hand, Bo Yi and Shu Qi are juxtaposed with Wen Wang who, though a symbol of virtue, ruled because the
hereditary right of his uncle had been breached. On the other, they are
juxtaposed with Wu Wang and his minister Taigong. Though Wu Wang is
a symbol of piety in carrying on his father's work and a man of virtue in
overthrowing Zhòu Xin, he did not mourn his father properly and killed
his hereditary lord, so they refused to serve him. Similarly, Taigong Wang,
renowned as a sage and appointed by Wen Wang because of his virtue,
is shown by contrast to the purity of Bo Yi and Shu Qi to have engaged
in complicity with a regicide.

Besides the version recorded in the *Shi ji*, there are two transformations of the story of Bo Yi and Shu Qi recorded elsewhere. The first occurs
in the *Hanfeizi* (4/12b), which states explicitly that Wu Wang yielded the
throne to Bo Yi and Shu Qi, though this is not recorded in any other text:

> In ancient times there were two men by the name of Bo
> Yi and Shu Qi. Wu Wang yielded all-under-heaven to them,
> but they did not accept it. They both starved to death at the
> mounds of Shouyang.

> 古有伯夷叔齊者武王讓以天下而弗受二人餓死首陽之陵

Since this account appears in isolation from other legends, it is
difficult to evaluate it in a transformational scheme, and its uniqueness

---

17. *Mengzi* 3/9b (2A.2), 10/1a–3a (5B.1), 12/7a–b (6B.6).

suggests that the names of Bo Yi and Shu Qi may be used carelessly, simply to symbolize the theme of refusal, especially since the speaker in the
passage wishes to emphasize his own service to the state. This account
does fit the transformation in which Wu Wang committed regicide, but
in that case Wen Wang stole the hearts of the people and thus threat-
ened the ruler.[18] If it is combined with the stories in which Wu Wang
carried his father's corpse into battle (lacked filial piety), then Wu Wang
would still need to absolve himself of the taint of usurpation. Hence the
transformation: Wu Wang yielded to Bo Yi and Shu Qi.

The other transformation of the legend of Bo Yi and Shu Qi occurs
only in the *Mengzi*, but there it is quite consistent with its context. There
are eight separate references given to Bo Yi, but none at all to Shu Qi, The
omission is particularly striking since Bo Yi and Shu Qi occur together
three times in the *Lun yu*. However, as mentioned above, in the transformation which dominates the *Mengzi* but is not developed in the *Lun
yu*, the actors simply go from one ruler to another. There is no abdication
and therefore no function for rule-refusers. The absence of Shu Qi from
the legend implies that the story of Bo Yi does not include the refusal to
rule the state of Gu Zhu. The *Mengzi* does not mention the story of Tai
Bo and Wang Ji, but to be consistent the people must be assumed to go
from the elder brother to the younger in this legend as well. If Tai Bo did
not give the rule to Wang Ji, then there would be no structural function
for a contrasting story of two brothers too pure to accept the rule from
one another. The *Mengzi* also makes no mention of the brothers starving
on Shouyang Mountain. Bo Yi appears as a symbol of integrity (*yi* 義)
who "went forward in times of order and retired in times of disorder"
(*Mengzi* 3/9b, IIA.2). Whether the disorder refers to the time of Zhòu Xin
or that of Wu Wang is not at all clear, but the following passage implies
that he did serve Wen Wang:

> Mencius said, "Bo Yi fled from Zhòu and settled on the edge
> of the North Sea. When he heard of the rise of King Wen he
> stirred and said, 'Why not go to him? I hear that the Western
> Lord takes good care of the aged.' Taigong fled from Zhòu and
> settled on the edge of the East Sea. When he heard of the
> rise of King Wen he stirred and said, 'Why not go to him? I

---

18. See *Hanfeizi* 12/5a, 15/7b. This argument is used to persuade Zhou against Wen Wang
in the *Shi ji* as well (*juan* 4, 116).

hear that the Western Lord takes good care of the aged.' These
two were the greatest old men of all-under-heaven, and they
turned to him. In other words, the fathers of all-under-heaven
turned to him. When the fathers of all-under-heaven turned
to him, where could the sons go? If any feudal lord practices
the government of King Wen he will certainly be ruling over
all-under-heaven within seven years."[19]

孟子曰伯夷辟紂居北海之濱聞文王作興曰盍歸乎來吾聞西伯
養老者太公辟紂距東海之濱聞文王作興曰盍歸乎來吾聞西伯
養老者二老者天下之大老也而歸之是天下之父歸之也天下之
父歸之其子焉往諸侯有行文王之政者七年之內必爲政於天下
矣 (*Mengzi* 7/10a–b, 4A.13; 13/9a, 7A.22)

Since this passage ends with Bo Yi and Taigong going to Wen Wang, we
cannot be sure whether Bo Yi refused to serve Wu Wang, but the implication is that both he and Taigong served the Zhou and contributed to their
uniting of all-under-heaven. This is consistent with the transformation
in which the people turn from one ruler to the other.

Period of Regency

During the period of foundation, the themes associated with rule by virtue and breach of heredity were explored and mediated. In the period of
regency, it is the themes associated with rule by heredity that are explored
and mediated, but in such a way that the final impulse to action lies
with rule by heredity—until, of course, the next period of foundation. The
general pattern is that established with respect to the Shang Dynasty,
but there is, once again, a further proliferation of figures representing
specific aspects of the legend themes. The graph of equivalents to the
period of regency in the Shang is as follows:

Yi Yin ⇒ Tai Jia   Zhougong ⇒ Cheng
  | |
Tai Jia   Guan, Cai

---

19. Translation by D. C. Lau, *Mencius*, 123. The same passage occurs in two chapters.

Here, Zhougong's "regency" for Cheng Wang parallels that of Yi Yin for Tai Jia, but he is challenged by his elder and younger brothers, Guan and Cai, rather than by the heir himself.

Zhougong, Guan and Cai, Cheng Wang:
The Regent, The Rebels, and the Ruler

Zhougong Dan 周公旦, "Dan, Duke of Zhou," was a younger brother of Wu Wang. Our texts speak of him as both military leader and minister, as they did Taigong Wang, but he is particularly associated with the campaigns consolidating the rule of Zhou rather than with the initial overthrow of the Shang. In later times, Zhougong became the most famous minister of the early Zhou period. There is also considerable historical evidence of his actual importance during the early Zhou, including bronze inscriptions that record his participation in the eastern campaigns to consolidate all-under-heaven.[20] Since he was a younger brother of

---

20. See Chen, "Xi Zhou," 144–50, 160–61. The question of whether or not Zhougong ruled in place of Cheng Wang does not seem to be solved by the inscriptions. Chen, 150, notes that Cheng Wang was not a child at the time of Wu Wang's death. Hayashi Taisuke came to the same conclusion from textual sources (see his *Zhougong*, 21–27). Chen, 149, says further that Cheng Wang also participated in the eastern campaigns, but neither would specifically disallow a "regency" during Cheng Wang's minority. Creel, in *Statecraft*, 69–80, generally accepts that Zhougong held the real power during Cheng Wang's reign, but he seems to base this assessment on the attribution of certain chapters of the *Shang shu* to Zhougong and on Warring States texts. Creel notes that the details, though abundant, are quite different in later versions and that there is little Western Zhou evidence. He accepts that there must have been a historical event because of this abundance of detail and explains away the lack of early evidence: "The fact that the Duke of Chou killed his own elder brother—a particularly deplorable event within the framework of Chinese custom— must have made this whole episode one on which men of the time had no desire to dwell" (70). I find this reasoning fallacious. The theme of Zhougong "killing his elder brother" is frequent in the Warring States texts, as we shall see below, but this does not mean it had become customary or palatable a few centuries later. Later writers would have even less reason for facing such a hard "fact." Nor is the abundance of detail any reason for accepting it as an early fact. The story was preserved, embellished, or made up because of its mythic significance. This includes both the affirmative (regency) and negative (fratricide) themes. Such themes cannot be taken as evidence of historicity, either positive or negative. Creel also notes the large amount of contemporaneous evidence concerning Shaogong and the lack of importance given to him in later texts. I would explain this by his lack of mythic importance, regardless of his "historical" importance in modern eyes.

Wu Wang, however, he could not play Yi Yin's roles of founding minister raised up from obscurity and regent. The former role was instead played by Taigong Wang, who was already an old man when raised up by Wen Wang. As founding minister, Taigong dominates the period of overthrow. Zhougong, however, dominates the following period, in which the rule of Zhou is consolidated.

Wu Wang's son Cheng Wang parallels Tai Jia as heir to the throne temporarily replaced by a regent. He differs from Tai Jia, however, in that he is never regarded as bad or rebellious; he is only *you* 幼 "young." Two other brothers of Wu Wang, Xian 鮮 and Du 度, whom he had enfeoffed respectively in Guan 管 and Cai 蔡, parallel Tai Jia in his role of rebellious member of the royal family. "Guan," as he is usually called, was older than Zhougong; "Cai" was younger. When Zhougong assumed the regency, the two brothers *yi* 疑 "suspected" his intentions and allied themselves with a son of the last Shang king in rebellion against him.[21]

Significantly, this is the first occasion in which a brother rather than a direct descendant of the ruler has rebelled against the regent. Dan Zhu, Shang Jun, Wu Guan, and Tai Jia were all filial descendants. Although we know from oracle bone inscriptions that fraternal succession was practiced in the Shang Dynasty, at least in the early period, in our texts, the crucial period of regency came with the first member of the *da zong* 大宗 "great lineage" after the founder, Tai Jia; the preceding rule of his uncles Wai Bing and Zhong Ren was virtually ignored. Nevertheless, at the beginning of the Zhou Dynasty, there could have been a question about whether the Zhou would follow the fraternal succession of Shang or the filial succession of the predynastic Zhou. The appearance in the legend set of both filial and fraternal heirs provides a model of the conflict and of an attempt to overcome it.

In the transformation in which Zhougong figures as a regent whose intention was to protect the hereditary descent of the Zhou ruling house, that descent was clearly filial. Zhougong symbolizes fraternal devotion and the precedence of filial hereditary right in his attitude toward Cheng Wang. Although he held the power of the government in his hands and was a man of virtue worthy to rule by the principles of the predynastic period, he nevertheless yielded the throne to Cheng Wang when he

---

21. *Shi ji, juan* 1, 132. *Juan* 33, 1518 is even more explicit, stating that Guan and his younger brothers spread rumors throughout the state that Zhougong would not bring advantage to Cheng Wang.

came of age. It is significant that the *Mengzi* feels it necessary to explain why such men as Zhougong, Yi, and Yi Yin did not become rulers like Shun and Yu.[22]

Even in this transformation, however, when Zhougong is compared to Guan and Cai, he appears to be a mediatory figure rather than simply a symbol of hereditary right. Disregarding Guan's fraternal claim to the throne, he is nevertheless Zhougong's elder brother. In protecting his nephew, Zhougong violated his obligation to his elder brother, just as Shun, in serving Yao as adopted son and regent, violated his obligation to his own father and brother. The *Huainanzi* (20/11b)[23] makes the parallel:

> Zhougong killed his elder brother; Shun banished his younger brother.

舜放弟周公殺兄

Consequently, Zhougong may be regarded as a usurper on either of two grounds. On the first, he usurped the rule from Cheng Wang; on the second, he replaced Guan as either ruler or regent. The *Xunzi* (4/2a) defends Zhougong as never intending to usurp the throne, but the terms of the defense show the possibility of the accusation:

> Therefore, for the branch to replace the main hereditary line was not a transgression; for a younger brother to punish his elder brother was not an act of violence.

故以枝代主非越也以弟誅兄非暴也

Similarly, in the passage from the *Shi ji* (*juan* 34, 1549) quoted in the last chapter, Zhougong cited the precedent of Yi Yin to defend himself against the suspicions of Shaogong. The transformation does not appear in a direct form, but the defense against it is evidence of the possibility of the argument. Indeed, it is this possibility that gives meaning and poignancy to Zhougong's return of the throne to Cheng Wang in the other transformations.

---

22. *Mengzi* 9/10b–12a (5A.6).

23. For other references to Zhougong's unbrotherly conduct, see *Huainanzi* 11/13a, 13/13b, 20/7a, *Mengzi* 4/10b (23.9), *Xunzi* 4/2b.

In summary, Legend Set 5 is once again a transformation of the themes of virtue and heredity. In this legend set, there are two founding kings—Wen Wang, who established the virtue of the dynasty, and Wu Wang, who overthrew the Shang. This affects the structure of the set, since Wu Wang was confirming his filial obligation to his father at the same time that he was breaching the right of the hereditary ruler. Thus, there can be no further mediation of a rule-refusal, though Bo Yi and Shu Qi's refusal to rule Gu Zhu contrasts with Wen and Wu Wang's succession to the rule of the state of Zhou. Bo Yi and Shu Qi's refusal to serve Wu Wang, who actually overthrew the Shang, further contrasts with Taigong Wang's willingness to aid him. In the period of regency, Zhougong Dan replaces the heir Cheng Wang and is challenged by his elder brother Guan and younger brother Cai. In returning the rule to Cheng Wang, he confirms the right of heredity, but he has nevertheless breached the position of his elder brother—once again, there is a mediation of the principles of heredity to balance the mediation of the principles of virtue depicted in the period of foundation.

6

The Philosophers

In the introductory chapter of this work, I hypothesized that the legends surrounding the critical periods of change or continuation of rule from Yao's transfer of rule to Shun to the foundation of the Zhou Dynasty serve as models to resolve an opposition between conflicting principles of rule by heredity and rule by virtue. Each legend has a deep structure of certain invariable elements, but may be transformed within a limited range, the transformation of one legend having implications for the entire system. I also suggested that ancient Chinese philosophers were at least intuitively aware of the structure and deliberately manipulated the system as a means of expressing political and philosophical ideas.

In the next chapters, I defined the essential elements of the legends in each set, traced their structural configuration, and demonstrated that the transformations that occur in the texts may all be derived from these elements. In each set, the same conflicting themes of rule by heredity and rule by virtue were posed and counterposed—as conflicts between king and minister, heir and sage, minister and recluse, regent and rebel—in a manner that appeared to resolve the conflict, though each set or slate in Lévi-Strauss's terminology was intertwined with the next in which the same conflict was again posed and mediated. In the course of this discussion, the reader may have noticed that certain transformations tended to be associated with certain texts. For example, the transformations in which Shun and Yu took the rule from Yao and Shun and in which Tang and Wu committed regicide occur most frequently in the *Hanfeizi* and the *Guben zhushu jinian*. In the *Xunzi* and the *Mengzi*, heaven changes the mandate and the people change their loyalties from one ruler to the other. The *Mozi* stresses the low position of the founding minister. The *Zhuangzi* celebrates the integrity of the rule-refusers.

In the following pages, I will analyze the transformations of the legends that occur in the various philosophical texts. These will include the *Mozi*, the *Lun yu*, the *Mengzi*, the *Xunzi*, the *Hanfeizi* (discussed together with the *Guben zhushu jinian*), and the *Zhuangzi*. Theoretically, each philosophical text should present a pattern of transformations consistent with its arguments and social attitudes. The Chinese philosophic texts of this period, however, were not the works of single men but were compiled over a period of time by the members of the school of the founder. There seems to have been no rigid concept of authorship. Some of the texts, such as the *Xunzi*, the *Hanfeizi*, and possibly the *Zhuangzi*, include sections by the philosopher after whom they are named. Others, such as the *Lun yu* and the *Mengzi*, include only the words of the philosophers as they were recorded by their disciples or their disciples' disciples. The arguments in the *Mozi*, on the other hand, may have no direct connection with Mozi at all. This is not a simple matter of forgery but rather of conception. The works included sayings, teachings, arguments, and stories associated with the founder of the school, but the attribution of a work to a philosopher did not mean that he himself wrote it. No distinction was drawn between the genuine and the apocryphal.

This manner of compiling philosophical works has created many problems for the modern historian, and much work has been devoted to the separation of the various layers of the texts. For the purposes of this study, however, that work is of little assistance. The texts are already fragmentary, and omissions of legends cannot be considered rejections. If the various layers of a text are separated, the remaining material is too sparse to yield any results. So in the following chapter I will examine each work as a whole and attempt to determine the pattern of transformations that characterizes it. The pattern may be contradicted by an occasional passage, but to the extent that the texts present a consistent philosophical viewpoint and mention the full range of transformations, they should also include a consistent system of transformations. These systems are discussed below.

The *Mozi*

The Mohist school was founded around 450 BC by Mo Di 墨翟 (ca. 479–390 BC) and died out soon after the repression of the philosophical schools in the Qin Dynasty.[1] Two of the primary philosophical tenets of the school were *jian ai* 兼愛 "universal love" and *shang xian* 尚賢 "honoring men of worth." According to the doctrine of universal love, men should care for the members of other families and states as they do for those of their own. By "honoring men of worth," the Mohists meant that men should he promoted and given office according to their merit and ability. These doctrines as well as those recommending frugality and cautioning against excessive display reflect an anti-aristocratic bias, so much so that modern scholars have suggested that the name Mo 墨 is not a surname, but means that Mozi was "tattooed"—that is, that he was a former convict. Whether or not this was true, the school seems to have consisted largely of craftsmen, and there is a suggestion in the text that Mozi himself was a wheelwright.[2] This bias against entrenched hereditary interests is reflected in the transformations of the legends that are recorded in the *Mozi*. The text is relatively consistent in its transformations, even though it includes three versions of many of the chapters, apparently derived from the three schools of the later Mohists. The Mohists claimed "history" as a criterion to test their theories, but this history is one in which the interests of virtue are regularly placed over those of heredity.

The doctrine of honoring men of worth is most frequently explained by citing the ancient kings' use of their founding ministers. Shun farmed, potted, and fished and was raised up by Yao from Fu Marsh (2/3a–b); Yi Yin was the personal servant of the lady of You Xin and was raised up by Tang from the kitchen (2/9b); Hong Yao and Tai Dian were raised up by Wen Wang from the fishing nets (2/15a). The low-status occupations and poverty of the ministers before they met their kings are continually stressed, and rulers are not only willing to take their ministers from the most unlikely places, they are willing to go to the man of virtue rather than wait for him to come to them (12/2a–b):

> Formerly, Tang was about to go to visit Yi Yin. He ordered Peng Shi Zhi Zi to drive the chariot. On the way there, Peng Shi Zhi Zi inquired, "Where are you going?" Tang said, "I am going to visit Yi Yin." Peng Shi Zhi Zi said, "Yi Yin is the humblest man

---

1. As stated in chapter 1, note 10, the dates for pre-Qin philosophers are from Qian Mu. The textual information in the following is largely taken from Cho-yün Hsü, *Ancient China in Transition*, 183–92. The date of the founding of the Mohist school is taken from the work of A. C. Graham, *Later Mohist Logic, Ethics, and Science*.

2. Graham, 6, n. 8.

under heaven. If your lordship wishes to see him, why do you not summon him to you? He would be honored." Tang said, "It is not something you know anything about. . . . Compare it to a fine doctor and good medicine. For you not to wish me to visit Yi Yin is to not wish me to be well."

湯將往見伊尹令彭氏之子御彭氏之子半道而問曰君將何之湯
曰將往見伊尹彭氏之子曰伊尹天下之賤人也君若欲見之亦令
召問焉彼受賜矣湯曰非女所知也……譬之良醫善藥也而子不
欲我見伊尹是子不欲吾善也

Here Yi Yin is called a *jian ren* 賤人 "humble man" (the opposite of a *gui ren* 貴人 "noble"), yet Tang is willing to go to him because he must promote the worthy in order to establish his rule.

In accordance with the principle of honoring men of worth, the *Mozi* defines the nonhereditary transfers of the predynastic period as the deliberate and conscious acts of the preceding ruler. Yao "bestowed the government" on Shun (*shou zhi zheng* 授之政, 2/3b), "gave over the government of all-under-heaven" to him (*yu jie tianxia zhi zheng* 與接天下之政, 2/9b) and "established him as son-of-heaven" (*li wei tianzi* 立為天子, 2/15b). These are the same passages that speak of raising up Shun and the other founding ministers from positions of poverty. There is no clear distinction between the investment of power in the minister and the actual abdication of the rule to him. Both are "honoring men of worth."

In accordance with the transformation in which the rulers of the predynastic era voluntarily gave the rule to their successors, we should expect that the succeeding rulers of the dynastic era took the rule from their predecessors but in so doing acted to punish them. This is the case in the *Mozi*. The *Mozi* promotes a doctrine of defensive but not offensive warfare. Nevertheless, it does accept punitive actions. Accordingly, the transfers of rule in the dynastic era are defined as punishment but not as offensive attack. In accordance with the *Mozi*'s stress on the common people rather than the upper classes or literati, the text stresses the crimes of Jie and Zhòu Xin against the people rather than their maltreatment of the remonstrating ministers. It describes their crimes in more graphic terms than those that occur in the other texts of this period. Zhòu Xin, for example, is said to have cast out the aged, mutilated and executed children, and cut up pregnant women (8/10b–11b). The evil ministers of Jie and Zhòu Xin who perpetrated these deeds were personally executed by Tang and Wu Wang (8/11b), but the remonstrating ministers are not discussed.

Their punishment, as in the *Mengzi* and the *Xunzi*, is heaven-sent. But although the people wished to be ruled by Tang and Wen Wang and went to them (9/3a–4a), heaven's will is demonstrated by supernatural omens rather than by the movement of the people. A belief in the supernatural is an important part of Mozi's philosophy, and this is reflected in the signs that appear to show that Jie and Zhòu Xin have lost heaven's favor and that Tang and Wen have gained it. At the end of the bad king's rule, for example, there were such ill omens as eclipses of the sun and moon, earth raining from the sky, ghosts moving about, the nine cauldrons changing places, and brambles growing in the roads (5/11b–13a). These, rather than the movement of the people, demonstrated the will of heaven. The new rulers fought against all odds (they had only one hundred chariots and four hundred men, 8/10b), and there is no suggestion that there was no warfare or that it was only the punishment of "one fellow."

The function of the rule-refuser, as stated above, is to emphasize the violation of virtue involved in the nonhereditary transfers. The refusal of office likewise serves to stress the breach of heredity implied by appointment by worth. The *Mozi* consistently promotes these breaches of the hereditary principle and consequently makes no mention of the recluses who refused to serve or to rule. Only Xu You is mentioned, and the context and parallels imply that he was a minister during the reign of Yao rather than a refuser (1/5b).

The themes of regency and the return of rule to the heir usually symbolize heredity over virtue. Accordingly, there are no direct references to either the predynastic or dynastic regencies in the text. This does not mean that the Mohists denied the legends of regency, but simply that they did not find it useful to discuss them. Zhougong does appear in the text as a "sage" (*sheng ren* 聖人) contrasted with the "man of violence" (*bao ren* 暴人) Guan Shu (12/9b), but his acting as regent for Cheng Wang is not mentioned. Indeed, his relationship with Guan Shu is described in highly unusual terms (11/15b–16a):

> Zhougong Dan found fault with Guan Shu and declined the position of one of the three dukes. He went east and dwelt at Shang Gai. Everyone called him mad, but later ages praised his virtue.

周公旦非關叔辭三公東處於商蓋人皆謂之狂後世稱其德

The rivalry I have hypothesized between Zhougong and Guan Shu is clearly demonstrated in this passage, but the reference is not at all clear. It appears to be a transformation of Zhougong's enfeoffment in Lu 魯 after Cheng Wang became king. Sun Yirang 孫詒讓 quotes Cai Yong's 蔡 邕 *Qin cao* 琴操 to the effect that because someone slandered Zhougong to the king, he fled to Lu where he died. It could also be a transformation of Zhougong's eastern campaigns. It differs from other accounts in stating not that Zhougong "punished" Guan Shu, but rather that he retired because of Guan Shu, who, it is further implied, held power in the state, if only temporarily. The other rebel members of the ruling family, Dan Zhu, Shang Jun, the Wu Guan, and Tai Jia, do not occur in the text.

The Lun Yu

The *Lun yu*, compiled for the most part within a generation or so after the death of Confucius (551–479 BC), slightly precedes the *Mozi* and is the earliest of our texts. There are very few references to legends in the *Lun yu*, and where they do occur, the references are brief and have little context. For this reason, the transformations in this text cannot be analyzed in detail. They are worth mentioning, however, because they differ substantially from those recorded in the later Confucian texts, the *Mengzi* and the *Xunzi*. In the *Mengzi* and *Xunzi*, change of rule is always attributed to the will of heaven or the changing loyalties of the people. This does not occur in the *Lun yu*. Transfers of rule are not discussed directly, and so there is no terminology by which to determine the transformation, but the references one finds to the predynastic period imply abdication, and those of the dynastic period, righteous force. Yao gives his dying charge to Shun, implying abdication to him. Shun gave the same charge to Yu (10/9a, XX.1).[3] Neither the refusers nor the bad sons of this period are mentioned. In the dynastic period, Tang offers himself to the Lord on High and declares that he will slay the guilty but spare the servants of the Lord. Presumably, he has overthrown Jie on behalf of heaven to punish the wrongdoers. Although Confucius reveres the Zhou, he does not discuss the transfer of rule except to say that the wronged ministers Weizi, Ji Zi, and Bi Gan were the "three humane men" of Yin (9/11a–b, XVIII.1).

---

3. This passage is not attributed to Confucius in the text, but is one of the *Shang shu*–like statements that make up this chapter. See Waley, 21.

Most important to Confucius is the role of the minister. Zhougong is the ideal to whom he looks back, the hero of whom he dreams. Once again, however, the text does not define precisely why. We may only assume it was because of his role of regent—the all-powerful yet perfectly loyal minister. Yi Yin is also mentioned, but in his role of founding minister (6/11b, XII.22):

> When Tang had all-under-heaven, he made a selection from among the multitude and raised up Yi Yin, and the inhumane went far away.

湯有天下選於眾舉伊尹不仁者遠矣

The *Lun yu* also includes the theme of refusal, but only with respect to the Zhou Dynasty. Two of Wen Wang's uncles who yielded to his father are mentioned. Confucius calls the eldest, Tai Bo 太伯, "most virtuous" (*zhi de* 至德) because he "declined all-under-heaven three times" and did not receive the praise of the people (4/11a, VIII. 1). Another uncle, Yú Zhong 虞仲 (i.e., Zhong Yong 仲雍), also appears in a series of men who withdrew from service (*yi min* 逸民), the most righteous of which were Bo Yi and Shu Qi, who "did not lower their ambitions or disgrace their persons" (不降其志不辱其身, 9/16a–b, XVII.8). Bo Yi and Shu Qi are frequently mentioned in the *Lun yu*, and Confucius particularly makes the point that though they were men of worth, they held no rancor against the Zhou. Since they "sought humaneness and obtained humaneness, why should they have felt wronged" (求仁而得仁又何怨乎, 4/4b, VII.14). Yú Zhong, on the other hand, appears to have complied with the exigencies of the time, but was not totally content. Confucius specifically declines to compare himself with this series of recluses, but he clearly respects their integrity. His ideal is one of pure virtue, of a man like Zhougong who used his virtue to support the hereditary ruler.

The *Mengzi*

The *Mengzi*, attributed by Sima Qian to Mencius (390–305 BC) himself, was probably written soon after the philosopher's death and is considered relatively free of later interpolations. The theory of the mandate of heaven (*tian ming* 天命) is especially well developed in the *Mengzi*, and the text specifically states that heaven demonstrates the change of mandate by the movement of the people. Modern scholars have often noted those revolutionary implications of Mencian philosophy that may be used to justify rebellion when the people feel that they have been oppressed. Compared to the *Mozi*, however, the *Mengzi* shows a bias toward the aristocracy and literati rather than the common people. A clear distinction is made between gentlemen who rule and those who give them their allegiance. Talk of rebellion is less of a "right" than a warning to the ruler. Further, though virtue is all-important, the conditions under which it may take precedence are strictly limited, and the transformations in which the people go from one ruler to the other are so phrased as to deny that the former kings ever acted deliberately to breach the rule of hereditary continuation.

In the *Mengzi*, heaven acts to change the rule and manifests its choice in the movement of the people. Only heaven can change the rule. The sage kings of the predynastic period did not abdicate:

> Wanzhang said, "Did it happen that Yao gave all-under-heaven to Shun?" Mencius said, "No. The son-of-heaven cannot give all-under-heaven to someone. . . ." [Mencius] said, "The son-of-heaven can commend someone to Heaven, but he is not able to cause Heaven to give him all-under-heaven. A feudal lord can commend someone to the son-of-heaven, but he cannot cause the son-of-heaven to give (a feof) to the feudal lord. A noble can commend someone to a feudal lord, but he cannot cause the feudal lord to give him noble (status). Formerly, Yao commended Shun to heaven, and heaven accepted him; he displayed him to the people and the people accepted him. Thus, it is said that heaven does not speak, it simply makes apparent with actions and deeds.

> 萬章曰堯以天下與舜有諸

> 孟子曰否天子不能以天下與人 . . .

> [孟子]曰: 天子能薦人于天不能使天與之天下諸侯能薦人于
> 天子不能使天子與之諸侯大夫能薦人于諸侯不能使諸侯與之
> 大夫昔者堯薦舜于天而天受之暴之于民而民受之故曰天不言
> 以行與事示之而已矣 (*Mengzi* 9/9a–b, VB.5)

Nor did the founders of Shang and Zhou commit regicide:

> (Wanzhang) said: "Is it permissible for a subject to assassinate his ruler?"

> (Mencius) said: "One who steals from others is called a 'thief'; one who takes away from right principles is called a 'mutilator.' Thieves and mutilators are called 'individuals.' I have only heard about the execution of the individual, Zhòu, never about the assassination of a ruler."

曰臣弒其君可乎

曰賊人者謂之賊賊義者謂之殘殘賊之人謂之一夫聞誅一夫紂
矣未聞弒君也。 (*Mengzi* 2/12a [IB.8])

The people went from one ruler to the other. There is no essential difference between the hereditary and nonhereditary transfers of rule. It is true that Tang and Wu acted to punish the individuals, Jie and Zhou, but in so doing, they were acting as rulers against criminals rather than as subjects against rulers. Although the *Mengzi* rather grudgingly admits that "Tang banished Jie and Wu Wang smote Zhou" (2/12a, IB.8), the text continually deemphasizes any violence that might have occurred in these transfers of rule. In one case, the *Shang shu* statement that "pestles swam in blood" when Wu Wang fought Zhòu Xin is dismissed as impossible, for how could it be so "when the most humane smote the most inhumane" (仁人無敵於天下以至仁伐至不仁而何其血之流杵也, 14/2a, 7B.3). Elsewhere, the text describes how the people grieved until the founding kings came to them but greeted them with joy when they came (6/6b–8b, 3B.5; 2/14a–b, IB.11; 14/2b 7B.4).

The *Mengzi*'s attitude toward the common people is also reflected in the transformations of the raising up of the founding ministers. The *Mengzi*, as discussed in chapter 3, specifically denies that Yi Yin would have disgraced himself by becoming a cook or Boli Xi would have sold himself for five sheepskins (9/14b, 5A.7; 9/16b, 5A.9). Taigong Wang was also a recluse by the Eastern Sea rather than a poor man raised up by Wen Wang (7/10a, 4A. 13; 13/9a, 7A. 22). The virtue of the true king is perfect, and he is able to attract men of worth into his service, but there is no question of his employing cooks or fishermen as his ministers, nor would gentlemen lower themselves to assume those positions.[4]

Since the true king attracts all men into his service and could neither abdicate nor usurp the throne, there can be neither rule-refusers nor minister-refusers. It is not only that they would serve the king; there is no breach of heredity and hence no structural function for a refuser. The only refuser who occurs in this text is Bo Yi, and he occurs alone, without Shu Qi. As discussed previously, Bo Yi is described in the *Mengzi* as a man who "went forward in time of order and retired in time of disorder" (3/9b, 2A.2). He went from the Eastern Sea with Taigong to serve Wen Wang (7/10a, 13/9a; 7A.22). Whether or not Bo Yi served Wu Wang after the death of Wen Wang is not stated in the text.

On the other side of the virtue-heredity axis, hereditary obligations are stressed. Shun's ambivalent position as Gu Sou's son and Yao's son-in-law is frequently referred to. The point is made that Shun would have abdicated and fled with his father if the latter had committed a murder while Shun was ruler (13/14a–b, 7A.35), and that he valued his parent's approval but not all-under-heaven (7/17a–b, 4A.28). Furthermore, Shun served Yao as regent (though Shun was not the actual ruler) for twenty-eight years. When Yao died, Shun yielded to Dan Zhu and only assumed the rule after three years' mourning when the people had turned from Dan Zhu to him (9/11a, 5A.6). Again and again, the text stresses that Shun respected his obligations to his own family and did not act to breach Dan Zhu's hereditary right.

Yi Yin's intentions toward Tai Jia were similar to those of Shun toward Dan Zhu, but in this case the people returned to the heir (13/12b, 7A.31):

> Gongsun Chou said "Yi Yin banished Tai Jia to Tong, saying, 'I do not wish to be close to the one who is intractable,' and the people were greatly pleased. When Tai Jia become good, Yi Yin restored him to the throne, and the people, once again, were pleased. When a prince is not good, is it permissible for a good and wise man who is his subject to banish him?"

---

4. One exception to this generalization is *Mengzi* 12/16b–17a (6B.15), which refers to the founding minister's previous low position as trials that Heaven sent down upon the ministers before it raised them up.

"It is permissible," said Mencius, "only if he had the motive of an Yi Yin, otherwise it would be usurpation."[5]

公孫醜曰伊尹曰予不狎于不順放太甲于桐民大悅太甲賢又反
之民大悅賢者之爲人臣也其君不賢則固可放與孟子曰有伊尹
之志則可無伊尹之志則篡也

Elsewhere in the text (9/11b–12a, 5A.6), Mencius explains why Yi, Yi Yin, and Zhougong never came to possess all-under-heaven—the sage must not only be virtuous but must also receive the presentation of the former ruler; conversely, only a Jie or a Zhòu Xin would be set aside by heaven. The duty of the sage is to respect heredity (Zhougong mistakenly enfeoffed Guan Shu, but this was because Guan Shu was his brother; see 4/10b, 2B.9), but he can accept the rule when virtue has been negated and the people have turned to him.

The *Xunzi*

The transformations in the *Xunzi*, attributed in large part to the philosopher himself (340–245 BC), are similar to those in the *Mengzi*, though less emphasis is placed on the changing mandate of heaven. The text tends to define the legitimacy of the ruler in terms of the loyalty of the people, rather than of the manner in which the people will turn peacefully from one ruler to the other. The *Xunzi*, like the *Mengzi*, denies that Yao and Shun declined the throne or that Tang and Wu Wang usurped the rule, but its argument is largely one of definition. Yao and Shun could not have yielded since their virtue was perfect and there was no one under heaven who did not give them his allegiance. This assertion involves a play on the term *rang* 讓, which implies both ritual abdication and yielding to superior force. Nor could Tang and Wu Wang have usurped the rule—Jie and Zhòu Xin were not true rulers. They had the accoutrements of rule (the registers of population and the rest), but the people obeyed Tang and Wu (12/2b–6b, 10b–15a).

As in the *Mengzi*, there cannot be any rule-refusers because there is no abdication. There are no examples of these in the *Xunzi* except in

---

5. Translated in Lau, 189.

juan 12, *pian* 篇18 (*Zheng Lun* 正論), which also differs from the rest of
the text because it refers to Yao bestowing the throne upon Shun.[6] In
the predynastic era, Dan Zhu and Shun's brother Xiang are mentioned
as men who could not be reformed even by the perfect virtue of Yao and
Shun, but "this was not the fault of Yao and Shun but the crime of Zhu
and Xiang" (是非堯舜之過朱象之罪也, 12/15a).

With regard to the dynastic period, the *Xunzi* follows the same
tradition that the *Mengzi* does in describing Jie and Zhòu Xin as "mere
fellows" punished by the new rulers, but unlike the *Mengzi*, it does not
stress the lack of violence in these overthrows. In *Xunzi*, Tang and Wu
Wang smote Jie and Zhòu Xin, just as Yao, Shun, and Yu smote the Huan
Dou, You Miao, and Gong Gong (10/13b–14b). The negative features of
the bad last kings mirror the positive ones of their successors. "Jie was
obsessed with Mo Xi and Si Guan but did not know the worth of Guan
Longfeng. His heart being deluded, his conduct was disorderly. Zhòu
was obsessed with Da Ji and Fei Lian but did not know the worth of
Weizi Qi" (桀蔽於末喜斯觀而不知關龍逢以惑其心而亂其行紂蔽於妲己
飛廉而不知微子啟). This reliance on concubines and evil ministers is
further contrasted with the use of Yi Yin and Taigong by Tang and Wen
Wang (15/2a–3a). This emphasis on how ministers were treated by the
last kings contrasts with the *Mozi*, which emphasizes instead the crimes
of those kings against the general population.

In accordance with the theory of the perfect transforming virtue
of the true king, there are no recluses or neglected men of worth. Even
in the dynastic era the founding kings do not "raise up" their ministers
from poverty, but only "use" them. The power of the king to attract sages
into his service replaces the theme of his willingness to raise them up.
As in the *Mengzi*, the importance of the minister is stressed, but no overt
sanction is given to the breach of heredity.

The treatment of the regency in this text corresponds to the treatment of the nonhereditary transfers of rule. The only regency that is mentioned is that of Zhougong, who assumed the rule in Cheng Wang's youth
in order to retain the rule of all-under-heaven for the Zhou (*Xunzi* 4/2a–b):

> When Cheng Wang was capped and became an adult, Zhou-
> gong returned the Zhou and gave back the registers. This
> showed that he had no intention of destroying the principle

of rule. Zhougong did not have all-under-heaven. To have formerly possessed all-under-heaven and then no longer to possess it, this was not abdication. Cheng Wang formerly did not possess all-under-heaven and then possessed it. This was not usurpation. The change of position and rotation of order was regular. Thus, for the branch to replace the main hereditary line was not a transgression. For the younger brother to punish the elder was not an act of violence. For prince and subject to exchange positions was not improper.

成王冠成人周公歸周反籍焉明不滅主之義也周公無天下矣鄉
有天下今無天下非擅也成王鄉無天下今有天下非奪也變勢次
序節然也故以枝代主而非越也以弟誅兄非暴也君臣易位而非
不順也

This argument resembles that in the *Mengzi* in which Yi Yin banished Tai Jia, but only for the purpose of instructing him. In both texts the people changed their allegiance from Jie and Zhòu Xin to Tang and Wu. Here they go from the heir to the regent and back to the heir, but in no case is there a deliberate breach of heredity or a change in the system. As the *Xunzi* states, this was neither abdication nor usurpation. The regent merely acted to preserve the house of the founding king.

The *Hanfeizi* and the *Guben Zhushu Jinian*

The arguments in the *Mozi*, the *Mengzi*, and the *Xunzi* tend to be directed to the ruler of a feudal state who wishes to become king. The ruler is encouraged to practice virtue and thus gain the mandate of heaven and the allegiance of the people. If he becomes like Yao, Shun, Tang, or Wu, he will also be able to achieve their power. The *Hanfeizi*, on the other hand, is directed to the established ruler who wishes to preserve his power and enlarge his state. The religious distinction between the son-of-heaven and the ruler of a state has been largely lost, and a rather cynical view of pragmatic politics has been substituted for the belief in the charismatic power of true virtue. This change is apparent in the transformations of the legends. The text is not entirely consistent, but there are two general trends. In the first place, the ruler is warned of the subversive power of virtue if practiced by his subjects. In the second, the former sage kings are shown to have practiced such subversion and committed regicide.

Since the *Hanfeizi* is written from the point of view of the entrenched ruler, the precedents of the previous nonhereditary transfers are regarded as a threat, especially when they are based on the principle of virtue. This threat is often shown by extending the transformations to their logical limits so that the virtuous ruler acts deliberately to usurp the throne, even using his virtue as a guise to aid his purpose. For example, in the *Hanfeizi* (16/3a) Confucius is said to have advised the Duke of She to please the near and attract the far:

> Yao's worth was the most excellent of the six kings. Yet as soon as Shun became his follower, he gathered everyone about him, and Yao no longer had all-under-heaven.

> 夫堯之賢六王之冠也舜一從而咸包而堯無天下矣

On the other hand, the text (15/8a) quotes Confucius as stating:

> How wise was Wen Wang. He let go one thousand li of land and gained the hearts of all-under-heaven.

> 智哉文王出千里之地而得天下之心

The critic, however, points out that he aroused Zhou's suspicion and was therefore imprisoned at You Li. In both cases, the "man of worth" was simply trying to gain the rule for himself.

Similarly, the abdication of Tang to Wu Guang was merely a design to rid himself of the taint of usurpation (7/5a). Those who refuse to serve the state present the greatest threat because they are beyond the power of reward and punishment (4/12b):

> Formerly there were Bo Yi and Shu Qi, who did not accept the rule when Wu Wang yielded it to them. Both men starved to death on Shou Yang mound. Subjects such as these do not fear heavy punishment, nor do they covet great rewards; they cannot be prohibited by chastisement nor moved by reward.

> 古有伯夷叔齊者武王讓以天下而弗受二人餓死首陽之陵若此
> 臣不畏重誅不利重賞不可以罰禁也不可以賞使也

The *Hanfeizi* (19/10b) accepts the tradition of the founding ministers. The king must have ministers on whom he can rely. The acquiescence of the people is, in itself, not enough:

Now those who do not know how to govern are bound to say, "Gain the hearts of the people." If by gaining the hearts of the people, one could thereby govern, then Yi Yin and Guan Zhong would be of no use—you would simply listen to the people.

今不知治者心曰得民之心欲得民之心而可以為治則是伊尹管
仲無所用也將聽民而已矣

On the other hand, "Tang got Yi Yin and become son-of-heaven with one hundred li [of land]; Huan Gong got Guan Zhong and was established as [one of the] five hegemons" (湯得伊尹一百里之地立為天子桓公得管仲立為五霸主, 4/12b). Conversely, ministers are urged to take Yi Yin and Boli Xi as their examples and be willing to become cook or captive if they can thereby obtain the ear of the ruler (4/5b). These ministers were not, of course, poor men waiting for a virtuous ruler but persuaders who could not otherwise obtain the patronage of the ruler. Yi Yin, for example, had gone seventy times to persuade Tang before he became a kitchen worker and carried the *ding*-tripod (1/7a).

Although the *Hanfeizi* provided much of the material used in the preceding discussion of transformations in which the predynastic rulers forced the rule from their predecessors and the dynastic rulers usurped the throne, the textual problems are extremely complex and the text often has internal discrepancies. The *Guben zhushu jinian*, on the other hand, records these transformations consistently and can often be used to clarify *Hanfeizi* references. Whereas the *Hanfeizi* hints at the subversion implied by Shun gathering the people around him and warns against the persuader who will tell the minister that "Shun forced Yao," the *Guben zhushu jinian* states explicitly that Shun imprisoned Yao (6). Similarly, Yi tried to take Qi's position from him and was killed by him (9). Finally, although the *Hanfeizi* warns that those who would cite the tradition of Yi Yin will turn their backs upon the law (5/9a), the *Guben zhushu jinian* (17–18) states that Yi Yin banished Tai Jia but that Tai Jia returned secretly to kill him.[7]

---

7. I believe this association between the transformations in the *Hanfeizi* and the *Guben zhushu jinian* may provide a clue to the nature of the *Guben zhushu jinian*. We know only that this text was buried around 300 BC. The *Hanfeizi* was compiled in the third century. Rather than being an "authentic" chronicle, the *Guben zhushu jinian* would seem to have specific associations with the Legalist school and may not be much earlier than its burial date.

The association of the *Guben zhushu jinian* with the *Hanfeizi* sheds light on the nature of this text. Although the history of the *Zhushu jinian* before it was buried in 296 BC is unknown, its *realpolitik* accounts of predynastic rulers imprisoning and forcing the rule from one another has led many pragmatic scholars to suppose that it is earlier than the more obviously mythical accounts of peaceful abdication and long regencies. Here, however, the "history" of the *Guben zhushu jinian* appears as another transformation within the range of possible transformations, consistent within itself, and closely associated with a third century legalist text, the *Hanfeizi*.

The *Zhuangzi*

In the *Zhuangzi* all political activity beginning with the abdication of Yao to Shun represents degeneration. An earlier period—such as that of Huang Di or Shen Nong, in which people knew their mothers but not their fathers, lived side by side with the animals, plowed and wove for their food and clothing, did not harm one another, and needed no governing—is taken as the ideal. Consequently, the text often points out the paradoxes of the nonhereditary transfers of rule in order to debunk the most esteemed rulers. For example (9/38a–b, *pian* 29):

> Yao was unfatherly, Shun was unfilial, Yu was withered on one side, Tang banished his ruler, Wu Wang smote Zhou, Wen Wang was imprisoned at You Li.

> 堯不慈舜不孝禹偏枯湯放其主武王伐紂文王拘羑里

Since the rule-refusers function to demonstrate the breach of virtue in nonhereditary transfers, they are explicitly said to have committed suicide, ashamed at the very suggestion that they might be willing to accept an abdication. The point is stressed. One of the refusers accuses Shun of having "wandered about in front of Yao's gate" (9/29a, *pian* 28). In the dynastic era, Wu Guang and Bian Sui are ashamed at the suggestion that they aid Tang in his regicide and castigate Yi Yin and Tang for their plots. Bo Yi and Shu Qi go to Wen Wang, who refrained from overthrowing Zhòu Xin, but they choose to starve to death rather than serve in Wu Wang's new dynasty.

Thus, although the philosophical texts contain certain omissions and occasional inconsistencies that may be related to textual problems, they do generally present consistent patterns of transformations that may be related to their political, philosophical, and social attitudes. And these transformations are related in the texts to the concepts that are expressed. Most striking are the differences between the *Mozi* and the later Confucian texts, the *Mengzi* and the *Xunzi*. The *Mozi*, consistent in its opposition to aristocratic privilege, expounds a doctrine of honoring men of worth and portrays the predynastic rulers and founding ministers as having been poor and of low social class before achieving power. The *Mengzi* and *Xunzi* expound a doctrine of the mandate of heaven that, by comparison with the *Mozi*, severely limits the circumstances in which hereditary right may be challenged; and the predynastic rulers and founding ministers in the *Mengzi* tend to be men of nobility in seclusion rather than men of low social class. The *Hanfeizi*, on the other hand, substitutes a cynical and mechanical view of political power for the belief in the charismatic power of virtue of the Confucian texts. It accordingly transforms the accounts to emphasize the violence and cunning of the earlier changes of rule. The *Zhuangzi*, rejecting politics, also debunks the ancient heroes. In each text, the transformations are regular and significant.

7

Conclusion

Claude Lévi-Strauss, in *The Raw and the Cooked*, found the opposition between nature and culture to be the key theme underlying the myths of certain South American Indian tribes. In this work, I have studied the manner in which the opposition between heredity and virtue—"the heir" versus "the sage"—is the key theme of ancient Chinese dynastic legends. The opposition between nature and culture is of universal significance, but it would seem to be of particular importance to primitive tribes such as those studied by Lévi-Strauss, which relied on hunting and food gathering for sustenance and whose members had a close relation in their daily life to animals and plants in their undomesticated state. It is essentially a theme suitable to those stages of civilization in which man is primarily concerned with the difference between the human and the animal and with the means by which man subjects nature to his civilizing processes.[1]

The opposition between virtue and heredity is also of universal importance. "Virtue," as I have used the term in this study, is essentially a response to the demands of the larger community or state, even when these demands conflict with the interests of one's family or kinship group. Heredity is the protection of family or kinship interests. This opposition is inherent in any human society that differentiates one nuclear family

---

1. Kirk has shown in *Myth* that the opposition between nature and culture is a widespread topic of myth and occurs in ancient Near Eastern European myths, but it does not seem to be the primary theme of the myths of these cultures. See also his *The Nature of Greek Myths* (Harmondsworth: Penguin, 1974), esp. 85–86.

or kinship group from another, but it increases in importance with the complexity of the political and social organization of the community. In the settled agricultural community of traditional China, with its complex system of kinship organizations existing alongside a political organization with a hereditary king and a nonhereditary officialdom, this opposition assumed an unusual importance. The themes of myths differ according to the concerns of the society that creates them; but, as I have tried to show in this study, the dynastic legends of ancient China functioned in the same way as the myths of the Bororo Indians—to mediate an inherent social conflict.

The period from which the legends I have studied were taken, the fifth to first centuries BC, was a particularly formative one in ancient Chinese history. Politically, it included the Warring States period and the beginning of the imperial era. The political system that characterized traditional China—a hereditary kingship accompanied by an officialdom based, in principle at least, on recruitment by merit—was taking form. The older aristocratic families had begun to be challenged by a rising technocratic class, a development that intensified the importance of the conflict between heredity and virtue. The philosophers who went from state to state hoping to convince the rulers to take their advice and accept their services were involved in this struggle and saw "history" in the light of their own interests as well as ideas. Intellectually, it was a time of great variety and excitement, a period in which "one hundred schools" of thought struggled for advantage. The primary concern of the philosophic schools was with ethics rather than metaphysics, with the defining of human relationships in terms of the family and state. Underlying many of the concepts debated—"loyalty," "benevolence," "filial piety," and "universal love"—was the very problem with which this study has been concerned, the need to reconcile the conflicting demands of virtue and heredity. Thus, their citations of history to illustrate these principles have provided the legend transformations on which this study is based.

The limitation of this study to texts dating from the fifth to first centuries BC and to legends from Yao to the regency of Zhougong is arbitrary. However, with the foundation of the Han, a number of changes began to take place that affected the usefulness of the texts for this type of analysis. From the Han Dynasty on, increasingly greater detail is recorded about the actual history of the period. This leaves the later writers with much less scope for transformation and makes the central themes of the historical situation less easy to determine. Additionally, as Confucianism became the orthodox philosophy of the court and the Con-

fucian texts came to be learned universally by rote, the legend transformations that appeared in those texts became increasingly dominant. After
the period of the "one hundred schools," philosophers in China never
again debated the philosophic basis of the state with such intensity and
variety of viewpoint. Finally, as cosmological beliefs and the five-element
theory became popular, political phenomena were interpreted more and
more uniformly in the light of Confucian assumptions; the underlying
ethical considerations were discussed much less. This cosmological over-
lay may not imply a change of structure, but it does make that structure
less easy to see or interpret.

In spite of these changes, the system of thought discussed in this
essay had important consequences for later China. It is beyond the pur-
view of this study to examine whether the same structural balance was
maintained in later legends of dynastic change, but the signs that 1 have
examined did continue to play a role in later Chinese thinking and even
to affect the course of Chinese history.

The manner in which legend themes could affect both history and
its interpretation can be seen, for example, in the stories of the foundation of the Han Dynasty. When Xiang Yu 項羽 revolted against the Qin
Dynasty, he did not immediately assume the rule himself but first set
on the throne a puppet king with rather more claim to legitimacy. When
he did finally have his puppet, the Emperor Yi, assassinated, his rival Liu
Bang 劉邦 accused him of regicide and took it as an excuse to punish
him. Liu Bang, on the other hand, achieved a sense of legitimacy by
obtaining the services of Zhang Liang 張良, a clever strategist of the same
type as Yi Yin and Taigong Wang. The connection with Taigong Wang is
made explicit by Zhang Liang's acquiring the *Taigong liu tao* 太公六韜,
the military work on which he based his strategy, from the "Yellow Stone
Duke," apparently an incarnation of Taigong Wang himself.

Even more clearly illustrative of the importance of these legend
themes is the story of Wang Mang 王莽, who briefly established the
Xin Dynasty (6 BC–AD 23). Wang Mang deliberately copied the ways
of ancient kings and tried to legitimize his usurpation in terms of the
legends of previous dynasties. Having achieved great power as a minister, he became regent for the young emperor Xiao Ping 孝平. While he
was still a regent, memorials to the throne (*Han shu, juan* 99) frequently
compared him to Yi Yin and Zhougong. He fostered this image, and
when he had his son Wang Yu 王宇 killed, he justified the act in terms
of Zhougong's execution of his brothers Guan and Cai while regent to
Cheng Wang. After Wang Mang finally assumed the throne, the terms

of comparison subtly changed. The memorials in the *Han shu* no longer speak of Zhougong but of Shun and Yu (when assuming the throne, Wang Mang made a point of tracing his ancestry back to Shun), for the desired pattern was no longer regency, but nonhereditary succession.

The influence of legend in the Three Kingdoms period can best be seen in terms of the Ming Dynasty historical novel *Sanguo zhi yanyi* 三國志演義 (*The Romance of the Three Kingdoms*). Indeed, *Sanguo zhi yanyi* takes much of its dramatic effect from the rival claims of the states of Wei and Han to dynastic legitimacy. Cao Cao 曹操 of Wei claimed to be the regent and then the successor of the Han child emperor he held captive. Liu Bei 劉備, on the other hand, claimed to be a scion of the royal house of Han. His claim to legitimacy was strengthened by his ability to attract the strategist Zhuge Liang 諸葛亮 into his service. Zhuge Liang was first described to Liu Bei by comparison with Taigong Wang and Zhang Liang, and Liu Bei was able to obtain his services only by going to him personally, in spite of the opposition of the impatient Zhang Fei 張飛—who, like Cheng Tang's charioteer, would have tried to summon the sage to attend on the ruler. After Liu Bei's death, Zhuge Liang even served his son as regent. These associations give the novel an added depth and imbue the fall of Han with a tragic sense that extends beyond the story of the individual characters.

Historical fiction, such as the *Sanguo zhi yanyi*, *Dong Han yanyi* 東漢演義, and *Fengshen yanyi* 封神演義, often takes critical periods of dynastic succession as its subject. Even *Shui hu zhuan* 水滸傳 (translated by Pearl Buck as *All Men Are Brothers*) is about a rebellion in which bandits claimed loyalty to an emperor befuddled by eunuchs and bad ministers. Historical fiction of this type, which makes up a large part of Chinese fiction, tends to exaggerate and play upon historical types in order to achieve its effect. For this reason it has often been criticized by Westerners for its excessive reliance on fictional stereotype and for its lack of emotional depth. This problem must be left for another study, but I suspect that much of the power and interest of this type of fiction for the Chinese reader lies in this very patterning—the use of variations upon stereotypes that are the descendants of the "signs" of an earlier era. I also suspect that this is a level of meaning not readily accessible to the non-Chinese reader.

The legend types continued to affect Chinese thought throughout Chinese history. They not only influenced literature, but were also a medium of political expression. As late as the founding of the Qing Dynasty (AD 1644), partisans of the previous dynasty starved themselves

to death in imitation of Bo Yi and Shu Qi, or otherwise committed suicide, rather than recognize the legitimacy of the new rulers. Even more
recently, the republican revolutionary Sun Yatsen claimed to derive his
philosophy from Zhougong.

Since 1949, Chinese history has been seen in terms of a Marxist
dialectic rather than a changing mandate of heaven. However, political
disputation still frequently takes place in terms of history, and many
of the old signs continue to be important. It is noteworthy that Mao
Zedong 毛澤東 looked back for an exemplar to the first Emperor of Qin
秦始皇帝, the one ruler in Chinese history who stepped outside of the
concept of the dynastic cycle and attempted to set up a dynasty that
would last "ten thousand years." During the anti-Confucian campaign
of the mid-1970s, criticism of Premier Zhou Enlai 周恩來 was disguised
as critique of the Confucian hero Zhougong. Besides having identical
surnames, Zhou's role could be interpreted as regent for the aging Mao
or—by his enemies—as that of potential usurper. Even more recently,
Mao's widow Jiang Qing 江青 has been described in terms previously
associated with wives of the bad last kings of dynasties.

Appendix 1

Charts

Key to the Charts

A → B	A passes the rule to B
C ← D	D takes the rule from C
E + F	E has the founding minister F
G ⇒ H	G rules in the stead of H
I ⇐ J	J rules in the stead of I
X, Y	X and Y

A
|
B   A contrasts with B such that A represents virtue as opposed to B and B represents heredity as opposed to A

A : B :: C : D   A is to B as C is to D

Chart A
Legend Sets

1. Tang Yao to Yü Shun	2. Yü Shun to Xia Yu	3. The Xia Dynasty	4. The Shang Dynasty	5. The Zhou Dynasty
Xu You	Shan Juan	Bocheng Zigao	Wu Guang, Bian Sui	Bo Yi, Shu Qi
|	|	Yi	|	|
Yao → Shun	Shun → Yu	Yu → Qi	Jie ← Tang + Yi Yin	Zhou ← Wen, Wu + Taigong
|	|	Wu Guan		
Dan Zhu	Shang Jun		Yi Yin ⇒ Tai Jia	Zhougong ⇒ Cheng
			|	|
			Tai Jia	Guan, Cai

Chart B
Ruler: Successor

Xu You	Shan Juan	Bocheng Zigao	Wu Guang, Bian Sui Yi Yin	Bo Yi, Shu Qi
YAO → *Shun*	**SHUN** → *Yu*	**YU** → *Yi* **QI**	**JIE** ← *Tang*	**ZHOU** ← Wen, *Wu* Taigong
Dan Zhu	Shang Jun	Wu Guan	Yi Yin Tai Jia	Zhougong Cheng
			Tai Jia	Guan, Cai

Chart C
Ruler: Founding Minister

Xu You	Shan Juan	Wu Guang, Bian Sui	Bo Yi, Shu Qi
YAO + *Shun*	**SHUN** + *Yu*	Jie **TANG** + *Yi Yin*	Zhou **WEN, WU** + *Taigong*
Dan Zhu	Shang Jun	Yi Yin Tai Jia	Zhougong Cheng
	Bocheng Zigao	Tai Jia	Guan, Cai
	Yi		
	+		
	YU		
	Qi		
	Wu Guan		

A: B :: **RULER** : *Founding minister*

Yao : Shun :: **Shun** : Yu :: **Yu** : Yi :: **Tang** : Yi Yin :: **Wen Wang, Wu Wang** : Taigong Wang

Chart D
Regent : Ruler

XuYou	Shan Juan	Bocheng Zigao	Wu Guang, Bian Sui	BoYi, Shu Qi
YAO ⇐ *Shun*	**SHUN** ⇐ *Yu*	Yi	Jie Tang YiYin	Zhou Wen, Wu Taigong
		YU ⇙		
Dan Zhu	Shang Jun	Qi	*YiYin* ⇒ **TAIJIA**	*Zhougong* ⇒ **CHENG**
		Wu Guan	Tai Jia	Guan, Cai

A : B :: **RULER** : *regent*

Yao : **Shun** :: **Shun** : Yu :: **Yu** : Yi :: **Taijia** : Yi Yin :: **Cheng Wang** : Zhougong

148

Chart E

Refusers and Rebels: Virtue and Heredity

XU YOU	SHAN JUAN	BOCHENG ZIGAO	WU GUANG, BIAN SUI	BO YI, SHU QI
Yao → Shun	Shun → Yu	Yu / Yi ← Qi	Jie ← Tang + Yi Yin	Zhou ← Wen, Wu + Taigong
Dan Zhu	*Shang Jun*	*Wu Guan*	Yi Yin ⇒ Tai Jia — *Tai Jia*	Zhougong ⇒ Cheng — *Guan, Cai*

REFUSERS (VIRTUE) : XU YOU, SHAN JUAN, BO CHENG ZI GAO, WU GUANG AND BIAN SUI, BO YI AND SHU QI
Rebels (heredity) : Dan Zhu, Shang Jun, Wu Guan, Tai Jia, Guan and Cai

Appendix 2

The Identities of Taigong Wang 太公望
in Zhou and Han Literature

The Problem

Taigong Wang 太公望 is one of many composite figures in early Chinese literature whose lives include both history and legend. These figures have a historical basis, but were more important to the early writers as exemplars of legendary themes. They were seen as actors in a recurring historical cycle and whatever their historic identity, their lives were molded by legend to demonstrate the appropriate theme. Since this theme was of more importance than the facts of their lives, differing regional legends and historical material are interspersed in the early literature without either writer or commentator taking note.

Even a superficial examination of references to Taigong Wang in Zhou and Han literature uncovers a variety of identities. Most prominently, he appears as an old fisherman fishing on the banks of the Wei River when he was discovered by King Wen of the Zhou Dynasty and raised to the rank of minister. Elsewhere, he appears as a butcher, a recluse, a persuader, and a boatman when he met the would-be king. In all of these accounts, he was a poor or obscure person with no family

This section was originally published in *Monumenta Serica* 30 (1972–73): 57–99, and is reproduced here by kind permission of the Monumenta Serica Institute. The material derives from a thesis presented in partial completion of the requirements for a master's degree at the University of California at Berkeley, June 1969. I would like to express my gratitude to my teachers who helped me with it, Cyril Birch, Peter A. Boodberg, Wolfram Eberhard, and David N. Keightley.

connections (except perhaps a wife who had thrown him out of the house). However, he is also described as a direct descendant of the chiefs of the four mountains (*si yue* 四嶽) whose ancestors were enfeoffed in Shen 申 and Lü 呂 and as a member of the Jiang 姜 tribe, a traditional ally of the Zhou.

The problem, then, is to separate the several distinct traditions concerning Taigong Wang and to analyze the interplay of history, legend, and philosophy that accounts for these contradictory identities. In the following paper, I will attempt to answer three principal questions: (1) Is there evidence of a historical person about whom the legends developed and if so who was he? (2) What are the different legend traditions; how did they develop and finally coalesce? (3) Why did the legends develop and why are they similar, that is to say, what is the role of Taigong Wang in early Chinese legend?

In order to determine the role of Taigong Wang, I have established a set of "founding ministers," singularly wise and talented men who were discovered in obscurity and raised to power by a future king or hegemon who thus proves his insight into human nature and worthiness to rule.[1] Hopefully, the isolation of this theme and the method of analysis established herein will be useful in understanding the interplay of history and legend in the lives of these and other such composite figures.

Determining Historicity

The accounts in the *Shi ji* 史記 of Taigong Wang as a fisherman, persuader or recluse before he met King Wen are so obviously dubious that Marcel Granet, comparing him with the Duke of Zhou (Zhougong 周公), wrote: "It is clear that the biography [of Zhougong] is made up of historical events and that of Lü Shang, of legendary events."[2] However, there are events in the biography of Taigong Wang that are usually accepted as historical, specifically certain events surrounding the overthrow of the Shang Dynasty by the Zhou and the enfeoffment of Qi, and some scholars have assumed that Taigong Wang was a historical figure.[3]

---

1. This set is incomplete since it includes only the names of ministers who are paralleled with Taigong Wang in Zhou and Han texts. Further study should establish a more complete set.

2. Translated from Marcel Granet, *Danses et légendes de la Chine ancienne*, v. 2, 406.

3. For example, Herrlee G. Creel, *Statecraft*, 343–44, 361–62.

The life of Taigong Wang includes legend and may also include history, but unfortunately there is little early evidence by which a historical identity may be determined. The only reference to Taigong Wang in a Western Zhou text or bronze inscription is in the *Shi jing* 詩經. Although this reference is early,[4] it is insufficient to determine a precise identity. Therefore, later texts such as the *Shi ji*, which are composite and include material from late and legendary as well as early and historical sources, must be used. In using such composite texts, however, the historical tradition must be systematically distinguished from the legendary tradition and carefully defined.

In order to determine the historical identity of Taigong Wang, and if indeed he existed, I first define as "historical" that information that may be placed accurately in a historical context, that is, any information that may be tested against and is not in conflict with a historical pattern determined by a number of texts, some of which are contemporaneous. This information is historical in type, but not necessarily in fact. Thus, we may know that a battle could have been fought at a certain place by two rival tribes or that a person held the appropriate social position to receive a fief, but lacking contemporaneous evidence, we cannot be sure that the battle was actually fought or the fief received. However, having separated this information, which is historical in type, we may then examine it to determine whether it forms a coherent whole and if so, the evidence for the antiquity of this tradition.

"Legendary" information, on the other hand, is that which is in conflict with historical reality (including information on the supernatural) or illustrates a recurring legendary theme. It tends to be anecdotal and cannot be related accurately to established historical patterns (often because it concerns primarily the persons immediately involved and has no larger historical consequences), but rather to a complex of legends of similar theme and the prevalent concepts of the period. Thus, the story that the Grand Duke was discovered by King Wen while fishing concerns primarily these two figures and violates the established pattern of appointing men of stature or noble birth, but it illustrates a recurring legendary theme in which a poor man is raised up by a future king thus proving his worthiness to rule.

The fact that the Zhou and Han texts tend to preserve the language of their sources and nomenclature is particularly useful in separating the different traditions about Taigong Wang. He has several names—Shi

---

4. See note 18 below for dating of the *Shi jing*.

Shangfu 師尚父 (Preceptor Father Shang), Lü Shang 呂尚, Lü Wang 呂望, Taigong Wang 太公望 (Grand Duke Wang or "Expected"), and simply Taigong 太公, the "Grand Duke." Only Shi Shangfu is used with the historical material, thus confirming the separation proposed on grounds of content and indicating that a single tradition has been isolated. (Since "Grand Duke," the name associated with his role in the ancestry of Qi 齊, is the most generally applied in the texts, I will use this name below when no particular role is indicated).

Using the above criteria as a guide, the historical identity of Taigong Wang may be determined. First the "historical" events in the life of the Grand Duke may be isolated from the legendary. Then, his role in these events and the antiquity of the tradition may be examined to form a coherent picture of his historical identity. Finally, this identity may be checked against the role of the Jiang tribe with relation to the Zhou at the time of the founding of the Zhou Dynasty.

Historical Events in the Life of the Grand Duke

The most extensive source of information about the Grand Duke is his biography in *juan* 32 of the *Shi ji*, entitled "The Hereditary House of the Grand Duke of Qi."[5] It includes three events in which the Grand Duke participates that are historical in type. These events involve the overthrow of the Shang, the ceremonial establishment of Zhou rule and the subsequent enfeoffing of feudal states. First is the battle at Meng Jin:

> The army went forth. Preceptor Father Shang held the yellow broadaxe in his left hand and took the white pennant in his right to urge on [the warriors]. He cried, "A green monster! A green monster![6] Together everyone! [Row your] boat oars as one. Heads off for the laggards!"

---

5. *Qi Taigong shijia* 齊太公世家, *Shi ji*, *juan* 32, 1477–81.

6. *Cang si* 蒼兕: *cang guang* 蒼光 in the reference to this story in *Lun heng* 論衡 17/11a. *Lun heng* describes this creature as a nine-headed water animal that subverts boats. E. Chavannes notes with approval Sima Zhen's 司馬貞 explanation that the term refers to an officer rather than a monster. As the latter, it reflects the unorthodox military methods of the Grand Duke celebrated in legend. He tries to scare his troops into speeding forward by evoking the image

Then King Wu is inaugurated:

> King Wu stood before the shrine of the tutelary gods and the
> assembled dukes offered him dew water. Kang Shufeng 康叔
> 封 of Wei 衛 spread out the multi-colored mat and Preceptor
> Father Shang led in the sacrificial beast. The scribe Yi recorded
> the incantation to inform the spirits of the punishment of the
> sins of [the Shang king] Zhòu . . .

Finally, the Grand Duke is awarded his fief:

> Thereupon, King Wu controlled the Shang and ruled the
> empire. He enfeoffed Preceptor Father Shang with Ying Qiu
> 營丘 in Qi.

These are the only passages in the biography in which Sima Qian
uses the epithet Shi Shangfu except for the rather vague statement that
King Wu "extended the government of Zhou and gave the empire a new
beginning. The advice [given in this regard] by Preceptor Father Shang
was extensive." Interspersed with these "historical" events are events
that illustrate legendary themes. Sima Qian records three contradictory
accounts of how Lü Shang or Taigong came to serve the Zhou. These
accounts illustrate the theme of the founding minister and will be discussed extensively in this context below.

   Another role of the Grand Duke is that of the unorthodox magician
who aids an otherwise righteous man in defeating an entrenched but
illegitimate ruler who cannot otherwise be defeated.[7] Taigong's lack of

---

of water monsters as well as by threatening them with punishment. In the "Basic Annals
of Zhou" (Zhou benji 周本紀 Shi ji, juan 4, v. 1, 120), Sima Qian 司馬遷 includes this passage in identical form, but omits the reference to cang si; thus, it may not have been in his
original source or he may have understood it as "green monsters" and doubted its historicity.

7. This is a recurring theme in later Chinese literature, of which the most famous example
is Zhu Geliang 諸葛亮 in the novel Sanguozhi yanyi 三國志演義. The Grand Duke as Jiang
Ziya 姜子牙 in the novel, Fengshen yanyi 封神演義 also plays this role. In the early texts
the craftiness of the Grand Duke's methods tends to be emphasized more than his ability
to control the supernatural, though he is said to have been "widely knowledgeable about
the occult." See the persuader legend below.

orthodoxy and superior understanding of the occult (*qi* 奇) are illustrated in the biography by his refusal to take note of an inauspicious divination taken just before the battle at Mu Ye 牧野 and a sudden storm which had arisen. This theme recurs in legends about the Grand Duke, both in variants of this story[8] and in other accounts of his aid to the Zhou king.[9]

The other events in the biography cannot be confirmed by their historical context, although they also cannot be related to recurring legendary themes. The statement that "King Wu . . . wrote the Great Harangue with the Grand Duke" is at variance with the predominant historical tradition in which King Wu alone wrote the Great Harangue[10] and in any case cannot be tested against an established historical pattern. More important, none of the events concerning the Grand Duke and the state of Qi after the original enfeoffment ceremony at the Zhou court are confirmed by other historical sources, and they appear to be in conflict with the established pattern. This impression is reinforced by Sima Qian's use of the epithet Taigong ("Grand Duke") rather than Shi Shangfu for these events, indicating that he is drawing his information from a different source.

The first event recorded by Sima Qian after the enfeoffment is an incident in which Taigong traveling leisurely toward his fief is warned:

> I have heard that time is difficult to obtain and easy to lose.
> The guest rests very peacefully. Perhaps he is not to arrive
> in his territory.

As a result, he dresses during the night and hurries on. This event is clearly anecdotal and concerns primarily the Grand Duke, but I do not know its thematic significance. When Taigong arrives in his territory, it is contested by the Lai Yi 萊夷. Troops attempting to establish a fief

---

8. Variants of the divination story occur in *Lun heng* 24/9b and 24/11a; of the storm story, in *Hanshi wai zhuan* 韓詩外傳 3/7b. The significance of this theme seems to have been debated in the Han Dynasty since both writers stress their belief that the Grand Duke rejected the interpretation, not the omens.

9. The Grand Duke's attitude toward omens and his unorthodox methods are also illustrated by a story in *Lun heng* 19/7a, according to which he fed a child cinnabar and taught him to say, "Yin is doomed." The enemy thought the child was a spirit and became disheartened. The "green monster" story discussed in note 6 is also part of this complex of legends.

10. *Shang shu* 尚書 (*Tai shi* 泰誓) 6/1a–5b; *Shi ji, juan* 4, v. 1, 120.

in Ying Qiu at this time could have fought the Lai Yi,[11] but this event is not recorded in any other text. Sima Qian concludes the section on the life of the Grand Duke by describing the virtues of his government of Qi and recording a mandate supposedly given him during the reign of King Cheng:

> When King Cheng of Zhou was young, Guan and Cai created disorder and the Huai Yi 淮夷 turned back upon Zhou. Duke Kang 康 of Shao 召 was sent to give a mandate to the Grand Duke which said, "East to the sea, west to the [Yellow] River, south to Mu Ling 穆陵, north to Wu Di 無棣, be they the five lords or the nine chiefs, you may certainly punish them."

Although the rebellions and campaigns in the East during the reign of King Cheng are historical,[12] this mandate is open to question. There are no other records of the Grand Duke's participation in these campaigns and the political significance of the mandate can be discerned from Sima Qian's following statement:

> Because of this mandate, Qi was able to punish and conquer and became a great country with its capital at Ying Qiu.

The *Zuo zhuan* 左傳 records that Guan Zhong 管仲 cited this mandate as justification for the invasion of Chu 楚.[13] Furthermore, if the Grand Duke was an old man in the reign of King Wen, he probably did not live into the reign of King Cheng. By Sima Qian's reckoning, he was over one hundred when he died.

The hiatus in the biography between the information about Shi Shangfu at the court of Zhou and that about the Grand Duke in Qi may be due to our lack of source material about Qi equivalent to that about Zhou, but the historical pattern indicates that the Grand Duke may not

---

11. Ying Qiu was in north central Shandong (modern Linzixian 臨緇縣), and the Lai Yi lived in the mountainous areas of central Shandong (Gustav Haloun, "Contributions to the History of Clan Settlement in Ancient China," 85).

12. See Chen Mengjia 陳夢家, "Xi Zhou tongqi duandai," 西周銅器斷代, pts. 1 and 2, *Kaogu xuebao* 9 (1955): 160–75 and 10 (1955): 66–83 (inscriptions 3–15).

13. *Chunqiu jingzhuan jijie* 春秋經傳集解 5/3b (Xigong, 4th year).

actually have taken possession of the fief in Qi. On the basis of bronze inscriptions, Chen Mengjia 陳夢家 states that the sons of the Dukes of Zhou and Shao took their fathers' fiefs while their fathers remained at the Zhou court. He argues by analogy that this was also true for the Grand Duke and his son Lü Ji 呂伋, the Duke Ding 丁.[14]

The events in the biography of the Grand Duke in which the epithet Shi Shangfu is used are not only historical in type. They are also recorded in the "Basic Annals of Zhou" (*Zhou ben ji* 周本紀) in almost identical language, including the epithet Shi Shangfu. The only other event in which he participates in the "Basic Annals" is the battle at Mu Ye 牧野. This event is also historical in type and the epithet Shi Shangfu is also used. No further mention of him is made in the "Basic Annals" except that "the Grand Duke Expected was preceptor" to King Wu. (This could derive from the same source since Sima Qian identified the two names and he may have found it redundant to say "the Preceptor . . . was preceptor"). Apparently, the events in the "Basic Annals" in which the "Grand Duke" participates derive from a single tradition in which he is called Shi Shangfu. Sima Qian's exclusive use of this tradition in the "Basic Annals" tends to support its historicity since he would naturally have used only the most reliable and historically relevant material for this section of the *Shi ji*, but probably used a wider range of material in the biography in order to give as full a portrait of the Grand Duke as possible.

---

14. Dinggong 丁公. Chen Mengjia, "Xi Zhou tongqi duandai," pt. 1 (*Kaogu xuebao* 9), 146. Contemporaneous evidence supports the view that the Grand Duke's son took a fief in Qi. He is called Qi Hou Lü Ji 齊後呂极 at the mourning ceremony of King Cheng in the *Shang shu* ("Gu ming" 顧命 ll/8a), and we know that a fief had been established from the inscription on the *Yi Hou Shi Gui* 宜候失歸 (excavated in 1954, Chen, 165, no. 5), which states that a Marquis of Qi (*Qi Hou*) feasted King Cheng when the king was on a tour of the Eastern regions. The view that he was the actual founder of the fief is further supported by Spring and Autumn Period records which mention him and his father as the ancestors of the house of Qi. Both the *Zuo zhuan* and *Yanzi chunqiu* 晏子春秋 refer to the two figures together as the founders of Qi, even though there are no recorded legends about the Duke Ding which would explain his prominence and the Grand Duke was officially considered the founder of Qi (*Chunqiu jingzhuan jijie* 20/15a, Zhaogong; 3rd year, 24/11a, Xianggong, 襄公 28th year; *Yanzi chunqiu jishi* [Beijing: Zhonghua shuju, 1962] *juan* 1, 65, *juan* 2, 108). R. Walker, "Some notes on the Yen-tzu Ch'un-ch'iu," *Journal of the American Oriental Society* 73 (1953): 156–62, thinks that this text predates the *Zuo zhuan* and is particularly associated with the state of Qi. From the *Ban Gui* 班歸 (rubbing only, Chen, 70–73, no. 12) and the *Ling Gui* 令歸 (Chen, 76–79, no. 15) inscriptions, we also know that he participated in the Eastern campaigns during the reign of King Cheng, thus the hiatus in the biography may be due to the telescoping of the lives of the Grand Duke and his son.

The impression that the Shi Shangfu events derive from a single tradition is strengthened by the use of this epithet in other Zhou and Han texts. It is always used in describing the battles at Meng Jin and Mu Ye,[15] though Taigong or Taigong Wang is sometimes used for the enfeoffment of Qi, probably referring not as much to the specific event as to the tradition that he was the founder of Qi. However, this epithet is never used for any event for which it is not used in the biography and tends to disappear altogether as the legendary aspects of the life of the Grand Duke become of more interest to later writers than the history of the overthrow of the Shang.

The Role of Shi Shangfu

We have seen that there is a distinct tradition concerning a Shi Shang-fu who participated in events surrounding the overthrow of the Shang Dynasty by the Zhou. Let us now examine his role in these events and coincidentally the evidence for the antiquity of the tradition.

The most strikingly "historical" events in the life of the Grand Duke are the battles at Meng Jin and Mu Ye, which were the decisive battles in the struggle between the Shang and Zhou.[16] Shi Shangfu appears to have been a commander who held symbolic as well as military author-ity in these battles. At Meng Jin he held the yellow broadaxe in his left hand and the white pennant in his right. The broadaxe and pennant are ritually significant and symbolize command or authority. Here, Shi Shangfu holds them "to urge on," or "harangue" as it is often translated (*yi shi* 以誓), the warriors; in the *Shang shu*, King Wu himself holds them at Mu Ye "to signal" (*yi hui* 以麾).[17]

Shi Shangfu was also the commander at Mu Ye. This tradition was recorded as early as the tenth or ninth century in the *Shi jing*:[18] "The grand-master (i.e., general) was Shangfu, he was an eagle, a hawk."[19]

---

15. *Lun heng* 17/11a; *Han shu* 漢書, *juan* 28, 1629.

16. *Shang shu* 6/1a, 6a ("Tai shi" 泰誓, "Mu shi" 牧師); *Shi ji, juan* 4, 120, 122.

17. *Shang shu* 6/6a.

18. According to W. A. C. H. Dobson's dating of the *Da ya* section of the *Shi jing*. See "Linguistic Evidence and the Dating of the Book of Songs," 323.

19. Translation of Bernhard Karlgren, "The Book of Odes," 66 (Mao 236).

The "Basic Annals" are more explicit: "King Wu sent Shi Shangfu with the one hundred officers to urge on the army."

Karlgren, recognizing the military role of Shi Shangfu at the battle of Mu Ye, notes that *Shi* should be understood here as "general." *Shi* has connotations of both military and moral authority[20] and is combined here in with *fu* in what appears to have been a Western Zhou title. This naming style occurs throughout the Western Zhou in bronze inscriptions.[21] However, it seems to have died out in the Eastern Zhou and was not understood by Han and later commentators.[22] Thus, the use of this title in the *Shi jing* and in the "historical" information about the Grand Duke is good evidence of the antiquity of the tradition.

Shi Shangfu not only held military authority on the field of battle, he also held ritual authority in the Zhou court. In court ceremonies, he participated with members of the Zhou ruling family, the Ji 姬, as an equal. He led in the sacrificial beast at the inauguration of King Wu, a ceremony in which all other participants except the scribe were members of the royal family.[23] In the subsequent enfeoffment ceremony, "Shi

---

20. As a military term, *shi* means "commander" and is defined in the *Shuowen* 說文 as "the leader of 2500 men." Creel, *Statecraft*, 304, states with regard to its usage in W. Zhou bronze inscriptions: "Where the context gives some clue as to function, *Shi* usually seems to be military, but whether this title was also used for civilian officers is debated and remains a question." *Shi* also connotes moral leadership, hence Chavanne's "précepteur" which I follow. In note 209, Creel says with regard to Taishi 太師, the position held by the Grand Duke: "Whether T'ai-shih was ever a military office seems to be uncertain. At times men holding this office appear to have wielded the highest power in the royal government."

21. Guo Moruo 郭沫若, *Liang Zhou jinwen ci daxi kaoshi* 兩周金文辭大系考釋 includes eight bronze inscriptions with five names in the form of *Shi . . . fu* (59b–61a, 70a, 78b, 121a, 154a). They are all Western Zhou and span the entire period (if we accept the opinion of Chen Mengjia and others that Shi Yongfu 師雍父 lived during the reign of King Cheng or King Kang). See Guo, 59b–61a; Chen Mengjia, "Xi Zhou tongqi duandai," pt. 5, 110. A few other titles are also frequently combined with *fu*, e.g., Bo 伯, Zhong 仲, Shu 叔. In the Ling Gui (Chen, pt. 1, 79), Dinggong is called alternatively Bo Dingfu.

22. In the Han Dynasty, Liu Xiang 劉向 interpreted each character of Shi Shangfu as an attribute of the Grand Duke (*Bie lu* 別錄 as quoted in *Maoshi zhushu* 毛詩註疏, 1339). In the Song Dynasty, Zhu Xi 朱熹 understood *shi* as a title, but considered Shangfu an appellation (*Shi jing jizhu* 詩經集注, 140).

23. The other participants were Kang Shufeng 康叔封 and Shaogong Shi 召公奭, younger brothers of King Wu who later received fiefs in Wei and N. Yan, respectively, and Mao Shuzheng 毛叔鄭 who is not clearly identified but appears to have been related to the king. According to *Fu Songben chongxiu Guang yun* 覆宋本重修廣韻, *juan* 2, 13b, the surname derives from King Wu's maternal uncle. Chen Mengjia, "Xi Zhou tongqi duandai," pt. 2 (*Kaogu xuebao* 1955), 71, identifies him as a son of King Wen.

Shangfu was the first to be enfeoffed,"[24] although the other four recipients of fiefs were brothers of the king.[25] In a highly ritualized society, the Grand Duke's position in these two family ceremonies probably indicates that he was accorded kinship status. This impression is strengthened by his son's status as chief mourner of King Cheng.[26]

Thus, Shi Shangfu commanded the forces in the major battles between Shang and Zhou and participated with members of the Ji family on important ritual occasions. If we examine the relations between the Jiang tribe and the Zhou at this time, we can see that Shi Shangfu's role as ally and kin of the Zhou rulers accurately reflects the tribal relationship. Apparently, he was not an unknown raised from obscurity, but the key figure in the close alliance of two powerful tribes.

Jiang and Zhou

There is general agreement, not only in the *Shi ji*, but in all Zhou and Han accounts, that the surname of the Grand Duke was Lü. The Lü, as Sima Qian indicates, were a ruling family of the Jiang 姜, a noble tribe that traced its ancestry to the *si yue* ("chieftains of the four mountain peaks") who served the predynastic ruler, Yao. When the Zhou Dynasty was founded, the Jiang had their home in north and western China, in the general area of the confluence of the Wei and Yellow Rivers.[27] This is in apparent conflict with Sima Qian's statement that the Grand Duke was a "man of the shores of the Eastern Sea," thus, a native of the Eastern coast of China. Sima Qian may be referring to the Grand Duke's close association with the state of Qi, centered on the Shandong peninsula, of which he was the reputed founder and revered ancestor. The *Zuo zhuan* states in this connection that he "represented the Eastern Sea."[28]

---

24. *Shi ji, juan* 4, 127.

25. Zhougong Dan 周公旦, Shaogong Shi, Shu Xian 叔鲜, and Shu Du 叔度 are listed with Shi Shangfu in the "Basic Annals" (ibid.) as the "meritorious ministers and advisory gentlemen" enfeoffed by King Wu, but they are all four brothers of the king.

26. *Shang shu* (Gu ming) ll/8a.

27. G. Haloun, 84, lists N. and N.W. Henan (the location of Lü and Shen) and S.W. Shansi as the original home of the Jiang. Qian Mu, "Zhou chu dili kao" 周初地理考, 1959–63, makes a convincing case that the state of Jin in Shansi Province was the original home of the Jiang. The state of Tai in Shensi was also populated by Jiang before the Zhou Dynasty (Haloun, 619–21).

28. *Chunqiu jingzhuan jijie*15/16b (Xianggong, 14th year).

Normally, such a statement of origin refers to the birthplace of a person's parents or the ancestral home of his family, but since the Grand Duke himself was revered as the ancestor of his family, it may mean the place where he and his descendants lived.

Otherwise, it is probably taken from the legend in which the Grand Duke was a recluse by the Eastern Sea and Bo Yi 伯夷 a recluse by the Northern Sea (south and north of Shandong, respectively), in order to avoid serving the last Shang king. This story is mentioned briefly in the biography and Mencius refers to it in similar language:

> The Grand Duke avoided [the Shang king] Zhòu and lived on the banks of the Eastern Sea. Hearing of the rise of King Wen, he roused himself and said, "Why not turn my allegiance to him?" (*Mengzi* 孟子 7/10b [and 13/9a])

Although Mencius states that the Grand Duke went east from the Shang court of Zhòu, a passage in *Lüshi chunqiu* 呂氏春秋 (14/8b) says that the Grand Duke was a native of the East. This is the only such assertion which I have found in a Zhou or Han text besides the biography and it seems to be a slightly different version of the same legend:

> The Grand Duke Expected was a gentleman of the Eastern Yi [tribe]. He wished to unite the world, but lacked his master. Hearing King Wen was virtuous . . .

The connection is clear. Eastern Yi is a transposition of living by the Eastern Sea, lacking a master, of avoiding the Shang ruler, Zhòu. The assertion that he was an Eastern Yi is in direct contradiction to Sima Qian's account in which he had to fight the Yi to take possession of his fief. In any case, the account imagines an unlikely degree of free travel among rival tribesmen, but this tradition could be the source of Sima Qian's assertion that he was "a man of the shore of the Eastern Sea."

The only other direct reference to the Grand Duke's place of origin is a remark in the *Li Ji* 禮記 that after the Grand Duke was enfeoffed in Ying Qiu, for five generations he and his descendants were returned to Zhou to be buried.[29] Although this statement may not be factual, it reflects an understanding that the native home of the Lü was within the confines of the Zhou state, which was centered in the Wei River Valley

---

29. *Zuantu huzhu Li ji* 纂圖互注禮記2/7a (Tan Gong 檀弓).

in Shaanxi, beginning with the reign of King Wen's grandfather, and extended over the area populated by Jiang.[30]

We may reasonably assume, then, that the Grand Duke was a member of the Jiang tribe. This does much to explain the important role which he played with relation to the Zhou rulers, for not only did the Zhou and Jiang occupy much of the same area after the Zhou moved down from Northern Shaanxi, they also maintained close ties of mutual benefit. The Zhou were the stronger and more numerous of the two, but dependent upon other tribes in extending their territory and eventually in conquering the Shang. The Jiang, by entering into alliance with the Zhou, were able to maintain much of their authority over their own territory and to reap some of the other rewards of the Zhou conquest.

This relationship between Jiang and Zhou is symbolized by the marriage of Jiang women to Zhou rulers. This marriage policy has been well documented by others and need not be treated in detail here.[31] According to legend, Jiang Yuan 姜原, whose name means "Origin of the Jiang," was married to the first ancestor of the Ji.[32] King Wen's grandfather (who "expected" Taigong Wang in the fishing legend) had a Jiang wife[33] and this marriage tradition continued in the early Zhou Dynasty.[34] Yi Jiang 邑姜, the wife of King Cheng[35] has been identified by commentators of the *Zuo zhuan* as the daughter of the Grand Duke.[36] Unfortunately, however, there is no early evidence to verify this.

---

30. *Shi ji, juan* 4, 114; see G. Haloun, 602–604 for identification of sites.

31. Fu Sinian 傅斯年, "Jiang Yuan" 姜原; Yang Yunru 楊筠如, "Jiang xingde minzu he Jiang Taigongde gushi" 姜姓的民族後姜太公的故事, 114–16, and Qi Sihe 齊思和, "Xi Zhou dili kao" 西周地理考, 70–71, all discuss this relationship. Shang rulers also contracted political marriages with women from rival tribes. See also Lin Chao, "Marriage, Inheritance, and Lineage Organization in Shang China," 2–4.

32. *Shi ji, juan* 4, 111.

33. Tai Jiang 太姜, ibid., 115.

34. Wu Qichang, comp., *Jinwen shizu pu* 金文世族譜, 2–3, records bronze inscriptions referring to Jiang wives for Kings Shao and Mu.

35. Chen Mengjia, "Xi Zhou tongqi duandai," lists three bronze inscriptions that refer to the Jiang wife of King Cheng (*Ling Gui*: pt. 2, 76, no. 15, *Zha Ci Qiong Yu* 乍册嬛卣: pt. 2, 117, no. 31; and *Shi Shu Sui* Qi 世叔隋器: pt. 3, 65). Guo Moro, 102b, also includes the *Cai Gui* 蔡簋. Creel, *Origins*, 130–31, points out that the powers exercised by the queen were normally functions of the king. The political power of this and other queens in the Western Zhou, if we accept Creel's interpretation, would help to explain the importance of the Grand Duke to the Zhou rulers since he was a prominent member of the queen's tribe, possibly her father.

36. *Chunqiu jingzhuan jijie* 22/14b (Zhaogong 12th year).

The Jiang tribe not only gave women in marriage to the Zhou rulers, but they entered into military alliance with the Zhou to overthrow the Shang and subsequently received several fiefs. The *Shang shu* attests to the assistance of Jiang forces at the battle of Mu Ye.[37] Subsequently, during the Western Zhou, the state of Jiao was ruled by members of the Jiang tribe, as were Tai (ruled by the Shen family) and Qi, which was governed by the descendants of the Grand Duke.[38]

A Historical Identity

In light of the alliance between Jiang and Zhou, the role of the Grand Duke becomes clear. He is the key figure in maintaining the alliance and acts as the representative of the Jiang to the Ji family. At Meng Jin 孟 津 and Mu Ye 牧野, he is acting as the head of his tribe in their military alliance with the Zhou. He holds a high ritual status because of the uncle relationship of the Jiang to the Zhou. Thus, at the inauguration of King Wu, he is acting as an elder within the Ji family and the fief of Qi is in recognition of the military and marital alliance of the Jiang with the Zhou.

Support for this conception of the Grand Duke as kin and ally of the Zhou appears in the *Zuo zhuan*. The tradition of an alliance between the Qi rulers and the Zhou is stressed in the *Zuo zhuan* in order to bolster the faltering authority of the Zhou. Nevertheless, we can see that in the Spring and Autumn Period, the ancestors of the Qi rulers were thought to have been kin and ally to the Zhou. Nine passages in the *Zuo zhuan* mention the Grand Duke or his son Duke Ding, all of which refer to them as the ancestors of the Qi rulers. The alliance with the Zhou in which the Shang are overthrown is invoked in five passages and two passages refer to kinship.[39]

There is too little evidence about Shi Shangfu's role within his own tribe to determine his precise identity in this respect. He may have been the head of a minor group of Jiang who took advantage of the rise of the Zhou to form a timely alliance, rather than the traditional

---

37. *Shang shu* 6/6a. See also *Shi ji, juan* 4, 122, and *Hou Han shu* 後漢書 (Beijing: Zhonghua shuju, 1965), *juan* 87, 2871.

38. Albert Herrmann, *An Historical Atlas of China*, 5.

39. *Chunqiu jingzhuan jijie*15/16b (Xianggong 14th year), 22/14b (Zhaogong 12th year).

leader of the Jiang tribe. This would explain Sima Qian's statement that the Grand Duke descended from a branch of the tribe that had been made commoners and also explain why his heritage was not commonly known. Whatever his precise position within his tribe, he was clearly an important leader of a powerful tribe.

Legends of Origin

When the historical tradition about the "Grand Duke" was isolated, we found evidence of a historical person, who was called Shi Shangfu and was a prominent member of the Jiang tribe, allied militarily and by marriage to the Zhou ruling family, the Ji. However, this identification is directly contradicted by accounts of the "Grand Duke" in which he is depicted as a man of obscure origin and lowly profession before he was discovered by the Western Lord of Zhou (King Wen) and raised to the rank of minister. Sima Qian includes three accounts of the origins of the Grand Duke in his biography, in which he is described as a fisherman discovered by King Wen while on a hunting trip, a recluse who came to the king's aid when he was imprisoned at You Li, and a traveling persuader who had been rejected by the other feudal lords. Outside of the *Shi ji*, there is a popular story that he was a butcher discovered by King Wen in the marketplace and one account that he was a boatman before he met the would-be king.

These accounts are not merely legendary events in the life of the Grand Duke, as suggested by Marcel Granet, since they are contradictory and occur separately except in a few cases where the fishing story has been combined with another legend. Sima Qian notes their contradictions and records them as alternate versions, giving the most credence to the fishing story (prefaced by *gai* 蓋 "it seems that" rather than *huo yue* 或曰 "some say"). Nor are they based on historical fact, as the identity implied by each of these accounts contradicts the historical identity isolated above. As will be shown below, they are distinct regional legends that grew up about or became attached to the historical figure Shi Shangfu in order to fit his life into the accepted pattern of dynastic change as a "founding minister."

In the following, I will attempt to isolate the different legend traditions and trace their development to their final coalescence. A chart of the historical tradition and three most prominent legends may be useful in understanding the more detailed analysis:

	Naming pattern	Place of origin	Date of origin
Historical person	Shi Shangfu	Wei River Valley	12–11th c. BC
Butcher legend	Lü Wang Taigong Wang Taigong	South—Chu No. Henan (cycle)	? (first recorded in "Tian wen," ca. 4th c. BC)
Fisher legend	Lü Shang Taigong	Wei River Valley	? (not recorded until Han Dynasty)
Recluse	Inconsistent	Eastern coast	Warring States

In tracing the development of these legends, the naming pattern proves useful again—in separating the various traditions and in tracing their coalescence. Geographical origin will be determined by the origins of the texts in which a legend is recorded, the sites mentioned in the legend, and indigenous local traditions concerning the legend. Chronological origin and development are indicated by broad discrepancies in the dates at which a legend or version of a legend is recorded and by thematic connections to a historical period.

The Butcher Legend

The butcher legend was recorded earlier than the legends in the *Shi ji* and rivals the fishing legend for popularity in Zhou and Han texts. I have found altogether ten passages in seven texts that make reference to some form of this legend: two in *Chu ci* 楚辭 ("Tian wen" 天問 and "Li sao" 離騷), two in *Huainanzi* 淮南子, one in *Zhanguo ce* 戰國策, two in *Hanshi wai zhuan* 韓詩外傳, two in *Shuo yuan* 說苑, and one in *Qian Han shu* 前漢書. In *Chu ci* and *Huainanzi*, the two texts of Southern origin, it is recorded as a simple story about a butcher who moved his knife in a singular way, which deeply impressed the future King Wen. *Qian Han shu* also refers to this story. In the Han anthologies besides *Huainanzi*, however, the butcher story is one episode in a cycle of stories about low positions held by the Grand Duke. The sites of Zhao Ge 朝歌 and Ji Jin 棘津 in Northern Henan are frequently mentioned in this cycle, indicating an affinity with this area. Finally, two passages from *Hanshi wai zhuan* and *Shuo yuan* include the fishing story as the final episode of the butcher cycle, anticipating the eventual loss of the butcher legend and universal acceptance of the fishing legend.

The independent origin of the butcher legend is clearly evident in its unusual naming pattern. Wang ("Expected") is consistently used as the given name of the butcher (seven passages) and Shang does not occur until the fishing legend has been added (one passage). Sima Qian understood Wang as a part of the epithet Taigong Wang ("Grand Duke Expected"). He explained that it was awarded to Lü Shang after King Wen found him fishing in the Wei River and meant that Lü Shang was "expected" by King Wen's grandfather. In this legend, however, it was evidently understood as his given name. It occurs with the surname Lü in four passages (Lü Wang) and with the title "preceptor" in one (Shi Wang).[40] Thus, the epithet Taigong Wang must have been understood as title and given name—Grand Duke, Wang—stylistically parallel to Duke of Zhou, Dan (Zhougong Dan 周公旦) and Duke of Shao, Shi (Shaogong Shi 召公奭), two figures with whom he is often grouped.

The legend of Wang the butcher seems to have originated in the South, sometime before the fourth century BC. It is first recorded in *Chu ci* where it appears in essentially the same form in "Tian wen" and "Li sao.""Tian wen" poses the question:

When Preceptor Wang was in the marketplace, how did Chang know him? When he drummed with his knife and a noise arose, why was the prince pleased?[41]

The similarity of Qu Yuan's 屈原 language in "Li sao" indicates that he was acquainted with the same tradition, but unfortunately his reference is too fleeting to answer the questions posed in "Tian wen":

By drumming with a knife, Lü Wang met Zhou Wen and got raised.[42]

---

40. The name Shi Wang 師望 is also used in *Yan tie lun* (*Yan tie lun jiaozhu* 鹽鐵論校注, 45) in a reference to the Grand Duke's military stratagems. This name also occurs in Western Zhou bronze inscriptions for a figure who lived during the reign of Gong Wang or at least after the reign of Kang Wang (see the *Shi Wang Ding*, Guo Moruo, 80a–b), but I have been unable to find any connection between the two figures.

41. *Chu ci tongshi* 楚辭通釋, 61.

42. Ibid., 19.

Both texts use the name Wang, the phrase "drumming with a knife," and mention Chang 昌, posthumously known as King Wen of the Zhou Dynasty.

The story implied in these two references is that a man named Wang ("Expected"), who belonged to the Lü family and held the title *shi*, preceptor or elder, was in a marketplace when it was visited by the future king. This Wang "drummed with his knife," creating a noise and so impressed Chang that he rewarded him, most likely with an office. Wang was probably a butcher, as later commentators have agreed, since there is no evidence to the contrary and he is clearly identified as such in the cyclical form of the legend, but precisely what he was doing when he "drummed with his knife" (*gu dao* 鼓刀) is not clear.[43]

Chu ci does not tell us what the butcher became after he was elevated, so we do not know whether the legend of Lü Wang the butcher merged with the story of Shi Shangfu before the fourth century BC. Shi Shangfu's role in aiding the Zhou was first mentioned five or six centuries earlier in the *Shi jing* and his surname, Lü according to the commentators, is the same as that of the butcher. Both are called "preceptor" and their given names, Shang (*diang*) and Wang (*miwang*)[44] have the same final and a desirative connotation similar to "hope" or "expect."[45] Thus, if we account for dialect differences, the names could have been confused.

Huainanzi, compiled in the court of Liu An 劉安, Prince of Huainan (d. 122 BC), follows the tradition recorded in *Chu ci*, but further identifies

---

43. The term *gu dao* probably does not mean simply butcher (*tu ye* 屠也) as stated by the commentators, since it does not occur in any early text except with reference to Lü Wang, but must refer to a precise movement made by Lü Wang to attract customers or the king or to the way in which he butchered. The only related term I have found is *zou dao* 奏刀 "to make music with a knife" which refers to the skill with which Cook Ding slaughtered a cow, producing a melodious hum, *Nanhua zhenjing* 南華真經 2/2a. *Gu* and *zou* are often used together in a compound. They may refer to two types of skill; or Cook Ding who was in harmony with the Way may have produced music and the Grand Duke who had not yet met his true fate, produced a racket (*yang sheng* 揚聲).

44. The reconstructions of Bernhard Karlgren, "Grammata Serica Recensa," 190 (#725) and 198 (#742).

45. The basic meaning of *wang*, according to *Shuowen*, is "one who has gone away looks forward to his return." It often means "to look from afar" or more abstractly, "to expect" or "hope for." The commentators have usually understood the *shang* in Shi Shangfu as meaning "exalted," but *shang* also has a desiderative connotation similar to *wang*, which is reflected in the *Shuowen* gloss, *shu ji* 庶幾. In *Songben Er Ya shu* 宋本爾雅疏, Xing Bing 邢昺 explains *shang* with reference to Mao 224 of the *Shi jing* as that which the heart hopes for (*xi wang* 希望).

Lü Wang as a butcher and with the roles of ally of Zhou and ancestor
of Qi played by Shi Shangfu and Taigong in the *Shi ji*. There are ten
passages in *Huainanzi* that mention the Grand Duke, two of which refer
specifically to the butcher legend and include language identical to that
used in *Chu ci*. One of them provides no additional information,[46] but the
other identifies him as a butcher (*tu* 屠) and "drumming with a knife" as
the manifestation of his virtue by which King Wen recognized his worth:

> The Grand Duke's drumming with a knife. . . . His excellence
> was contained in it. . . . He left the butcher and beverage
> seller's market. (*Huainanzi* 13/15a)

By examining all ten passages, we can see that the compiler of
Huainanzi not only considered this figure a butcher, but consistently used
the pattern of nomenclature common to all references to the butcher
legend found in other works, and that he identified him with the preceptor of Kings Wen and Wu and the ancestor of Qi. In this text, he
is called Lü Wang, Taigong, and Taigong Wang, but never Lü Shang or
Shi Shangfu. Although the name Shi Shangfu never occurs, this role is
implied in two passages that refer to the defeat of Zhòu, the last king of
the Shang Dynasty and in one that refers to his plans (*mou* 謀), which
allowed King Wu to succeed.[47] His role as ancestor of Qi is implicit in
two other passages in which he is juxtaposed with the Duke of Zhou,
Dan, the ancestor of Lu.[48]

The brief reference in *Qian Han shu* is late (latter half, first century
AD), but seems to derive from the same tradition: "The Grand Duke suffered the hardship of drumming with a knife."[49] However, the Eastern
Han commentator of *Huainanzi*, Gao You 高誘, a native of Zhu Jun 瘃
郡 in modern Zhu Xian 瘃縣, because of geographical or chronological
distance, was better acquainted with the fishing legend or the butcher
cycle culminating with the fishing episode. Thus, although the text of
Huainanzi includes only the butcher tradition, after the phrase "drumming with a knife" quoted above, he explains: "The Grand Duke expe-

---

46. *Huainanzi* 19/2b.

47. Ibid., 6/4a, 12/19b, 21/6b.

48. Ibid., 10/7b, ll/2a.

49. *Han shu, juan* 64下, 2826.

rienced the hardships of being a butcher and a fisherman, but finally became the assistant of King Wen."

In another passage (17/6a), he identifies Lü Wang by stating that he "drummed with a knife and fished with a line," although *Huainanzi* states explicitly that Lü Wang "entered Zhou" by "drumming with a knife" (19/2b). Since both fishing and drumming with a knife were supposedly the means by which the Grand Duke attracted King Wen and became his minister, the two stories are logically inconsistent. However, because the theme is the same and its illustrative value of more importance to the early writers than the details of the legend, the two traditions were readily combined.

Chu ci and *Huainanzi* only mention a single episode in the background of Lü Wang, but the other five passages in Zhou and Han texts that refer to the butcher legend all include a larger cycle of deprivations or degradations. These passages all use the term *butcher* (*tu*) rather than "drummed with a knife." Four of the five specify Zhao Ge as the place where he was a butcher and mention Ji Jin, though they differ about the nature of his activity there. Three of them further refer to his wife or her family casting him out.

The exact relationship of this cycle to the "drumming with a knife" episode is not clear. The switch from a single episode capsulized as "drumming with a knife" to a series of episodes in which the term *butcher* is used indicates that the development was not simply progressive. The single episode and the cycle are closely related since the naming pattern is the same and one passage in *Huainanzi* used both terms. Furthermore, the single episode is always interpreted by later writers in terms of the cycle, indicating that it did not give rise to a different later tradition. However, there are indications of a geographic difference. The two sites mentioned in the cycle, Zhao Ge and Ji Jin, are both in Henan Province, north of the Yellow River, whereas the *Chu ci* poems and *Huainanzi* are associated with regions south of the Yellow River. However, the difference is not conclusive since Zhao Ge was the last Shang capital and the state of Chu had an early connection with the Shang Dynasty.[50] *Huainanzi* was also compiled under the direction of a Han prince. Nevertheless, the two versions of the legend are probably regional variants of a legend

---

50. Te-kun Cheng, *Archeology in China*, v. 3 (*Chou China*), 12 states, "Ch'u was an inheritor of Shang culture." For further references on the links between Chu and Shang, see Creel, *Statecraft*, 218, n. 99.

that was accepted over a large area including both the state of Chu and Northern Henan.

The earliest record of a cycle of degradations suffered by the Grand Duke is in *Zhanguo ce* (3/83a–b). This cycle has some unusual aspects, but follows the normal pattern of the butcher cycle by referring to the Grand Duke as a "butcher," cast out by his wife, and including the place names Zhao Ge and Ji Jin:

> The Grand Duke Expected was a cast out husband in Qi, a discarded butcher at Zhao Ge, the rejected minister of Zi Liang子良, and an unemployed slave at Ji Jin.

The emphasis of this passage on the Grand Duke's failure in every walk of life before he became preceptor of King Wen is unusual. That the Grand Duke could not succeed in any position except minister of the Zhou kings may be the import of the legend cycle, but it is not explicitly stated in the other versions. The other references to Ji Jin mention that he "hired himself out," "greeted guests," or "sold food," but never suggest that he could not even sell himself as a slave. That he was the "rejected minister of Zi Liang" is also not mentioned in other texts,[51] nor is he known to have failed as a butcher.[52] The most typical examples of the butcher cycle occur in two other Han anthologies, *Hanshi wai zhuan* and *Shuo yuan*. Both of these passages are emphatic about his degradation before he served the Zhou, but not to the extent of stating explicitly that he was a failure at even the meanest of tasks. *Hanshi wai zhuan* (7/4b) states:

> When Lü Wang was fifty, he sold food at Ji Jin; at seventy, he was a butcher at Zhao Ge; but at ninety, he became the preceptor of the Son of Heaven; this is because he met King Wen.

Similarly, *Shuo yuan* (8/5a):

> The Grand Duke Expected was a husband cast out by his old wife, a butcher's assistant at Zhao Ge, and a person who

---

51. I have not found it elsewhere nor has the commentator, *Zhanguo ce* 3/83b.

52. The commentator explains that *fei* 廢 "discarded" refers to rotten meat which he refused to sell, but this line seems to be parallel to the preceding lines, so I have taken it as "discarded butcher."

greets guests at Ji Jin, but at seventy he was minister to Zhou and at ninety he was enfeoffed in Qi.

These two anthologies also include passages in which the fishing legend had expanded into an area in which the butcher legend had previously been accepted and the resulting confusion was reconciled by expanding the cycle:

> When the Grand Duke Expected was young, he was a live-in son-in-law; when old, he was thrown out. He slaughtered cattle at Zhao Ge, hired himself out at Ji Jin, and fished in Pan Stream. King Wen elevated and made use of him. [Then] he enfeoffed him in Qi (*Hanshi wai zhuan* 8/14b).

This passage follows the standard pattern of the butcher cycle, except for the addition of the fishing story. The statement that he was a "live-in son-in-law"[53] who was thrown out when old explains the "cast-out husband" of the other cycles. He was so poor that he lived with his wife's family rather than bringing her into his; then, when he was old and useless, he was cast out.

The *Shuo yuan* passage (8/1b) simply refers to Lü Shang as a "fisherman and butcher" (*diao tu* 釣屠), but it is particularly significant because it uses the name Lü Shang. This is the only passage referring to the butcher story that uses the name "Shang" and all but one include "Wang." When the fishing story was simply added as an episode at the end of the butcher cycle, "Wang" was still used, but here fishing and butchering are on an equal level and "Shang" is used. The fishing legend seems to be gaining dominance and with it, the name Lü Shang.

Persuader and Recluse

Besides the fishing legend, the biography of the Grand Duke in the *Shi ji* includes two stories of how the Grand Duke came into the service of the Zhou. In one of these the Grand Duke was a traveling persuader; in the other, a recluse by the Eastern Sea:

> Some say the Grand Duke was widely knowledgeable [about the occult] and once served Zhòu, [king of the Shang Dynasty].

---

53. I have taken this translation from James Hightower, *Han Shih Wai Chuan*, 279.

Zhòu was without the Way, [so] he left him[54] and travelled around as a persuader to the various lords, without success until finally he turned westward to the Western Lord of Zhou. Others say Lü Shang was a hermit gentleman who was in seclusion by the sea coast. When the Western Lord of Zhou was seized at You Li 羑里, Sanyi Sheng 散宜生 and Hong Yao 閎夭 who had long known of him, summoned him. And, indeed, Lü Shang was saying, "I have heard that the Western Lord is virtuous and also likes to care for the elderly; why should I not go to him!" The three men sought out beautiful women and rare things which they presented to [the Shang king,] Zhòu in order to ransom the Western Lord. Therefore the Western Lord was able to leave and returned to his territory.[55]

The persuader legend is relatively late since the phenomenon of persuaders who traveled to the various feudal courts in search of employment did not occur until the late Chunqiu or Warring States periods. It never seems to have gained popularity as only one other extant text refers to the Grand Duke as a persuader:

Lü Shang went to King Wen three times and thrice he entered Yin, but he could not reach an understanding until later when he met King Wen. (Guiguzi 鬼谷子 2/6b)

This passage is not explicit, but it implies that the Grand Duke was a persuader who was rejected by the Western Lord (later King Wen) and the last Shang king until finally he met King Wen under different circumstance—perhaps by butchering at Zhao Ge or fishing in the Wei River. The latter is especially likely since this legend eventually gained dominance.

The recluse legend is related thematically to the persuader legend and reflects the conditions of the same late period.[56] The Grand

---

54. *Qu zhi* 去之 This is ambiguous and may mean either that the Grand Duke left Zhòu or that Zhòu dismissed the Grand Duke.

55. This story also appears in the "Basic Annals" of Yin and Zhou of the *Shi ji* (*juan* 3, 106 and *juan* 4, 116), but the "ministers of the Western Lord and the followers of Hong Yao" are said to gather up the gifts. Neither Sanyi Sheng nor Lü Shang are mentioned (though Sanyi Sheng is discussed elsewhere in these chapters). For Hong Yao, Sanyi Sheng and Nangong Kuo 南宮括 with the Grand Duke, see *Shang shu da zhuan* 尚書大傳 2/17b–18a.

56. Yang Yunru, 109–10, discusses the influence of the Warring States Period on this legend. See also James Crump, *Intrigues of the Warring States*, 1 for a discussion of persuaders.

Duke travels from the Shang kingdom where he has refused to serve an unworthy king to the Eastern coast and then returns to aid a virtuous feudal lord, much like a wandering persuader going from one court to another, albeit a highly principled one who will only serve a ruler who follows the Way. His eremetism also reflects the thought and conditions of the Warring States Period, certainly not those of the warring tribes at the beginning of Western Zhou.

The earliest reference to this legend is in *Mencius* (late fourth and early third century BC), where it occurs in two identical passages.[57] The story here, as discussed above, is that Bo Yi and the Grand Duke became hermits by the Northern and Eastern Seas, respectively, in order to avoid Zhòu, but hearing of the rise of King Wen, decided to go to him, remarking that he respected the elderly.

In the third century BC, this legend was recorded in *Lüshi chunqiu* and in the Han Dynasty, it was recorded in *Xin xu* 新序 as well as in the *Shi ji* biography. *Xin xu* (10/9b) and the biography are not significantly different from *Mencius* except that they specify the time at which the Grand Duke went to King Wen. Since they differ from each other in this regard,[58] the time was probably not an essential part of the legend even in the Han Dynasty. *Lüshi chunqiu* (14/8b), however, shows a significant development. As explained above, this passage is an interpolation of the same legend:

> The Grand Duke Expected was a gentleman of the Eastern Yi.
> He wished to unite the world, but lacked his master. Hear-
> ing that King Wen was virtuous, he fished in the Wei River
> to see [if it were so].

Here, fishing is described as the means by which the Grand Duke finally met King Wen, just as fishing was added to the end of the butcher cycle and in the persuader legend the Grand Duke finally met King Wen by some unknown means. The other legends are rather awkward with the addition of the fishing legend, but it is a logical way of reconciling the conflicting accounts when the fishing legend had encroached upon areas where the other legends were better known.

---

57. *Mengzi* 7/10a–b, 13/9a.

58. The biography specifies after King Wen was seized at You Li; *Xin xu*, after he settled the dispute between the peoples of Yú 虞 and Rui 芮.

The Eastern coast is the identifying feature of the recluse legend and its most likely place of origin. Not only is it the site where the legend takes place, but there is also an indigenous tradition in this area about the Grand Duke, including sites where he is said to have lived during his hermitage.[59] The inclusion of only the recluse legend in Mencius also points to an Eastern origin since Mencius was a native of Zou 鄒, a small state, not directly on the sea coast, but in the Eastern region. He also served in the court of Qi, in Shandong.

The Fishing Legend

Ultimately, the recluse, butcher, and perhaps the persuader legends merged with the fishing legend. Sima Qian already tended to accept this legend. After the Han Dynasty, it was generally acknowledged and acquired elaborate symbolic overtones, including a story that the Grand Duke (called Jiang Ziya 姜子牙) fished with a straight, unbaited hook. Few of these elaborations are included in the Zhou and Han texts, and the information about it during this period is surprisingly sparse, though it is included in a number of texts. Besides the three passages quoted above (two of which included the fishing legend as the culmination of the butcher cycle and one as the device by which the recluse went to King Wen) and the passage in the biography, there are six references to this legend in four texts: one in *Shuo yuan*, two in *Lüshi chunqiu*, one in *Lun heng*, and two in *Shi ji* (one of these also appears in *Zhanguo ce*). The account in the biography is by far the most extensive:

> It seems that Lü Shang had been in difficult straits and was very elderly[60] when he sought the Western Lord of Zhou by the device of a fishing line. When the Western Lord was about to go out hunting, he had a divination made. It said, "Your catch will be neither a grey dragon, nor a yellow dragon, neither tiger nor bear, but your catch shall be the supporter of a hegemonic king." Thereupon, the Western Lord of Zhou

---

59. *Shi ji, juan 99*, 2715; the *Zhengyi* 正義 commentary refers to a house and temple in Sujou Haiyan District 蘇州海燕.

60. This vague reference to hardship may indicate that Sima Qian was acquainted with the butcher cycle preceding the fishing legend, but was dubious of its authenticity.

went hunting and, indeed, he met the Grand Duke on the north bank of the Wei. He spoke with him and was extremely pleased, so he said, "Of old our [forefather], the Grand Duke,[61] said, 'When a sage comes to Zhou, then Zhou shall flourish.' Are you really he? Our Grand Duke expected you long ago." Therefore he called him "Grand Duke Expected." He carried him with him [in his carriage] and they returned together. Then he installed him as preceptor.

The fishing legend appears to have originated in the Wei River Valley and spread into other areas with Zhou culture. According to the biography, Lü Shang fished on the north bank of the Wei River, and other texts mention small tributaries of this river that would not be known outside the immediate region.[62] There is also an indigenous tradition of considerable antiquity about the fishing legend in this area, including sites where the Grand Duke is said to have fished.[63] This valley was inhabited by the Zhou as well as the Jiang and the credence given it by Sima Qian who made use of official court records reinforces the view that it was accepted by the Zhou.

The similarity of the naming style in the fishing legend and the Zhou historical tradition is further evidence that the Zhou accepted this legend. Sima Qian uses the name Lü Shang in the biography and in two other references to the fishing legend.[64] This name and the epithet "Grand Duke," which Sima Qian uses further on in the fishing account ("the Western Lord . . . met the Grand Duke on the banks of the Wei"), are particularly associated with this legend. Of the four other passages that refer to this legend, three use the name "Grand Duke." The fourth uses both "Lü Shang" and "Grand Duke" in the same relation to one another as Sima Qian:

---

61. Literally, "our antecedent lord, the Grand Duke." This presumably refers to King Wen's grandfather, the Ancient Duke, Dan Fu who was called the Grand King (Taiwang 太王) after the Western Lord began to be called King Wen.

62. The Pan Stream and Zi Spring are often given as sites where Lü Shang fished. *Shui jing zhu* 水經注31/11a, in discussing this legend, explains that the Zi Spring is in the Pan Stream which flows into the Wei River. This is in modern Shaanxi Province, Baoji District.

63. See n. 62 above and G. Haloun, 620.

64. *Shi ji, juan 79, 2406; juan 83, 1477.*

The Grand Duke caught an enormous fish on a fishing line. When he slit it[s stomach] he found a letter which said, "Lü Shang enfeoffed in Qi." (*Lun heng* 22/12a)

Here, as in the *Shi ji*, he is called "Grand Duke," but his proper name is thought of as "Lü Shang." Thus, his given name is the same as in the historical tradition and in the dynastic ballad of the Zhou recorded in the *Shi jing* (Shi Shangfu).

A theoretical reconstruction is that in the Wei River Valley where the fishing legend originated this figure was called "Lü Shang" or "Grand Duke," but farther south where the butcher legend grew up, he was called "Lü Wang" or "Grand Duke, Wang." At some time Shang and Wang were phonetically similar in the two regions and both legends were associated with the same historical figure. Later, when cultural unity increased, the legends began to encroach upon each other and confusion resulted. In order to reconcile the contradictions, the legends were combined and the naming patterns merged. Thus, although the name Lü Shang is never used in the fishing legend (it occurs only as an epithet awarded by King Wen, never in a description of him), it is used when the fishing story is added to the butcher cycle and when it is combined with the recluse legend.[65] After the fishing legend gained acceptance, the name Shang, which was associated with it and consistent with the Zhou records of a Shi Shangfu, was maintained. The name Wang, which was also associated with this figure, could not be discarded altogether, so it came to be regarded as an epithet rather than a name. The story that Taigong Wang was an epithet meaning "Expected by the Grand Duke" is improbable since Lü Shang himself is called "Grand Duke," but it is an effective rationalization to explain the confusion about the names.

The development of the fishing legend is difficult to trace since the earliest reference is in *Lüshi chunqiu* (third century BC) and all of the extant references seem to reflect a comparatively late form. There is no evidence of sequence in the texts, but there is a dichotomy in the interpretations about whether the Grand Duke was a fisherman attempting to make a living or a gentleman fishing to while away the time or to attract the Western Lord. The first interpretation would seem to be the basic folk legend and is thematically parallel to the butcher legend, but

---

65. The recluse legend has no consistent naming pattern, perhaps because of its relatively late origin.

it is reflected in only one passage, which suggests that the Grand Duke
both farmed and fished:

> For farming, the Grand Duke could not till well enough; fish-
> ing, he could not fill his net; but for governing the world, he
> had more than enough knowledge. (*Shuo yuan* 17/4b)

This is very much like the story of the butcher who was of no value
to his wife's family and a failure at every degrading task, but uniquely
suitable to be the minister of King Wen.

The other interpretations of the fishing legend are much closer in
theme to the recluse legend. *Lüshi chunqiu* (18/19b) refers to fishing as a
kind of eremetism: "The Grand Duke secluded himself by fishing with a
line." This interpretation allows the Grand Duke to have been a gentleman or scholar-persuader rather than a simple fisherman and must have
been looked upon with more favor by the gentlemen who recounted this
story in the feudal courts. The difference in interpretation is reflected in
the terminology. Whereas *Shuo yuan* uses the term *wang* 網 "net," the
means by which a fisherman would obtain his catch, *Lüshi chunqiu* and
the other texts all use the term *diao* 釣 "hook" or "to fish with a line,"
the means by which a gentleman would fish.[66]

The interpretation in the Grand Duke's biography and *Lüshi chunqiu* that the Grand Duke was fishing to attract the Western Lord allows
the Grand Duke to have held a higher social status than that of a simple
fisherman. As the story develops, this interpretation becomes even more
emphatic. When he fishes with a straight or unbaited hook, he is clearly
fishing only for a very special fish—one that wishes to be caught, the
Western Lord—for he certainly could not have hoped to catch his dinner.

Boatman—Similarity of Theme

In the above, I have traced the most popular legends about the origins
of the Grand Duke and shown how they finally merged with the fishing legend. There is one other extant legend—that the Grand Duke was
a boatman. This legend cannot be traced since it is found in only one
passage, which appears in almost identical form in *Xunzi* (8/12a–b) and

---

66. *Lun yu* 論語 4/7b states, "The master angled, but did not use a net."

Hanshi wai zhuan (4/9b). This passage is particularly interesting because of its stress on the Grand Duke not being a relative, as the historical evidence indicates, but raised out of poverty solely because of his ability:

> Now King Wen . . . took [Taigong], a boatman, raised him up from the ranks and employed him. Why did he favor him? Because he was a relative?! No, he was of a different clan. Because he was an old friend?! No, he had never known him before. Because of the beauty of his appearance?! No, [Taigong] was a toothless old man of seventy-two. So in using him King Wen wished to set up the Precious Way, to make clear the Precious Name, and with him to govern the empire to the benefit of the Middle Kingdom. All this he was unable to do alone. Therefore raising up this man, he employed him; and in fact the Precious Way was set up, and the Precious name was made clear. They governed the world together . . ."[67]

Although the Grand Duke is a boatman in this passage, any of the other legends we have examined could be substituted and it would make equally good sense. Whether the Grand Duke was a boatman, a butcher, a recluse, a persuader, or a fisherman, he was unrelated to the Western Lord and had nothing to offer him but his ability. His worth was not easily discernable but the Western Lord perceived it, determined to use him, and was thus able to establish his rule over the world. The legends about the Grand Duke all have a common theme—an unknown was raised and employed by King Wen and his son, King Wu, and aided them in founding the Zhou Dynasty.

The integrity and unique talent of the Grand Duke or the perception and virtue of the future king may be stressed more in one legend than another, but the theme remains the same. If the Grand Duke was a man of low birth or previously unsuccessful, the king's perception in recognizing his worth and his virtue in being willing to use him in spite of his low standing tend to be emphasized, though the Grand Duke's integrity in following the Way rather than seeking after a higher position is still apparent. The Grand Duke's lack of previous success may also show that he was unsuited for any other task, but uniquely suited

---

67. Translated by James Hightower, *Han Shih Wai Chuan*, 289–90.

to serve King Wen. If the Grand Duke is a man of higher class who has rejected the service of an unworthy ruler, his own integrity and the ability of the future king are emphasized, though the king must still have the virtue to be willing to use him.

The butcher legend particularly exemplifies the perception and virtue of King Wen and the Grand Duke's unique talent. In its earliest form, King Wen demonstrates his extraordinary perception by recognizing the Grand Duke's worth from the way he chopped meat; and his virtue, by his willingness to employ him in spite of his background. As the cycle develops, Lü Wang's poverty and obscurity are emphasized and this in turn shows not only King Wen's insight, but the Grand Duke's unique suitability to be his minister. He fails at job after job as he is fated to be minister of King Wen and no other task matches his capabilities.

That the Grand Duke was uniquely suited to be the minister of King Wen is also stressed in the version of the fishing legend in which he was a poor farmer and fisherman. The passage in *Shuo yuan* (17/4b) expressly states that he was a poor farmer and fisherman because he was concerned with greater matters: "Devoting himself to large things, he assuredly forgets the small." Thus, the man who is worthy to be founding minister must wait for the opportunity to arise and his success in other tasks or lack of it is no measure of his talent. The recluse legend stresses the integrity of the Grand Duke and the virtue of King Wen. In this legend, the Grand Duke becomes a recluse in order to avoid serving the wicked king Zhòu. When he hears of the rise of the Western Lord, however, he goes to him and helps him to overthrow the Shang. King Wen's ability to attract a virtuous minister and his willingness to rely upon his advice is more striking in this legend than his perception of the Grand Duke's extraordinary ability, though this element is still present. The Grand Duke's integrity in not serving a lesser man is also stressed and in this case it is the conscious integrity of a political man rather than that of a sage bound by his fate. Even more important in this legend may be a rejection of the idea that such a good minister might come from the ranks of the poor and uneducated.

The persuader legend expresses both the integrity of the Grand Duke and the virtue and insight of King Wen, but since the Grand Duke is unsuccessful instead of from a low social position, it is undramatic. The integrity of the Grand Duke is shown by his leaving the Shang court because Zhòu was "without the Way." He then tries to find service with another feudal lord, but not one will appoint him because they have neither the insight to recognize his ability nor the virtue to employ a man who follows the Way.

The version of the fishing legend in which the Grand Duke is seeking to attract King Wen is the most complete expression of all the aspects of the theme, partly because the identity of the Grand Duke is so vague. King Wen's perception of human nature and virtue in employing ministers according to their ability is dramatically demonstrated by his immediate recognition that an old man he finds fishing on the riverbank is a sage that his grandfather had foreseen and by his employment of the old man as his preceptor. However, since the Grand Duke is really not simply a fisherman, but a sage who is attracted by the virtue of King Wen, the king's ability to attract virtuous men and the Grand Duke's integrity in waiting for him are also demonstrated.

The Founding Minister—From Obscurity to Fame

The legends about the origins of the Grand Duke seem to have grown up independently, but they all have a common theme of an unknown raised to a position of power by the Western Lord of Zhou. There is some disagreement about the original social status of the Grand Duke and consequently differing emphasis on the poverty of the Grand Duke and insight of the Western Lord or the Grand Duke's integrity and the Western Lord's virtue to which he was attracted. This disagreement may reflect the different uses of the legend. The original legends were probably about men of the lower class raised up by the future king. The gentry (shi 士) class, many of whom rose from lowly backgrounds in the Chunqiu and Warring States Periods,[68] may have been particularly interested in these legends to justify their own authority though somewhat uncertain about the degree of poverty portrayed in the legends, but the noblemen must have preferred to view the legendary figure as a man of the upper class who had fallen or put himself into a position of poverty or obscurity. Nevertheless, the legends were generally accepted and the theme expressed in them is not specific to the Grand

---

68. Cho-yün Hsü, *Ancient China in Transition*, 24–52, discusses the changes in social stratification in this period. This increased mobility may have been responsible for the popularity of these legends in Zhou and Han texts.

Duke, but is a theme common to ministers of founding kings or great hegemons.[69]

The theme of the founding minister is an expression of one aspect of the concept of the dynastic cycle, the exchange of power, which was thought to be a manifestation of the removal of heaven's mandate from an unworthy ruler and its bestowal upon a man of virtue. The unworthy ruler or "bad last king" had certain bad attributes that caused his downfall and loss of mandate. One of these is that he neglected and abused upright officials and favored sycophants and corrupt officials.[70] The good first king, on the contrary, used upright officials and rejected sycophants. His founding minister is a dramatic expression of his ability and virtue. The would-be king "knows men" (*zhi ren* 知人) and "uses" them (*yong ren* 用人). He shows this by "raising" (*ju* 舉) a man from obscurity and relying upon him heavily. This is his "founding minister," traditionally a man who is so talented that he alone can help the future king to obtain his rule, but plunged in obscurity either because no one else has had the insight to recognize his ability or because he has found no one else worthy of his services. The founding minister is the ideal of a good minister just as the first king is the most perfect of kings, and this accounts for the ambivalence about his social position.

This theme explains why so many different legends of a similar nature grew up about the origins of the Grand Duke and why they were so easily merged. The concept of the dynastic cycle was such that the founding king was expected to have such a minister. The two other most important ministers of Kings Wen and Wu, the Dukes of Zhou and Shao,

69. M. Granet, *Danses et légendes*, v. 2, 393–403, "Les fondations des dynasties," recognizes this theme and uses the term "ministre-fondateur" which I have translated as "founding minister." He considers the Duke of Zhou the "ministre-fondateur" of Zhou, apparently because he became more prominent historically as the chief minister of the early period of the Zhou than did the Grand Duke. The Grand Duke, however, meets the thematic criterion better. Granet, himself, notes that the Duke of Zhou was a member of the Zhou royal family and therefore could not have the characteristic trait of a founding minister—being "captured" in seclusion (or obscurity)—which is attributed to Lü Shang, 409. The Duke of Zhou is best known as the regent of King Cheng, the third Zhou king, and for preserving the line of succession, whereas the Grand Duke is best known as the assistant of the first two kings, Wen and Wu, who aided them to found the dynasty. The regency is specific to the Duke of Zhou and not a repeated theme associated with the founding of dynasties. The story of the sage raised out of obscurity who aids his ruler to found a new dynasty is repeated at the founding of the Shang and Zhou Dynasties and the characteristic of the founding minister.

70. Arthur F. Wright, "Sui Yang-ti: Personality and Stereotype," 173.

could not be fitted into the pattern of obscurity since both were brothers of the king. Although the Grand Duke may have been related to the
royal family by marriage, his clan name was different and his parentage
was not well known. Therefore, he was the most suitable candidate for
the role of founding minister, and regional legends either grew up about
him or extant legends became associated with him to fit his background
to the popular expectations of a founding minister. Since the theme was
of primary importance and the details of the Grand Duke's life relatively
unimportant, the legends were readily combined.

The influence of the founding minister theme on the Grand Duke
can be shown by examining his role in Zhou and Han literature. Zhou
and Han writers were not particularly interested in the details of the background of the Grand Duke. They show no qualms at the contradictions
of the different legends, merging them readily and without discussion.
They seldom discuss the individual legends, so most of the information
presented above had to be garnered from brief identifications after the
Grand Duke's name, meant to serve more as emphasis than explanation. However, they do frequently cite the names of the Grand Duke to
illustrate a theme or prove a point, often with a list of others thought to
illustrate the same theme. These lists of names may provide the key to
understanding the role of the Grand Duke. If we examine the identity of
these figures, we find that they form a larger complex of founding ministers, and if we examine the theme expressed in the passages that list
the names, it is the necessity of having such a minister to achieve power.

The role of the Grand Duke should be the same as that of other
persons whose names are listed in a parallel fashion with his. Therefore,
I have attempted to isolate all of the passages in the major philosophical
texts of the Zhou and Han periods in which the Grand Duke's name is
given as a parallel to others. I have not included contemporaries, people
factually related to the Grand Duke, or people whose lives are juxtaposed
rather than paralleled to that of the Grand Duke.[71] By following these

---

71. Contemporaries include the Dukes of Zhou and Shao and Bo Yi. People factually related
to him include, for example, lists of descendants or ministers of Qi. Juxtaposed to him are
people such as Zuo Qiang 左强, the evil minister of the last king of Shang or Wu Zixu
伍子胥, contrasted as an unsuccessful but wise minister. Stylistically, these names may
appear similar, but the intent is to contrast rather than parallel. An interesting study might
also be made of these, but they are not nearly so common. In a few cases, I have had to
make arbitrary decisions about which passages should be included, but these were few
and would not have significant effect on the results.

guidelines, I was able to isolate thirty-six passages in twelve texts or, discounting duplicates (listed in parentheses below), thirty-two passages:[72]

Guiguzi 2/6b
Hanfeizi 5/6b, 17/7a
Hanshi wai zhuan 5/3b, 7/4b, 8/4b, (5/15a), (8/14b)
Huainanzi 13/7a, 13/15a, 19/2b
Lüshi chunqiu 4/5a, 17/14b, 18/19b, 24/3a, (2/8b)
Lun heng 3/1b, 6/10b, 14/4a, 30/11a
Mengzi 14/19a
Mozi 1/5b
Shuo yuan 8/1b, 8/5a, 8/5b, 17/4b, (17/12b)
Xin xu 2/1a, 4/1b, 5/1a
Xunzi 7/19a, 9/3a, 15/3a, 20/2b
Zhanguo ce 3/83a, 4/58a

The names listed in these thirty-two passages are remarkably consistent. At least one of the three names mentioned most frequently occurs in twenty-eight of the passages. The nine names listed below are those which occur at least three times.[73] The dynasty or state which they served is placed in parentheses.

Yi Yin 伊尹	23 passages (Shang 商)
Guan Zhong 管仲 (or Guan Yiwu 管夷吾)	14 passages (Qi 齊)
Boli Xi 百里奚	11 passages (Qin 秦)
Sunshu Ao 孫叔敖	5 passages (Chu 楚)
Gao Yao 皋陶	4 passages (Xia 夏)

---

72. In determining duplicates, I have discarded those passages where the names listed were identical or almost so, but included *Lüshi chunqiu* 4/5a which is textually related to *Xin xu* 5/la and *Hanshi wai zhuan* 5/15a, but has a different list of names.

73. I have only included those names listed three times in order to exclude names that may be listed twice because of copying. However, the name of Fu Yue 傅說, the convict minister of Wu Ding 武丁, the Shang king who rejuvenated his dynasty, occurs twice and probably belongs in this list of founding ministers.

Shun 舜	3 passages (Tang Yao 唐堯)
Xu You 許由	3 passages (Yú Shun 虞舜)
Jiu Fan 咎犯	3 passages (Jin 晉)
Ning Qi 甯戚	3 passages (Qi 齊)

These figures and the Grand Duke served all of the founding kings before the Han Dynasty and four of the five hegemons.[74] Shun, Xu You, and Gao Yao served the three "august" (predynastic) rulers (*san huang* 三 皇), Yao, Shun, and Yu 禹, respectively. Gao Yao, Yi Yin, and the Grand Duke are the founding ministers of the three dynasties, Xia, Shang, and Zhou. Guan Zhong and Ning Qi served the great hegemon, Duke Huan of Qi. Boli Xi served Duke Mu of Qin; Jiu Fan, Duke Wen of Jin; and Sunshu Ao, King Zhuang of Chu. A fifth minister of a hegemon is not consistently named, but neither are the early texts consistent in naming the fifth hegemon. These four technically might not be considered "founding ministers" since they did not serve founding kings, but the hegemons were so highly respected in these texts that they are accorded the same status as the founding kings.[75]

A detailed examination of the legends surrounding these figures is beyond the scope of the present paper. However, their role in these texts may be discerned from the brief identifying descriptions that occur after the names in many of the thirty-two passages. These almost always refer to their obscurity or degradation before they met their ruler—the key motif in the founding minister theme.

Yi Yin is described in these passages as a servant of the lady Xin (*You Shen Shi* 有莘氏 betrothed to Tang, the founder of the Shang Dynasty),[76] as having carried the *ding*-tripod,[77] and as a cook[78] (or, just as the Grand

---

74. No Han figure is mentioned more than once, indicating that most of the passages were originally composed before the beginning of the Han Dynasty. This is probably because the discussion of how rule is founded was more vital to the feudal courts of the Warring States Period than to the ministers of Han.

75. M. Granet, *Danses et légendes.*, also recognized this. See v. 1, 80–84, for his discussion of Boli Xi and Guan Zhong as "ministers-fondateur."

76. The times at which Xu You and Gao Yao lived differ in the early texts, but in all three passages here Xu You is referred to as minister of Shun. Gao Yao is mentioned both as minister of Shun and of Yu.

77. *Hanshi wai zhuan* 7/4b; *Shuo yuan* 8/5a.

78. *Hanshi wai zhuan* 7/4b; *Huainanzi* 13/15a, 19/2b.

Duke's fishing is described as a kind of eremetism, having "secluded himself in the kitchen"[79]). Since the founding minister is the mechanism by which a virtuous ruler achieves power in a decadent state, it is not perfectly applicable to the peaceful transfer of rule from one virtuous man to another, as from Yao to Shun or Shun to Yu. Thus, since the Shang was the only dynasty before the Zhou that, according to popular belief, was founded by overthrowing a previous dynasty, Yi Yin is the only perfect parallel to the Grand Duke and most frequently mentioned with him. Guan Zhong and Boli Xi, the ministers of the two great hegemons of Qi and Qin, are mentioned next most often and usually together (nine passages). Guan Zhong who was a prisoner[80] is most characteristically described as "bound and tied"[81] and in one passage called a "thief."[82] His rival for founding minister to Duke Huan, Ning Qi,[83] is described as a "cart-puller" who "beat the cart shafts and sang"[84] or simply as "singing"[85]—for this is the means by which Duke Huan recognized his worth. Boli Xi, a "slave"[86] or a "beggar,"[87] "sold himself for five rams' skins"[88] and herded or fed oxen.[89]

Sunshu Ao and Jiu Fan, the two other ministers of hegemons, are less perfect examples of the founding minister, but elements of the theme do occur. Sunshu Ao's degradation is referred to in a passage that states that he was slandered while serving Chu.[90] (The story of Sunshu Ao does not fall quite within the standard pattern since both Chu's suc-

---

79. *Shuo yuan* 8/1b.

80. *Lüshi chunqiu* 18/19b.

81. *Zhanguo ce* 3/83a.

82. *Hanshi wai zhuan* 7/4b; *Huainanzi* 19/2b.

83. *Shuo yuan* 8/5a.

84. The legend of Ning Qi is mentioned in "Li sao" with the butcher legend of Lü Wang, but there is only one brief reference to Ning Qi in the *Shi ji*. Guan Zhong is not mentioned at all in *Chu ci*, but is discussed at length in the *Shi ji*. Thus, the legend of Ning Qi may have been regional—from the same southern area as the butcher legend—and that of Guan Zhong may have been a rival legend, from the area of the fishing legend.

85. *Shuo yuan* 8/5a.

86. *Huainanzi* 13/15b.

87. *Shuo yuan* 8/1b.

88. *Zhanguo ce* 3/83a.

89. *Zhanguo ce* 3/83a; *Hanshi wai zhuan* 7/4b; *Shuo yuan* 8/5a.

90. *Hanshi wai zhuan* 7/4b; *Huainanzi* 13/15a.

cess and its ultimate failure are attributed to its use or lack of use of
Sunshu Ao.) None of the passages that list the name of Jiu Fan include
descriptive epithets, and the motif of obscurity or degradation does not
seem to occur in his life. However, in one passage, Duke Wen, himself,
is described as "planting rice."[91] The total dependence of the ruler on
his minister is also a strong element in Jiu Fan's life. In one instance,
he even had to inebriate Duke Wen in order to make him return to his
state instead of abandoning himself to the search for pleasure.[92]

The discovery of Shun by Yao is the prototype of the theme of
the discovery of a virtuous unknown by a wise ruler. He becomes ruler
rather than minister, but this passage of rule also establishes the principle
that rule may pass to a worthy man rather than an unworthy son. Here
Shun is described as having "farmed on the north slope of Mt. Li."[93]
Identifying epithets do not occur in these passages for the other two
pre-Shang ministers, Xu You and Gao Yao. Xu You was a recluse and a
farmer during the reign of the predynastic ruler Yao, whom he refused
to serve. Gao Yao, however, seems to be included simply because he
was minister of Shun and Yu. I have not found any record of obscurity
or degradation in his life.

The role of the Grand Duke, then, is that of founding minister to
Kings Wen and Wu. As a founding minister, he was thought to have been
raised from obscurity by a future king and to have aided him to found his
rule. The importance of this theme to the concept of the establishment
of power can be seen not only by its recurrence at every new dynasty
or hegemony, but directly from the themes expressed in these thirty-two
passages. These passages stress the necessity of such a minister for the
establishment of rule or else explain the mechanics of the phenomenon
of the founding minister.

By far the most common theme (sixteen passages) is that a *founding king or hegemon must have a virtuous minister in order to establish his
rule*. The virtuous ministers of the founding kings are cited to illustrate
this theme and, as shown above, these are almost all men raised from
obscurity. The theme is most commonly expressed by the formula:

---

91. *Shuo yuan* 17/4b.

92. *Shi ji, juan* 39, p. 1658.

93. *Shuo yuan* 17/4b.

X (ruler) got A (founding minister) and then he became king
or hegemon;

Y got B and then he became king or hegemon;

Z . . .

The implication is often, "If you take me, then you too may become
king." Many of the passages, however, are more general discussions of
the theory of power. *Xunzi* (7/19a), for example, states the importance
of the sagacious minister to the king who wishes to establish his rule
very explicitly: "If one can get the right person, then the world may be
taken; if one loses the right person, the tutelary temple will be lost."
Thus, the future king must have an appropriate minister or he cannot
rise. For King Wen, this was the Grand Duke. This minister is uniquely
suited to aid the would-be king and must be discovered by him, usually in obscurity. To meet this criterion the legends of the Grand Duke's
obscure origins arose.

There are three other themes that occur regularly. Each of these
concerns some aspect of the founding minister theme. The theme that is
mentioned second most often (five passages) is: *for a sage to meet the right
ruler depends on fate* [*ming* 命] *or time* [*shi* 時]. This theme is the obverse
of the above and is usually used to explain why a certain sage, such as
Confucius, was not appointed rather than to explain why certain rulers
met with such outstanding success. In the fishing legend, the Grand
Duke was fated to meet King Wen by the Wei River. In some versions
he was aware of his fate and that is why he went there to fish. Conversely, some sages are not fated to meet a superior ruler, not because
of lack of virtue, but because the time is not right. As *Hanshi wai zhuan*
(7/4a) explains: "Meeting or not meeting [a ruler] is [a matter of] time."
Similarly, *Lun heng* (3/1b), in explaining why some virtuous ministers met
a violent death and others, such as Yi Yin and Lü Wang were promoted,
states: "Fate is the ruler of fortune and misfortune."

The two other themes concern the character attributes of the future
ruler and his founding minister that were cited above as key elements of
the founding minister motif. Three passages are about the ability of the
ruler to recognize the worth of a man who has not yet achieved merit.
Huainanzi (13/15b) explains this trait in terms of the prototypes of Yao
and Shun: "Knowing his virtue without his having achieved merit, this

is how Yao knew Shun." The integrity, unselfishness, or humility of the founding minister who has not yet achieved success is the topic of four passages. *Huainanzi* (19/2b) explains: "The position occupied by the sage is not for his own pleasure."

In sum, the king must have insight and the sage must be humble. Then, if the time is right, they will meet and new power be established over the world. This theme is both explicitly stated and demonstrated by legends about every new dynasty and great hegemony. The founding of the Zhou had to be fitted into this pattern and the role of the Grand Duke is that of the founding minister, a sage who is raised from a humble position by a future ruler and aids him to establish his rule.

Conclusion

At the base of the legends about Taigong Wang is a historical figure, Shi Shangfu, a member of the Jiang clan. The Jiang and the Zhou were allied militarily and through marriage; the Grand Duke represented the Jiang in this alliance with the Zhou. Although his historical role implies that he was an esteemed figure within a powerful clan, sometime in the Zhou Dynasty legends grew up in which he was raised out of poverty or obscurity by the future King Wen. These legends are all quite different in their particulars—the Grand Duke was a butcher, a fisherman, a recluse, a persuader, or a boatman—and they have distinct regional origins. The butcher legend is associated with the South, the fishing legend with the Wei River Valley, and the recluse legend with the Eastern coast. In tracing the development of these legends, we find that they are of similar theme and thus readily combined in the early texts. Broader study shows that this theme is not only common to the various legends about the Grand Duke, but recurs in legends about a set of "founding ministers" who helped first kings and great hegemons to establish their rule. These ministers are grouped together in the early literature to show the necessity of having such a minister to achieve power. Thus, the legends of the Grand Duke as a founding minister grew up to fit the founding of the Zhou into the accepted pattern for the change of power.

In isolating the motif of the founding minister, certain problems have arisen that cannot be solved without a more complete study of the whole group of founding ministers and further reference to other legend motifs about the origins of power. Chronology is one such problem. The motif of the founding minister was certainly not static and must have developed over a period of time. However, an exact chronology can only be established by studying a larger group of interrelated legends with a larger number of references which can be placed in time. Philosophical import is another. I have mentioned the apparent disagreement of Warring States philosophers about the social status of Taigong Wang. The philosophical import of the motif might be more precisely determined by studying the different treatment of these legends by the various philosophical schools. Finally, there is the problem of the political function and use of the legends. The legends tended to legitimize rule and conscious use of the concept of the founding minister may have been made by some of the rulers.

Postscript

Taigong Wang is mentioned in several of the Warring States period bamboo-slip manuscripts written in the script of the Southern state of Chu that have been discovered since this article was first published. I will not attempt to analyze them herein. However, *Qiong da yi shi* 窮達以時 ("Failure and success depend on the season") from Guodian 郭店 Tomb One, Jingmen 荊門, Hubei Province, is particularly worth mentioning because it includes a list of founding ministers. As the title given by the scholars who transcribed it indicates, its theme is timeliness. Thus, each minister is said to have been raised up while they were laboring because they happened to meet the future king or hegemon who recognized worth. Taigong is called Lü Wang, and he is said to have been a slave (or shopkeeper) and watcher of the gates at Ji jin before he met King Wen while butchering oxen at Zhao Ge. This corresponds with the territory naming pattern of the butcher legend discussed above.

The list of founding ministers and the rulers that discovered them in this manuscript presents a problem. It begins with Shun meeting Yao, and then refers to Shao Yao 邵謠 meeting Wu Ding 武丁, the king who restored the Shang Dynasty around 1300 BC. The name Shao Yao is easily read as a variant of Gao Yao, but the legend reference is the story of building earthen walls associated with Fu Yue 傅說 who served Wu Ding. It is possibly a mistake, but since Yi Yin is omitted from the list too, the confusion is more likely to be due to a missing section of text, either because of "eyeskip" by a copyist or because a slip is missing. The other founding ministers in the list are Guan Yiwu, Sunshu (Ao), and Boli (Xi).[94]

Two manuscripts now in the Shanghai Museum collection are especially relevant for understanding the historical development of the legend of Taigong Wang. They are *Ju zhi wang tianxia* 舉治王天下, which includes subsections assigned the titles, "Gu Gong jian Taigong Wang 古公見太公望" ("The Old Duke visits the Grand Duke Expected") and "Wen Wang fang zhi yu Shangfu juzhi 文王訪於尚父舉治" ("King Wen enquires of Shangfu about raising and governing"), and *Wu Wang jian zuo* 武王踐阼 ("King Wu ascends the throne"). I take both manuscripts as Warring States period compositions. Both make extensive use of the name Shi Shangfu beyond the limitations of the military context described above, as well as Taigong Wang. This is probably because of the name Shi Shangfu recalled Taigong's role as a strategist in the defeat of the Shang.[95] *Wu Wang jian zuo* is particularly significant for in understanding the development of the legend of Taigong Wang as a type of military wizard in later times. Moreover, it includes the historical in which the Yellow Emperor and Zhuan Xu precede Yao and Shun, that is found in the *Shi ji* and other Han texts but is extremely rare in the Warring States period. However, the manuscripts include many complex problems of reconstruction, so detailed analysis must await further study.

94. *Guodian Chu mu zhujian* 郭店楚墓竹簡, 145–46 (Slips 4–5). For translations and discussion of this manuscript, see Dirk Meyer, *Philosophy on Bamboo*, 53–76 269–82; Scott Cook, *The Bamboo Texts of Guodian*, 429–64.

95. For *Qiong da yi shi*, see Jingmenshi Bowuguan 荊門市博物館, ed. *Guodian Chu mu zhujian* 郭店楚墓竹簡, 27–28, 145–46. For *Wu Wang jian zuo* and *Ju zhi wang tianxia*, see Ma Chengyuan 馬承源, ed. *Shanghai Bowuguan cang Zhanguo Chu zhushu* 上海博物館藏戰國楚竹書, vol. 7 (2008), 13–29 and 148–68, and vol. 9 (2012), 59–95 and 189–236.

Bibliography

Primary Sources

Unless otherwise noted, the Chinese editions cited are the unpunctuated Sibu congkan 四部叢刊 editions published by Commercial Press in Shanghai, 1919–1922. These are cited in the form: *juan* 卷/page number a (*shang* 上) or b (*xia* 下). Other editions of primary sources cited herein include:

Chu ci buzhu 楚辭補注. Edited by Hong Xingzu 洪興祖. Shanghai: Commercial Press, n.d.

Chu ci tongshi 楚辭通釋. Edited by Wang Fuzhi 王夫之. Shanghai: Zhonghua Shuju, 1959.

Chunqiu Zuo zhuan jinzhu jinyi 春秋左傳今注今譯. Edited by Li Zongtong 李宗侗. Taipei: Taiwan Commercial Press, 1970.

*Fu Songben chongxiu Guang yun*覆宋本重修廣韻. Shanghai: Commercial Press, 1930.

*Guben zhushu jinian jijiao dingbu*古本竹書紀年輯校訂補. Edited by Fan Xiangyong 范祥雍. Shanghai: Xin Zhishi, 1956.

Guo ce kan yan 國策勘研. Edited by Zhong Fengnian 鐘鳳年. Yenching Journal of Chinese Studies, Monograph, no. 11. Beijing, 1936.

Guodian Chu mu zhujian 郭店楚墓竹簡. Edited by Jingmenshi Bowuguan 荊門市博物館. Beijing: Wenwu, 1998.

Hanfeizi jishi 韓非子集釋. Compiled by Chen Qiyou 陳奇猷. Beijing: Zhonghua Shuju, 1958.

Han shu 漢書. Beijing: Zhonghua Shuju, 1962.

Huainan honglie jijie 淮南鴻列集解. Edited by Liu Wendian 劉文典. Shanghai: Commercial Press, 1933.

Laozi jiaogu 老子校詁. Edited by Ma Xulun 馬敘倫.Beijing: Guji Chubanshe, 1956.

Lun heng jiaoshi 論衡校釋. Edited by Huang Hui 黃暉. Shanghai: Commercial Press, 1964.

Lüshi chunqiu jishi 呂氏春秋集釋. Compiled by Xu Weiyu 許維遹. Beijing: Wenxue Guji Kanxingshe, 1955.

Lüshi chunqiu jiaoshi 呂氏春秋校釋. Edited by Yin Zhongrong 尹仲容. Taipei: Zhonghua Congshu, 1958.

Maoshi zhushu 毛詩註疏. Shanghai: Commercial Press (Guoxue jiben congshu), 1940.

Mengzi yizhu 孟子譯注. Edited by Yang Bojun 楊伯峻. Beijing: Zhonghua Shuju, 1960.

Mengzi jizhu 孟子集註. Edited by Zhu Xi 朱熹. Shanghai: Commercial Press, 1938.

Mozi jiangu 墨子閒詁. Edited by Sun Yirang 孫詒讓. Shanghai: Commercial Press, 1936.

Shanghai Bowuguan cang Zhanguo Chu zhushu 上海博物館藏戰國楚竹書. Edited by Ma Chengyuan 馬承源. Shanghai: Shanghai Guji, 2000–.

Shi ji 史記. Beijing: Zhonghua Shuju, 1959.

Shi jing jizhu 詩經集注. Edited by Zhu Xi 朱熹. Shanghai: Guangyi Shuju. 1939.

Song ben Er ya shu 宋本爾雅疏, Xing Bing 邢昺. Shanghai: Hanfenlou, 1922.

Xunzi jianshi 荀子簡釋. Ed. Liang Qixiong 梁啟雄. Beijing: Guji Chubanshe, 1957.

Xunzi jijie 荀子集解. Edited by Wang Xianqian 王先謙. Shanghai: Commercial Press, 1936.

Yan tie lun jiaozhu 鹽鐵論校注. Edited by Wang Liqi 王利器. Gudian Wenxue Chubanshe, Shanghai, 1958.

Yanzi chunqiu jishi 晏子春秋集釋. Compiled by Wu Zeyu 吳則虞. Beijing: Zhonghua Shuju, 1962.

Zhuangzi jishi 莊子集釋. Compiled by Guo Qingfan 郭慶藩. Taibei: Heluo, 1974.

Zhuangzi buzheng 莊子補正. Edited by Liu Wendian 劉文典. Shanghai: Commercial Press, 1947.

Secondary Sources

Allan, Sarah. *Buried Ideas: Legends of Abdication and Ideal Government in Early Chinese Bamboo-Slip Manuscripts*. Albany: State University of New York Press, 2015.

———. "The Identities of Taigong Wang in Zhou and Han Literature." *Monumenta Serica* 30 (1972–73): 57–99.

———. "The Myth of the Xia Dynasty." *Journal of the Royal Asiatic Society* 2 (1984): 242–56.

———. "Shang Foundations of Modern Chinese Folk Religion." In *Legend, Lore, and Religion in China*, edited by Sarah Allan and Alvin P. Cohen, 1–21. San Francisco: CMC, 1979.

————. *The Shape of the Turtle: Myth, Art, and Cosmos in Early China.* Albany: State University of New York Press, 1991.

————. "Some Preliminary Comments on the X Gong Xu." In *The X Gong Xu,* Special Issue of the *International Research on Bamboo and Silk Documents: Newsletter,* edited by Xing Wen (2003): 16–22.

————. *The Way of Water and Sprouts of Virtue.* Albany: State University of New York Press, 1997.

Benoist, Jean-Marie. *The Structural Revolution.* London: Weidenfeld and Nicolson, 1978.

Chao, Lin. "Marriage, Inheritance, and Lineage Organization in Shang China." Taipei: Yichih Press, 1970.

Chen Mengjia 陳夢家. *Yinxu buci congshu* 殷墟卜辭總述. Beijing: Kexue Chubanshe 科學出版社, 1956.

————. "Xi Zhou tongqi duandai" 西周銅器斷代. *Kaogu xuebao*考古學 9 (1955): 137–75 (pt. 1); 10 (1955): 69–142 (pt. 2); 1956, no. 1: 65–114 (pt. 3); 1956, no. 2: 85–94 (pt. 4); 1956, no. 3: 105–14 (pt. 5); 1956, no. 4: 85–122 (pt. 6).

Cheng, Te-kun. *Archeology in China,* vol. 3 (*Zhou*). Cambridge: Cambridge University Press, 1963.

Chmielewski, Janus. "Notes on Early Chinese Logic." *Rocznik Orientalistyczny* 26.1 (1962): 7–21, 26, no. 2 (1962): 91–105, 27, no. 1 (1963): 103–121, 28, no. 2 (1965): 87–111, 29, no. 2 (1965): 136–39, 30, no. 1 (1966): 31–52.

Conrady, August. *T'ien Wen.* Leipzig: Asia Major Library, no. 2, 1931.

Cook, Constance A. "The Sage King Yu and the Bin Gong *xu* 爾公盨." *Early China* 35 (2012–2013): 69–103.

Cook, Scott. *The Bamboo Texts of Guodian: A Study and Complete Translation.* Ithaca: Cornell University East Asia Program, 2012.

Creel, Herrlee G. *Studies in Early Chinese Culture.* Baltimore: Waverly, 1937.

————. *The Origins of Statecraft in China.* Chicago and London: University of Chicago Press, 1970.

Descola, Philippe. *Beyond Nature and Culture.* Chicago: University of Chicago Press, 2013.

Dobson, W. A. C. H. "Linguistic Evidence and the Dating of the Book of Songs," *T'oung Pao* 51 (1964): 323–34.

Dubs, Homer, trans. *The History of the Former Han Dynasty.* Baltimore: Waverly Press, 1955.

Eberhard, Wolfram. *Local Cultures in South and East Asia.* Leiden: E. J. Brill, 1968.

Falkenhausen, Lothar, von. *Chinese Society in the Age of Confucius (1000–250 BC): The Archaeological Evidence.* Los Angeles: Cotsen Institute of Archaeology at UCLA, 2006.

Forke, Alfred, trans. *Lun heng: Philosophical Essays of Wang Ch'ung.* New York: Paragon Book Gallery, 1962.

Fu Sinian 傅斯年. "Jiang Yuan" 姜原. *Bulletin of the Institute of History and Philology* 2 (1930), pt. 1: 130–35.

Graham, A. C. *Later Mohist Logic, Ethnics and Science.* Hongkong: Chinese University Press, 1978.

Granet, Marcel. *Danses et Légendes de la Chine Ancienne.* 2 vols. Paris: Presses Universitaires de France, 1959.

———. *La Pensée Chinoise.* Paris: La Renaissance du Livre, 1934.

Gu Jiegang 顧頡剛, ed. *Gu shi bian* 古史辯. 7 vols. Beijing and Shanghai: 1926–1941.

Guo Moro 郭沫若. *Liang Zhou Jinwen ci daxi kaoshi* 兩周金文辭大系考釋. Beijing: Kexue, 1957 (originally published in Tokyo: Bunkyūdō, 1935).

Haloun, Gustav. "Contributions to the History of Clan Settlement in Ancient China," *Asia Major* 1 (first series) 1 (1924): 76–111, 587–623.

Hawkes, David, trans. *Ch'u Tz'u: The Songs of the South.* New York: Beacon, 1962.

Hayashi Taisuke 林秦輔. *Zhougong* 周公. Translated and edited by Qian Mu 錢穆. Taipei: Commercial Press, 1967.

Herrmann, Albert. *An Historical Atlas of China.* Chicago, 1966.

Hightower, James Robert, trans. *Han Shih wai chuan: Han Ying's Illustrations of the Didactic Application of the Classic of Songs.* Harvard-Yenching Institute Monograph Series 11. Cambridge, MA, 1952.

Hsü Cho-yun. *Ancient China in Transition.* Stanford: Stanford University Press, 1968.

Hung, William, ed. *Chunqiu jingzhuan yinde* 春秋經傳引得. Harvard-Yenching Institute Sinological Series, Supplement No. 11. Peking: Harvard-Yenching Institute, 1937.

Kang Youwei 康有為. *Xinxue weijing kao* 新學偽經考. Peking: Guji chubanshe, 1956.

Karlgren, Bernard. "Grammata Serica Recensa," Stockholm: *Bulletin of the Museum of Far Eastern Antiquities* 29 (1957).

———, trans. "The Book of Odes." Stockholm: *Bulletin of the Museum of Far Eastern Antiquities* 17 (1945).

———, trans. "Legends and Cults in Ancient China." Stockholm: *Bulletin of the Museum of Far Eastern Antiquities* 18 (1946).

———, trans. "The Book of Documents." Stockholm: *Bulletin of the Museum of Far Eastern Antiquities* 22 (1950).

Kirk, G. S. *Myth: Its Meaning and Function in Ancient and Other Cultures.* New York: Harper and Row, 1970.

Lau, D. C. *Mencius.* Harmsworth: Penguin, 1970.

Legge, James, trans. *The Confucian Classics.* Hong Kong: Hong Kong University Press, 1960.

Lévi-Strauss, Claude. *Structural Anthropology.* New York: Doubleday, 1967.

———. *The Raw and the Cooked.* New York: Harper and Row, 1970.

————. *The Savage Mind*. Chicago: University of Chicago Press, 1966.

Liao, W. K., trans. *The Complete Works of Han Fei Tzu*. London: Arthur Probsthain, 1959.

Loewe, Michael. *Crisis and Conflict in Han China, 104 B.C. to A.D. 9*. London: George Allen and Unwin, 1974.

Maspero, Henri. "Légendes Mythologiques dans le Chou King." *Journal Asiatique* 204 (1924): 11–100.

Meyer, Dirk. *Philosophy on Bamboo: Text and the Production of Meaning in Early China*. Leiden: Brill, 2012.

Morgan, Evan, trans. *Tao the Great Luminant*. Shanghai: Walsh and Kelly, 1934.

Needham, Joseph. *Time and Eastern Man*. Royal Anthropological Institute Occasional Paper, no. 21. London: Royal Anthropological Institute, 1965.

Piaget, Jean. *Structuralism*. New York: Harper Torchbook, 1971.

Puett, Michael. *The Ambivalence of Creation: Debates Concerning Innovation and Artifice in Early China*. Stanford: Stanford University Press, 2001.

Qi Sihe 齊思和, "Xi Zhou dili kao" 西周地理考, *Yanjing xuebao* 燕京學報, 30 (1946): 63–106.

Qian Mu 錢穆. *Xian Qin zhuzi xinian* 先秦諸子系年. Hong Kong: Hong Kong University Press, 1956.

Qian Mu, "Zhou chu dili kao" 周初地理考, *Yanjing xuebao* 燕京學報, 10 (1931): 1955–2008.

Shima Kunio 島邦男. *Inkyo bokuji kenkyū* 殷墟卜辭研究. Hirosaki: Chūgokugaku Kenkyūkai, 1958.

Thompson, Paul M. *The* Shen tzu *Fragments*. London Oriental Series 29. Oxford: Oxford University Press, 1979.

Waley, Arthur, trans. *The Book of Songs*. New York: Random House (Vintage paperback), 1966.

Walker, Richard L. "Some Notes on the *Yen-tzu ch'un-ch'iu*." *Journal of the American Oriental Society* 73 (1953): 156–63.

Watson, Burton, trans. *Han Fei Tzu: Basic Writings*. New York: Columbia University Press, 1967.

————, trans. *The Complete Works of Chuang Tzu*. New York: Columbia University Press, 1964.

Weightman, John. "A Visit to Lévi-Strauss." *Encounter*, February 1971.

Wilhelm, Richard, trans. *Frühling und Herbst des Lü Bu We*. Jena: Eugen Diederichs, 1928.

Wright, Arthur F. "Sui Yang-ti: Personality and Stereotype." In *Confucianism and Chinese Civilization*, edited by Arthur Wright. New York: Atheneum, 1964.

Wu Qichang 吳其昌. *Jinwen shizu pu* 金文世族譜. Shanghai: Commercial Press, 1936.

Yang Yunru 楊筠如. "Jiang xingde minzu he Jiang Taigongde gushi" 姜姓的民族後姜太公的故事. In *Gu shi bian*, v. 2, edited by Gu Jiegang, 109–17.

Zhang Guangzhi 張光直. "Tan Wang Hai yu Yi Yin de jiri bing zai lun Yin-
    shang wangzhi" 談王亥與伊尹的祭日並再論殷商王制. *Zhongyang Yanji-
    uyuan Minzuxue Yanjiusuo jikan* 中央研究院民族學研究所集刊 35 (1973):
    111–27.
Zhang Xincheng 張心澂. *Wei shu tongkao* 偽書通考. Shanghai: Commercial Press,
    1954.

Index

Page numbers for main references are in bold

Made in the USA
Las Vegas, NV
28 September 2022

56174024R00132